One
Quiet Moment

One
Quiet Moment

Dr. Lloyd John Ogilvie

HARVEST HOUSE PUBLISHERS
EUGENE, OR 97402

ONE QUIET MOMENT

Copyright © 1997 by Harvest House Publishers
Eugene, Oregon 97402

Library of Congress Cataloging-in-Publication Data

Ogilvie, Lloyd John.
    One quiet moment / Lloyd John Ogilvie.
        p. cm.
    ISBN 1-56507-535-8
    1. Devotional calendars.   I. Title.
BV4811.0356   1997
242'.2—dc20   96-35337
                                                                            CIP

Printed in the United States of America

97 98 99 00 01 02 / BG / 10 9 8 7 6 5 4 3 2 1

To
Antoinette and Senator Mark Hatfield

Whose magnificent impact on America
is empowered by their daily prayers.

Preface

These are personal prayers for daily devotions at the beginning of each day of the year. They are written in the first person singular to express our deepest hopes and hurts, delights and difficulties.

Over my 40 years of pastoral ministry I have listened to the needs and aspirations of people. These prayers articulate the longing for a profound, intimate relationship with God. They are not just my own personal prayers, but my wording of the prayer requests I have heard from people through the years. Therefore, these prayers are not in stained-glass language. They are meant to be an honest, open expression of those who seek to know and serve God.

Portions of a few of the prayers were first prayed at the opening of the United States Senate and then personalized for inclusion here. This especially would be true for prayers for the nation, patriotism, citizenship, and special national holidays. The need for a spiritual awakening in America is a consistent theme. My hope is that these prayers will help prepare your mind and heart for God's blessing on our beloved nation.

You will note that there is no formal ending to these prayers. For good reason. My desire is that the prayers will be "prayer starters" for you and will instigate further prayer during your quiet time and throughout the day. A good ending, if you want to insert one after you have added your own extended prayer, might be, "To be continued throughout the day, in Jesus' name."

I am grateful for the assistance of Susanne Lorenzini in typing and editing the prayers for inclusion in the manuscript. Also, I appreciate the encouragement for this project from Kathy Rust, who formerly worked as my Assistant. And, as with all my books through the years, my wife Mary Jane has been the faithful, enthusiastic cheerleader.

Now, my prayer is that *One Quiet Moment* will help fill all the hours of your days with joy and peace.

—Lloyd John Ogilvie
Washington, D.C.

JANUARY
1

Then you shall call, and the LORD will answer; you shall cry, and He will say, "Here I am."

— ISAIAH 58:9

Almighty God, You said through the prophet Isaiah that when I call, You will answer, and while I am speaking, You will hear. I thank You that prayer begins with You. It originates in Your heart, sweeps into my heart, and gives me the boldness to ask for what You desire to give.

In my communion with You, Lord, may the desires of my heart be honed by Your greater desires for me. Then, Lord, grant me the desires of my heart. And may my human understanding be surpassed by Your gift of knowledge, my inadequate judgment with Your wisdom, and my limited expectations with Your vision.

May this day be one continuous conversation with You. I ask this not just for my own peace and security, but for my responsibility to loved ones and friends around me. The margin of human error is an ever-present concern. So I yield my mind, heart, will, and imagination to be channels for the flow of Your divine guidance. Without Your help I will hit wide of the mark. But with Your power, I cannot fail.

JANUARY
2

*Let us draw near [to God] with a true heart in
full assurance of faith.*

— HEBREWS 10:22

Sovereign Father, as I begin this new day filled with
responsibilities and soul-sized issues, I am irresistibly
drawn into Your presence by the magnetism of Your love
and my need for your guidance. I come to You at Your invitation; in the quiet of intimate communion with You,
the tightly wound springs of pressure and stress are released and a profound inner peace fills my heart and
mind.

I hear again the impelling cadences of the drumbeat
of Your Spirit calling me to press on in the battle for truth,
righteousness, and justice. My mind snaps to full attention, and my heart salutes You as Soverign Lord. You have
given me a mind capable of receiving Your mind, an imagination able to envision Your plan and purpose for me,
and a will ready to do Your will.

Help me to remember that no problem is too small
to escape Your concern and no perplexity is too great to
resist Your solutions. I know You will go before me to
show me the way, behind me to press me forward, beside
me to give me courage, above me to protect me, and
within me to give me wisdom and discernment.

Lead on, oh King Eternal . . . in Your all-powerful
name.

JANUARY
3

Speak, LORD, for your servant hears.

— 1 SAMUEL 3:9

Almighty God, I dedicate this day to do justly, love mercy, and walk humbly with You. I am challenged by the realization that the Hebrew meaning of "walk humbly" is "to walk attentively." And so I commit my mind and heart to listen attentively to You.

Speak to me so that what I speak may be an echo of Your voice, which has sounded in the depth of my receptive soul. In the din of the cacophony of voices demanding my attention and the pressure of self-seeking forces willfully dominated by self-interest, help me to seek to know and do Your will for what is best for those around me.

Lord, grant me the greatness of a mind tuned to the frequency of the Spirit's guidance. Free me of any tenaciously held opinions that may not have been refined by careful listening to You. Be with me, lest I forget to listen to You.

JANUARY
4

O LORD, our Lord, how excellent is Your name in all the earth. . . . What is man that You are mindful of him, and the Son of Man that You visit him? For You have made him a little lower than the angels, and You have crowned him with glory and honor. You have made him to have dominion over the work of Your hands.

—PSALM 8:1,4-6

Gracious God, ultimate Sovereign of our Nation and Lord of our lives, I am stunned again by Your majesty and the magnitude of the delegated dominion You have entrusted to me. I respond with awe and wonder and begin this day with renewed commitment to serve You.

In a culture that often denies Your sovereignty and worships at the throne of the perpendicular pronoun, help me to exemplify the greatness of servanthood. You have given me a life full of opportunities to serve and enabled me to live at full potential for Your glory. I humble myself before You and acknowledge that I could not breathe a breath, think a thought, make sound decisions, or press on to excellence without Your power. You alone are the One I seek to please. I have been blessed to be a blessing. And so I greet this day with, "Life's a privilege!" intentionality and "How may I serve?" incisiveness. Grant me grace and courage to give myself away to You and to others with whom I work this day.

JANUARY
5

*You are my rock and my fortress; therefore, for
Your name's sake, lead me and guide me.*

— PSALM 31:3

Almighty God, You have promised strength for the
work of this day, power to handle the pressures, light for
the way, patience in problems, help from above, unfading
courage, and undying love. In the stresses and strains of
living, often I sense my wells have run dry. Life has a way
of de-powering me, depleting my resiliency, and draining
my patience. People can get me down and perplexities stir
me up.

Lord, I pray for a fresh flow of Your strength—
strength to think clearly, serve creatively, and endure consistently; strength to fill up diminished human resources;
silent strength that flows from Your limitless source, quietly filling them with artesian power.

You never ask me to do more than You will provide
the strength to accomplish. So make me a riverbed for the
flow of Your creative Spirit. Fill this day with serendipities, unexpected surprises of Your grace. Be Lord of every
conversation, the unseen guest at every meeting and the
guide of every decision. In the name of Him who is the
way, the truth and the life.

JANUARY
6

God forbid that I should glory except in the cross of our Lord Jesus Christ.

—GALATIANS 6:14

Give God the glory! —JOHN 9:24

Lord, forgive me when I try to grasp the glory for myself. It's so easy to take pride in my accomplishments and what I've accumulated in my self-made kingdom of thingdom. Help me to not miss the real purpose of life: to know You and emulate Your love, justice, and righteousness. Help me turn from all my lesser goals of grandisement and focus my life on Your ultimate calling.

I commit this day to seeking that which delights You. I want to give You the glory for all I have and am, and for the opportunities to serve You by being a servant to others and caring for what You have entrusted to me.

Make me an example of what it truly means to live life to Your glory and honor. Help me to point to You as the source of all that You have provided and all that You have enabled me to accomplish.

To You be the glory!

JANUARY
7

You are our Father; we are the clay, and You our potter; and all we are the work of Your hand.

— ISAIAH 64:8

Holy Father, You created me for Yourself and I realize my heart will remain restless until it rests in You. I confess my ambivalence. I want You to be Lord of my life, and yet sometimes I sense reservation within me. I want Your direction in my life, but at times I feel troubled about losing my own control. I need Your love and yet fear the implications of loving others as You have loved me. I pray for America to be a great nation under Your sovereign reign, but there are times when I am reluctant to ask You to begin a vital spiritual awakening in my own heart.

Yet I am willing to be made willing. Help me to see what my life could be if I loved You with all my heart and removed the self-erected obstacles to trusting You completely. I want to open my mind to think magnificently with the wisdom of Your Spirit, commit my will to seek the guidance of Your Spirit, and face the challenges of this day with the power of Your Spirit.

JANUARY
8

*My grace is sufficient for you, for My strength
is made perfect in weakness.*

— 2 CORINTHIANS 12:9

Thank You, Father, for receiving me as I am with
unqualified grace. Thank You for the strength, security,
and serenity You provide in the midst of strain and stress.
To know You is my greatest privilege, and to grow in the
knowledge of Your will is my greatest need. My plans and
ways are insufficient; bless me with Your eternal strength
and wisdom. My vision is incomplete; bless me with Your
hope.

Thank You for enabling me to make the most of this
day. Empower me to emulate Your faithfulness in my responsibilities and relationships today. May I be a person
on whom others can depend. Help me to say what I mean
and mean what I say. I want each decision to be guided by
You. Give me light when my vision is dim, courage when
I need to be bold, decisiveness when it would be easy to
equivocate, and courage when others are tempted to be
discouraged.

JANUARY
9

Call to Me, and I will answer you.

— JEREMIAH 33:3

Almighty God, as I begin a new day filled with opportunities masquerading as complex problems, I claim Your promise, "Call to Me, and I will answer you, and show you great and mighty things which you do not know" (Jeremiah 33:3). I know that no matter how intense my problems, You are with me. The bigger the problem, the more all-encompassing Your abiding presence will be. And the more complex the problem, the greater will be the wisdom You offer. Equal to the strain of each problem will come the strength You give.

Thank You for this time of quiet with You in which I can receive the peace of knowing that I am loved and forgiven, the healing of the hurts of harbored memories, the answers to problems that often seem unsolvable and the vision for solutions that otherwise would be beyond my human understanding. I praise You that to know You is my greatest joy and to serve You is life's greatest delight. I pray this in the name of Him who came to give us abundant life.

JANUARY
10

I will bless the LORD at all times; His praise shall continually be in my mouth. My soul shall make its boast in the LORD; the humble shall hear of it and be glad. Oh, magnify the LORD with me, and let us exalt His name together.

— PSALM 34:1-3

Lord, what You desire from me You inspire in me. You use whom You choose; You provide for what You guide; You are working Your purposes out and know what You are about. I trust You with all my heart. Inspire me with Your Spirit and use me.

I praise You for the challenges of this day, which will force me to depend more on You. I know that You will never forget me; help me to never forget to ask for Your help. Set me free of any worry that will break my concentration on what You have given me to do today.

Keep me mindful of the motto of abundant living: "Without You we can't; without us You won't." Think Your thoughts through me, speak Your truth through my words, radiate Your love through my actions. When this day is finished the only thing that will really matter is hearing You say, "Well done, good and faithful servant."

JANUARY
11

Be kindly affectionate to one another with brotherly love, in honor giving preference to one another.

—ROMANS 12:10

Gracious Father, You have given me the privilege of caring for others. Each is a never-to-be repeated miracle. You have called me to a ministry of intercession and to release Your blessings when I pray for others.

Lord, I entrust to Your care my loved ones and friends—especially those who are confronting difficulties or illness. Help me to be sensitive to the needs of the people I meet today. Enable me to be to others what You have been to me. Help me to live this day as if it were the only day I had left.

If there is any kindness I can show, any affirmation I can give, any care I can impart, Lord, help me to express it today. May I be an encouragement and not a burden; a source of courage and not of cynicism. This is the day You have made, and I plan to rejoice and be glad in it. In the name of Him who gave us the Commandment, "Love one another as I have loved you."

JANUARY
12

Holy, holy, holy is the LORD of hosts; the whole earth is full of His glory!

—ISAIAH 6:3

Praise and honor be to You, Lord most high. Lord of creation, recreate my heart to love You above all. Ruler of the universe, I invite You to reign over me as my personal Lord.

As I begin this new day, I confess with humility that I am totally dependent on You, dear God. I could not breathe a breath, think a thought, or carry out my responsibilities without Your constant and consistent blessing. I praise You for the gifts of intellect, education, and experience. Most of all, I thank You for the gifts of Your Spirit, which make it possible to live supernaturally. Beyond the level of talent and training You alone are the source of wisdom, discernment, knowledge, and prophetic vision.

All that You have done in me has been in preparation for what You want to do through me now. I am here by Your divine appointment. Thank You, Lord, for the gift of life!

JANUARY
13

Bless the LORD, O my soul: and all that is within me, bless His holy name! Bless the LORD, O my soul, and forget not all His benefits.

—PSALM 103:1-2

Father, You have created me to glorify You and enjoy You forever. You have developed in me the desire to know You and have given me the gift of faith to accept Your unqualified love.

You turn my struggles into stepping stones. I know Your promise is true: You will never leave me nor forsake me. You give me strength when I am weak, gracious correction when I fail, and undeserved grace when I need it most.

And just when I think there is no place to turn, You meet me and help me return to You. I love You, Lord. My heart overflows with gratitude. My mind, emotions, and will are like parts of an orchestra. Tune them to bless Your name.

May my thoughts, attitudes, and actions this day be an expression of my grateful worship to You.

JANUARY
14

Behold, I make all things new.

— REVELATION 21:5

Father, the psalmist expresses my need: "As the deer pants for the water brooks, so pants my soul for You, O God. My soul thirsts for God, for the living God" (Psalm 42:1-2). Nothing and no one can satisfy my inner restlessness. I praise You for this longing to reaffirm my relationship with You. My primary purpose is to know and love You. And yet, yesterday there was so much that distracted me from serving You and disturbed my commitment to putting You first. Forgive me for the things I said and did when my priorities got messed up.

Last night I went to sleep before I'd finished praying. No wonder I didn't sleep soundly and woke up feeling unrested. But here I am with a new day heavy on my hands. Then it occurs to me that the only way for today to be different from yesterday is to get it off my hands by committing it unreservedly to You.

Thank You for the freedom to close the door on yesterday and walk through the open door of opportunity You have set before me today. I surrender the needs of the day ahead and trust You completely. "I can do all things through Christ who strengthens me" (Philippians 4:13)!

JANUARY
15

Martin Luther King, Jr. Day

Almighty God, You are the Lord of history who calls great leaders and anoints them with supernatural power to lead in times of social distress when Your righteousness and justice must be reestablished. Along with my fellow Americans of all races, I celebrate today the birthday of Martin Luther King, Jr.

I praise You, O God, for Dr. King's life and leadership in the cause of racial justice. You gave him a dream of equality and opportunity for all people which You empowered him to declare as a clarion call to all America.

As the memory of this truly great man and courageous American is honored, I ask You to cleanse any prejudice from my heart and help me to press on in the battle to assure the equality of education, housing, job opportunities, advancement, and social status for all people regardless of race and creed. May I take part in this ongoing challenge to assure the rights of all people in this free land. Help me to start in my circle of influence, where I work, and in my church and community.

God has not given us a spirit of fear, but of power and of love and of a sound mind.

—2 TIMOTHY 1:7

Spirit of the living God, fall afresh on me. Peel back the icy fingers of the fist of fear that holds my heart in the grip of grimness . . . that makes me cautious when faced by great challenges, and causes me to be timid in life's testing hours.

I open my mind, heart, will, and body to the infilling of Your power. Infinite Intelligence, grant me power to understand Your solutions to my problems. Unlimited Love, fill my heart with healing love from which deeper affirmation of others may flow. Liberating Spirit, set me free from the bondage of will so intent on what I want that I often miss the guidance You have for me. Artesian Strength, energize my body for the arduous pressures of the day ahead.

Spirit of life, help me pull out all the stops so You can make great music of joy in my soul. Radiate Your hope through me. Make me a positive person who is expectant of Your best for me and those around me. Give me the authentic charisma that comes from Your grace gifts of wisdom, knowledge, discernment, and love. And so, lead on! This is the day that You have made. I will rejoice and be glad in it!

Present your bodies a living sacrifice, holy, acceptable to God, which is your reasonable service.

—ROMANS 12:1

Gracious Lord of all life, help me never to separate what You have joined together.

All of life is sacred to You. Forgive my imposed dichotomy between the sacred and the secular. Every person, situation, and responsibility is sacred because everyone and everything belongs to You. Give me a renewed sense that all that I have and am is Your gift. May I cherish the wonder of life You have entrusted to me. I want to live with an attitude of gratitude. Therefore I make a renewed commitment to excellence in everything I do and say.

You have taught me the inseparable relationship between intimacy with You and the integrity of my life. You've shown me that authentic intimacy results when the real I meets the true You in an honest, open, unpretentious relationship. It's when I come to You as I am that You whisper in my soul, "You are loved now!" Then the consistent experience of Your unqualified love gives me the courage to be genuine, loyal, and faithful to You in my relationships with others and the responsibilities You have entrusted to me.

The body is one and has many members, but all the members of that one body, being many, are one body, so also is Christ.

— 1 CORINTHIANS 12:12

Almighty God, You are the source of unity in the midst of diversity. Enable me to accept my awesome calling to live and work together peaceably with my brothers and sisters in Christ. Help me to communicate my convictions without censure of those who might not fully agree with me. Free me from any false assumptions that I might ever have a corner on all truth. Unsettle within me any pious posturing that pretends that I alone can speak for You.

You created me in Your image; help me never to return the compliment. May I restrain from adopting the spirit of judgment so prevalent in our society. Forgive me when I presume Your authority by setting myself up as a judge of the worth of those who disagree with me.

At the same time, Lord, I know You have not called me to indulgence when it comes to seeking truth. Nor do You encourage me to buy into the mindset of appeasement and tolerance, where everything is relative and there are no absolutes. What You do ask is that with other believers I will seek what is Your best for this world and work to achieve that with them. To that goal I commit this day.

I delight to do your will, O my God, and Your law is within my heart.

— Psalm 40:8

Almighty God, Creator, Sustainer and Lord of all, You who have brought light out of darkness and have created me to know You, I praise You for Your guidance.

As I begin this day, I acknowledge my total dependence upon You. Revelation of Your truth comes in relationship with You, and Your inspiration is given when I am illuminated with Your Spirit. Therefore I want to prepare for the decisions I make this day by opening my mind to the inflow of Your Spirit.

I confess that I need Your divine intelligence to invade my thoughts and Your light to flood upon the dimness of my understanding. I know that my life and the lives of those around me will be shaped by the decisions I make.

And so I say with the psalmist, "Show me Your ways, O LORD; teach me Your paths. Lead me in Your truth and teach me, for You are the God of my salvation; on You I wait all the day" (Psalm 25:4-5).

JANUARY
20

Commit your works to the LORD, and your thoughts will be established.

— PROVERBS 16:3

Gracious Lord, Your Spirit is impinging on me, hovering around me, ready to enter me and give me power to live this day to the fullest. You have shown me that commitment is the key that opens the floodgate and receives the inflow of Your incredible resources for living today to the fullest. Remind me that there is enough time and You will provide enough strength for what You have called me to accomplish today.

Lord, may this day be one of constant conversation with You. Help me to listen as You give me Your insight, discernment, wisdom, and vision. Help me to focus my attention on Your solutions to my problems. I now commit this day to being a day in which I work with freedom and joy.

I picture myself free of worry and anxiety, and able to enjoy the day as it unfolds. It's wonderful to know that this vision for today is exactly what You desire for me. Thank You for giving the day and showing the way.

JANUARY

21

Pray without ceasing.

— 1 THESSALONIANS 5:17

Almighty God, You have promised that if Your people will humble themselves and seek Your face and pray, You will answer and heal us.

Lord, I know you have called me to be salt and light in the bland neglect and darkness of what contradicts Your vision for this world. Give me courage, then, to be accountable to You and Your commandments—even when it means I might not receive the approval of those around me.

Lord of new beginnings, help me to be among those who encourage others to a spiritual awakening. Count me among those of Your children who pray for the needs of those whose understanding is darkened.

Help me to repent of the pride and selfishness that prevail in our society, and to manifest—in an infectious way—a justice and righteousness that honors You as the one true Sovereign of our nation. I know that renewal must begin with repentance and humility. I am ready Lord; begin with me.

JANUARY
22

If you really fulfill the royal law according to the Scripture, "You shall love your neighbor as yourself."

— JAMES 2:8

Gracious God, help me to get inside what is happening to others so that I may see with their eyes, think with their minds, and feel with their hearts. Strengthen me to be as kind to others as I want them to be to me. Empower me, by Your Spirit, to be as faithful to others as You have been to me in spite of my shortcomings and failures.

Help me to make the same allowances for others as I would want them to make for me. Help me to express the same empathy to others as I would want them to express when I hurt. And help me to understand others as I would want to be understood.

I commit this day to seeking to be to others the giving and forgiving love You have been to me . . . through Him who taught the secret of serving others.

JANUARY
23

God is able to make all grace abound toward you, that you, always having all sufficiency in all things, have an abundance for every good work.

— 2 CORINTHIANS 9:8

Father, I claim this promise from Your Word as I begin this new day. Thank You for Your amazing grace, Your unqualified love, and the forgiveness that flows from Your heart into mine, filling up my diminished reserves.

Enable me, this day, to clarify my priorities and commit myself to seek first Your will and put that above all else. It is liberating to know that You will supply all my need, in all sufficiency, to discern and do what glorifies You. Grant me wisdom, Lord, for the decisions of this day. I ask this not for my personal success, but for the sake of Your kingdom.

Your mighty abundance is for the purpose of making me a channel for Your work in the world. You provide for what You guide. The great need in the people around me is for Your grace. May I abide in You so I can abound in Your grace. May Your grace be on my face!

JANUARY
24

Be strong in the Lord and in the power of His might.

— EPHESIANS 6:10

Almighty God, I praise You for empowering me to stand with strength and courage in the midst of spiritual warfare. I come to the armory of Your presence to be suited up with Your whole armor for today's battles of the mind and spirit.

Thank You for the breastplate of righteousness, which makes me secure in Your unqualified love and forgiveness. Shod my feet with the preparation of the gospel of peace and help me to stride forward with the inner calm of Your perfect peace, which surpasses all understanding. Give me the shield of faith to quench the fiery darts of satanic influence. Place over my head the helmet of salvation and protect my thoughts from distorted half-truths and confused direction. And help me to grasp the sword of the Spirit . . . Your words of guidance for hand-to-hand battles with evil. On time and in time, whisper in my soul the exact word of encouragement and strength I need.

Lord, I gladly accept Your whole armor as You prepare me for today's battles—in the name of the One who vanquished evil and is my victorious Savior.

JANUARY
25

Do not fear, for I am with you.

— GENESIS 26:24

Lord God, You are infinite, eternal, unchangeable and the source of wisdom, holiness, goodness, and truth. Today I come to You with two biblical admonitions. I am told that the fear of the Lord is the beginning of wisdom (Proverbs 9:10), but also that I am not to fear (Genesis 26:24). Help me to distinguish between the humble awe and wonder that opens me to the gift of Your guidance, and the negative panic that so often grips my soul when problems arise.

Give me a profound reverence for You that keeps me on the knees of my heart. May I never presume that I am adequate for a day's challenges until I have received Your strength and vision. Give me the confidence that comes from trusting in Your reliability and resourcefulness. I know You will never let me down because You always endeavor to lift me up.

Lord, liberate me from all the fears that haunt me: the fear of the past, the fear of failure, and the fear of what is ahead. I may not know what the future holds, but I do know that You hold the future. And that's why I can replace my every fear with total confidence in You who never leaves nor forsakes.

JANUARY
26

My tongue shall speak of Your righteousness and of Your praise all the day long.

—PSALM 35:28

Gracious God, You have made praise the secret of opening my mind and heart to You . . . the key to unlocking the mysteries of Your will . . . and the source of turning difficulties into opportunities. When I praise You even for life's tight places and trying people, I am strangely liberated. You have made praise the highest form of committing to You my needs.

I begin this day, then, with praise to You for the blessings I neither deserve nor could earn, and for the problems in which You will reveal Your supernatural guidance and power. I dedicate this day to be one in which I constantly give You praise in all things—especially the perplexities that force me to seek You and Your limitless grace.

Most of all, my heart is filled with praise for You, dear God, for who You are as my Father, Lord of my life, and indwelling power. Praise to You Father, Son and Holy Spirit!

JANUARY
27

Who may ascend into the hill of the LORD?
. . . He who has clean hands and a pure heart.

— PSALM 24:3-4

Gracious God, whose dwelling place is the heart that longs for Your presence and the mind that humbly seeks Your truth, I eagerly ask for Your guidance in the work I do this day. I confess anything that would hinder the flow of Your Spirit in and through me. Heal any broken or strained relationships that would drain off creative energies into the eddies of anxieties. Lift my burdens and resolve my worries. Then give me a fresh experience of Your amazing grace, which will set me free to live with freedom and joy.

Now Lord, I am ready to live this day with great confidence, fortified by the steady supply of Your strength. Give me the courage to do what I already know of Your will so that I may know more of it for the specific challenges of this day.

In disagreements or conflict, help me to listen attentively to others. May I never think I have an exclusive corner on the truth. Enable me to be open to aspects of the truth You will provide through the voices of those who may differ with me. My dominant desire is for Your best in my life and the lives of others You have given me in my family, my friends, or those with whom I work. Make me a responsible communicator of Your encouragement and hope.

JANUARY
28

*Delight yourself also in the LORD, and He shall
give you the desires of Your heart.*

— PSALM 37:4

Father, You have shown that You want to guide what
we pray so that You can grant us the desires of our hearts.
I want to begin this day with King Solomon's response to
Your question, "Ask! What shall I give you?" (2 Chronicles 1:7). Solomon asked for an "understanding heart,"
and confessed his inadequacy and need for strength to fulfill his responsibilities.

It's moving to know that the Hebrew words for "understanding heart," literally translated, refer to a "hearing
heart." Solomon wanted to hear both Your voice and the
voices of the people who came to him with their needs.
He wanted to be able to respond and speak to those needs
out of the depth of wisdom that came from a heart tuned
to Your Spirit's supernatural power.

Lord, make me one who longs to have a wise and
understanding heart. May I be one who listens carefully to
Your heart speaking to my heart. Help me to listen to You
today and always!

JANUARY
29

You will keep him in perfect peace, whose mind is stayed on You, because he trusts in You.

—ISAIAH 26:3

Jehovah Shalom, I thank You for this marvelously direct and uncluttered promise. You seek to give me profound inner peace, but sometimes I find it difficult to stay my mind on You. I want to focus on You, yet often my attention wanders. I want to listen to You, but my heart sometimes is cluttered with the static of distracting voices. I want to trust You, but years of self-reliance make it difficult to wait patiently for Your answers.

You alone, Lord, can keep my mind stayed on You. All I can do is ask for the miracle of a day lived in constant awareness of Your abiding presence. May this be a day filled with spectacular moments during which You keep my mind focused, my heart calm, and my will alert to Your will. Lord of peace, help me keep my mind on You.

In the name of the Prince of Peace, who promised, "Peace I leave with you, my peace I give to you; not as the world gives do I give to you. Let not your heart be troubled, neither let it be afraid" (John 14:27).

JANUARY
30

The earth is the LORD's, and all its fullness, the world and those who dwell therein.

— PSALM 24:1

Creator and Sustainer of all, I humbly accept Your calling to be a diligent steward of the resources and riches You have so bountifully given to me. You have blessed me with opportunities and provided for my material needs. I ask for only one thing more, Lord: a grateful heart.

May I turn to You, then, when it comes time to decide how to use the resources You have entrusted to me. Help me to know how best to care for what is really Yours . . . for the benefit of Your children, Your kingdom, Your world. And enable me to do what is best with the blessings You give me today.

Fill my grateful heart with generosity. Help me give myself away to serve others. May I share what I've learned from You without pious superiority and the lessons of life without arrogance. All through this day I want to point away from myself to You—the Author of my life story.

JANUARY
31

*Teach me Your way, O LORD; I will walk in
Your truth.*

— PSALM 86:11

Gracious God, my source of spiritual, intellectual,
and physical strength, I thank You for a fresh new day in
which I have the privilege of serving You. You are the
source of all that I have and all that I am, and I want to
show my gratitude by making my every thought, word,
and action today a gift to You.

Lord, it's so great to be alive! I trust You to guide me
so that all I do is in keeping with Your will. Take command
of my mind and my words so that Your wisdom and
Your truth prevail in the choices I make. Help me to live
this day to the fullest . . . for Your glory.

Help me pull out all the stops so You can make
great music in my soul. Radiate Your hope through me. I
commit this day to live without reservations. Anoint me
with Your power. May the fruit of Your indwelling presence
shine forth in love, joy, peace, patience, kindness,
goodness, faithfulness, gentleness, and self-control. It's
going to be a great day, and I thank You in advance.

FEBRUARY
1

*It is He who has made us, and not we our-
selves; we are His people and the sheep of His
pasture.*

— PSALM 100:3

Gracious Father, Your lovingkindness draws me to
You, Your faithfulness opens my mind and heart before
You, and Your omniscience motivates me to seek wisdom
from You. I know that it is in a relationship of complete
trust in You that revelation of Your will is released.

Help me to press on to the challenges of this day in
a manner worthy of Your high calling for my life. It is with
humility, Lord, that I seek Your great power so that I
might do great things for You today.

Take charge of the control center of my brain.
Think Your thoughts through me and send to my nervous systems the pure signals of Your peace, power, and
patience. Give me a mind responsive to Your guidance.

Guide my tongue so that I may speak truth with
clarity, without rancor or anger. May my discussions with
others be an effort to reach agreement rather than simply
to win an argument. Make me a mediator of Your grace to
others. May I respond to Your nudges to communicate
affirmation and encouragement.

I want to march to the cadences of Your drumbeat.
Help me to catch the vision of Your will for my life. Invade my heart with Your calming Spirit, strengthen it
with Your powerful presence, and imbue it with Your gift
of faith to trust You to bring Your best for my life.

FEBRUARY
2

The LORD of hosts has sworn, saying, "Surely, as I have thought, so it shall come to pass, and as I have purposed, so it shall stand."

—ISAIAH 14:24

Almighty God, I have known grim days and great days. Some days are filled with strain and stress, while on other days everything goes smoothly and successfully. Life can be simply awful or awfully simple. Today, I choose the awfully simple, but sublime, secret of a great day: Your work, done in Your power, achieves Your results, in Your timing. I reject the idea that things merely work themselves out, and ask You, dear Lord, to work out things.

Before me is a new day filled with more to do than I can accomplish in my own strength. Give me the power of sanctified imagination to envision a day in which the tasks that are truly important get done. Pull my anchors out of the mud of procrastination, lift my sails, and remind me that it is the set of my sails and not the gales that determines where I shall go.

You have given me this day, Lord, and I intend to live it to the fullest with Your guidance, by Your power, and for Your glory.

FEBRUARY

3

Having been justified by faith, we have peace with God through our Lord Jesus Christ, through whom also we have access by faith into this grace in which we stand, and rejoice in hope of the glory of God.

—ROMANS 5:1-2

Lord God, You are the source of righteousness and are always on the side of what is right. I confess that there are times when I assume that I know what is right without seeking Your guidance.

Give me the humility to be more concerned about being on Your side than trying to recruit You to be on my side. Clear my mind so I can think Your thoughts. Help me to wait on You, to listen patiently for Your voice, to seek Your will through concentrated study and reflection. And free me from the assumption that I have an exclusive on the dispatches of heaven, and that those who disagree with me must also be against You.

I commit this day, Lord, to seeking what is best for those around me. Thank You for allowing me the privilege of a right relationship with You through faith in Christ. Through Him I have access to Your grace and can live with the assurance that tribulation produces perseverance, and perseverance character, and character hope. This hope does not disappoint because of Your love poured out in my heart through the Holy Spirit! (Romans 5:3-5, adapted).

FEBRUARY
4

Do not be overcome by evil, but overcome evil with good. —ROMANS 12:21

Gracious God, there are five vandalizing words that confuse, hurt, and deplete—words that cause discouragement, cut the slender thread of hope, and give that bottomless inner feeling of frustration. Those words are, "It won't make any difference."

As I come to You in prayer, I hear Your voice sounding in my soul, encouraging me to believe that I really can make a difference. Help me to realize that You have all power and are ready to use me in the relationships and responsibilities You've granted to me.

Thank You, too, that what You have given me to do this day can be an expression of my worship of You. I can rest assured in the knowledge that my work is not wasted, insignificant, or useless. Give me a fresh burst of enthusiasm, and help me to make my motto these five words of determination: "I am making a difference!" Praise the Lord!

FEBRUARY
5

*Whatever you ask in My name, that I will do,
that the Father may be glorified in the Son.*

— JOHN 14:13

Almighty God, I praise You that it is Your will to give good things to those who ask You. You give strength and power to Your people when they seek You above everything else. You guide the humble and teach them Your way. Help me to humble myself as I begin this day so there will be no need for life to humiliate me because of any vestige of arrogance in me. I ask You for the true humility of total dependence on You.

Lord, You know what I need before I ask You, and yet, You encourage me to seek, knock, and ask in my prayers. I know that when I truly seek You and desire Your will, You will guide me in my petitions. Thus I ask for the wisdom of Your Holy Spirit to prevail in all the decisions that I make this day. May I enter into no venture in which I would be embarrassed to have You present; may I resist no opportunity in which I sense You calling me to be faithful and obedient to You. I pray this through Him who taught us true humility: even Christ our Lord.

FEBRUARY
6
━━━

O God of our salvation, You who are the confidence of all the ends of the earth . . . You make the outgoings of the morning and evening rejoice.

—PSALM 65:5,8

Lord, on this day I know I am likely to face challenges and decisions beyond my own knowledge and experience. I dare not press ahead on my own resources. In the quiet of this magnificent moment of conversation with You I commit this day; I want to live it to Your glory.

Bring me wholly in step with Your Spirit as I fulfill my responsibilities throughout this day. Make my heart one with the psalmist, who said, "Blessed be the Lord, who daily loads us with benefits, the God of our salvation!" (Psalm 68:19). Lord, anoint my mind with the benefits of vision and discernment. Thank You in advance for these blessings.

I claim the promise given through Isaiah: "Your ears shall hear a word behind you, saying, 'This is the way, walk in it'" (Isaiah 30:21). May Your guidance be that decisive in the decisions I must make today. I am thankful that there is no limit to what can be accomplished when I give You the glory.

FEBRUARY
7

I will remember the works of the Lord; surely I will remember Your wonders of old. I will also meditate on all Your work. . . . Who is so great a God as our God?

—PSALM 77:11-13

Gracious God, so often I come to You listing out my urgent petitions. With lovingkindness and faithfulness, You guide and provide. You bless me beyond my expectations and give me what I need on time, and in time. My prayer today is for a much better memory of how You have heard and answered my petitions in the past.

I thank You, Lord, for the gift of life, for my relationship with You, for Your grace and forgiveness, for my family and friends, for the privilege of work to do well, for problems and perplexities that force me to trust You more, and for the assurance that You can use even the dark threads of difficulties in weaving the tapestry of my life.

Knowing how You delight to bless a thankful person, I thank You for Your strength and care today. Thank You not just for what You do, but for who You are—blessed God and loving Father. In that confidence I ask for Your providential care throughout this day. In the name of Him who said, "Lo, I am with you always" (Matthew 28:20).

FEBRUARY
8

*Let each of you look out not only for his own
interests, but also for the interests of others.*

— PHILIPPIANS 2:4

Almighty God, before me is a brand new day filled
with opportunities to live out my calling as a servant. I
trust You to guide me so that all I do and say will be to
Your glory.

You are the magnetic and majestic Lord who draws
me out of self-centeredness to worship You. In Your presence I can see the people of my life as they are—in need
of You and Your kindness and affirmation expressed
through me.

Father, help me to be sensitive to what is happening
to people around me. I know there are unmet needs beneath the surface of the most successful and the most self-
assured. I know that today I will meet some who are
enduring hidden physical or emotional pain, others who
are fearful of an uncertain future, and still others who
carry burdens of worry for families or friends. May I take
no one for granted, but instead, be a ready communicator
of Your love and encouragement. Make me aware of these
concerns of others, available to express Your care, and articulate with Your hope. I pray this through Christ, who
gave us the key of self-sacrifice to set us free from the dun-
geon of selfishness.

FEBRUARY
9

*In this is love, not that we loved God, but that
He loved us and sent His Son to be the propitiation for our sins. Beloved, if God so loved us,
we also ought to love one another.*

—1 JOHN 4:10-11

Almighty Father, whose chosen dwelling is the
mind that is completely open to You and the heart that is
unreservedly responsive to You, I thank You that my desire to find You is because You already have found me. My
prayers are not said in an effort to get Your attention, for
You have gotten my attention.

You always are before me with anticipatory, providential initiative. My longing to know Your will is because You have wisdom and guidance prepared to impart
to me. You place before me certain people and their problems and potential because You want to bless them
through my prayers as well as uplifting words and actions.

You have solutions to unfold and implement
through me. I am amazed: You know what I need before I
ask You, but have ordained that in my asking You will
draw me into closer fellowship with You and reveal Your
power in answer to my prayers.

FEBRUARY
10

The LORD is on my side; I will not fear. What can man do to me?
—PSALM 118:6

Lord, this contemporary rendering of the Twenty-Third Psalm provides me with a prayerful confession of faith to begin this day:

> The Lord is my strength, I shall not panic;
> He helps me relax and rest in quiet trust.
> He reminds me that I belong to Him
>   and restores my serenity;
> He leads me in my decisions and
>   gives me calmness of mind.
> His presence is peace.
> Even though I walk through the valley
>   of the fear of failure,
> I will not worry, for He will be with me.
> His truth, grace, and lovingkindness
>   will stabilize me.
> He prepares release and renewal in
>   the midst of my stress.
> He anoints my mind with wisdom;
> My cup overflows with fresh energy.
> Surely goodness and mercy will be
>   communicated through me,
> For I shall walk in the strength of my Lord,
>   and dwell in His presence forever. Amen.

FEBRUARY
11

*Great is the LORD, and greatly to be praised;
and His greatness is unsearchable. . . . I will
meditate on the glorious splendor of Your
majesty.*

—PSALM 145:3,5

Father, help me to think magnificently about You—
Your glory and grace, Your greatness and goodness, Your
peace and power. I acknowledge that my prayer is like dip-
ping water from the ocean with a teaspoon. Whatever I
receive of Your infinite wisdom and guidance, it is infini-
tesimal in comparison to Your limitless resources. So I
come humbly and gratefully to receive from You . . . to
draw from Your divine wisdom what I need for today's decisions and opportunities.

Help me, Lord, to keep Your perspective in what I
say and do. Equip me with fervent diligence and fresh enthusiasm. I commit this day to loving and serving You
with all my heart, soul, mind, and strength. Help me to
draw on the spiritual riches You have given me. May I not
live like a pauper when You have placed at my disposal
unqualified grace, unlimited joy, unfettered hope, and un-
ending peace. Through Christ, who became poor that
through His poverty we might become rich (2 Corinthians 8:9).

FEBRUARY
12

As you have therefore received Christ Jesus the Lord, so walk in Him, rooted and built up in Him and established in the faith, as you have been taught.

—COLOSSIANS 2:6-7

Gracious Lord, You have placed within me a conscience as the voice of my deep inner self. Over the years, my conscience has been shaped by what I have learned to be true and right. I thank You for a conscience rooted in the Ten Commandments and guided by Your Spirit. I know that You are the Potter, and my conscience is the clay. Please... will You mold my values after Your way? Refine my conscience, and purify any dross until You can see Your own nature reflected in the refined gold of Your priorities of righteousness, justice, and mercy.

Father, continue to speak to me through my conscience. And may I work out in my actions what You have worked into the fiber of my character. I commit myself anew to seek Your guidance and follow it this day. Alarm me with a divinely inspired discomfort when I drift from You. Disturb me with discontent when I settle for less than truth and honesty. Expose any hypocrisy or slick manipulation of others. Give me a cleansed conscience that will keep me sensitive to You... through Christ, our liberating Lord and Savior.

You are my God, and I will praise You; You are my God, and I will exalt you.

— PSALM 118:28

Holy Father, as I begin this new day I want to reaffirm my commitment to exalting You by seeking to uphold righteousness in my life. I know that righteousness comes from being right with You. That's why I want to humbly confess whatever may keep me from being in a right relationship with You both in my personal life and my work. Forgive me for the idols of my heart.

I also acknowledge that righteousness involves how I treat other people. Forgive me when I am insensitive to their needs. How will I be righteous in my decisions and actions without seeking and then doing Your will? Forgive me, Lord, for any self-sufficiency that makes it difficult for me to be accountable to You.

In this bracing moment of a fresh encounter with You, I gratefully accept that it is by faith in You that I am made righteous in You. I realize Your utmost desire is that I humbly trust You and follow Your guidance in all that I say and do. Empower me today, Lord, to do what You would want me to. Show me the way!

FEBRUARY
14

*I have called upon You, for You will hear me,
O God. . . . Show Your marvelous lovingkindness by Your right hand, O You who save those
who trust in You.*

—PSALM 17:6-7

Lord, I am greatly encouraged to know that even as great a leader as Abraham Lincoln expressed his dependence on prayer to sustain him in difficult and challenging times. He said, "I have been driven many times to my knees by the overwhelming conviction that I had nowhere to go but prayer. My own wisdom and that of all about me seemed insufficient for the day."

Thank You, Father, for the gift of prayer. When problems pile up and pressures mount, I am so grateful that I, too, have a place to turn. And You are there waiting for me, offering Your grace for grim days and Your strength for my struggles. How good it is to know that I am not alone. I can be honest with You about my insufficiencies and discover the sufficiency of Your wisdom given in very specific and practical answers to my deepest needs.

Help me to spend more time listening to Your answers than I do in my lengthy explanations to You of my problems. I dedicate this day to seeking Your guidance, following Your direction, and doing my best to serve according to Your will.

FEBRUARY
15

The LORD is my strength and my shield; my heart trusted in Him, and I am helped; therefore my heart greatly rejoices.

— PSALM 28:7

Almighty God, You know what I seek before I ask You, and yet, You encourage me to seek, knock, and ask. I know that when I truly seek You and really desire Your will, You will guide me in what to ask.

I anticipate that this day will be filled with challenges that will test my knowledge and experience. I know that I dare not trust in my own understanding. In the quiet of this moment, then, fill my inner well with Your Spirit. My deepest desire is to live today for Your glory and by Your grace.

I praise You that it is Your desire to give good gifts to your children. You give strength and courage when we seek You above everything else. You guide those who are humble and teach them Your way. Your inspiration opens our minds and astounds us with new insight and fresh ideas we would not conceive without Your blessing.

Indeed, You are my strength and my shield. May my heart trust and rejoice in You today. Through Him who came that our joy may be full.

FEBRUARY
16

Your Father knows the things you have need of before you ask Him.

—MATTHEW 6:8

Almighty God, infinite, eternal, and unchangeable, full of love and compassion, abundant in grace and truth, I praise You for being the faithful initiator and inspiration of prayer. I need not search for You because You have already found me; I need not ask for Your presence because You already are impinging on my mind and heart; I need not convince You of my concerns because You know what I need even before I ask.

Lord, give me today a humble and receptive mind. Awe and wonder grip me as I consider that You want to use me to accomplish an aspect of Your plan in this world. Because of the inadequacy of my understanding, I come before You and ask that You infuse me with Your wisdom.

You have given me this quiet moment to receive the Holy Spirit, Your indwelling presence. I confess that my most urgent need is for a fresh infilling of the Spirit. As You have freed me to acknowledge my emptiness, please, Lord, fill me with power for Your glory's sake.

FEBRUARY
17

Be kindly affectionate to one another with brotherly love, in honor giving preference to one another . . . distributing to the needs of the saints, given to hospitality.

—ROMANS 12:10,13

Father, the day ahead is filled with details that can easily confuse and misdirect me. Reveal Your will for what is best for me to do today. I yield my mind to think, and then communicate Your thoughts. Invade my attitudes with Your patience so that I will be able to work effectively with others—especially those who differ with me. Help me to listen to others as attentively as I want them to listen to me.

You have revealed in Scripture, through the generations, and in my own experience, that You pour out Your power when there is unity, mutual esteem, and oneness.

Bless me with Your Spirit so that I may disagree without being disagreeable, share my convictions without being contentious, and lift up truth without putting others down. Help me to seek to convince without coercion, persuade without power moves, motivate without manipulation. May I trust You unreservedly and encourage others unselfishly.

FEBRUARY
18

Cast your burden on the LORD, and He shall sustain you.

— PSALM 55:22

Almighty God, I have great concerns on my heart today, yet I know You are a great Lord who can help me with those concerns. My work, unfinished projects, and unresolved perplexities weigh heavily on me. Uncertainty about the future and my inability to solve everything reminds me of my human limitations. And worries about loved ones and friends occupy my thoughts.

Help me to cast my burdens upon You, and stop trying to manage my burdens in my own strength. In this quiet moment of prayer I deliberately commit each one of my burdens, large or small, into Your gracious care. Help me not to snatch them back. And give me an extra measure of Your wisdom, insight, and discernment as I tackle the challenges of this day.

Make this a productive day in which I live with confidence that You will guide my thinking, unravel my difficulties, and empower my decisions. I am ready for this day, Lord, and I intend to live it with freedom and joy.

FEBRUARY
19

I delight in Your law.

— PSALM 119:70

Sovereign God, I praise You for my accountability to You. You are a God of judgment as well as grace. If You did not care, life would have no meaning. I thank You that You have given me the basis on which I will be judged each hour, and at the end of each day. You want me to know what is required of me so I can pass Your daily examination with flying colors.

Your commandments are in force as much now as when You gave them to Moses. I know that You require me to do justly, love mercy, and walk humbly with You. Integrity and faithfulness have not gone out of style; nor has absolute trust in You ceased to be the secret for personal peace. Help me to trust in You daily, and judge me by the extent that I have put my trust in You for guidance in making my decisions.

Gracious God, as I receive Your judgment, I also seek Your forgiveness and a new beginning. May Your forgiveness give me the courage to seek first Your rule and righteousness. In the name of Jesus, who died that I might know, that in spite of everything, I am loved and forgiven.

FEBRUARY
20

Rejoice in the Lord always. Again I will say, rejoice!

— PHILIPPIANS 4:4

Almighty God, I thank You for this moment of quiet in which I can reaffirm whose I am and why I am here. Once again I commit myself to You as Sovereign Lord of my life. I spread out before You the specific tasks I must fulfill today, and I claim Your presence and guidance in all my thoughts, words, and actions. Help me to draw on the supernatural resources of Your Spirit, which can give me divine wisdom, penetrating discernment, and indomitable courage.

Thank You for my emotions. With them I can feel life to the fullest. But You know how my feelings get burdened down with the impressions of human need. Open my eyes to Your great goodness and providing care. I trust You, Lord, and claim the promise that You will be with me always. So, now and all through this day, I want to rejoice in You while I live in my circumstances. Accept my rejoicing praise now as I review the specific people and situations for which I can rejoice immediately so that eventually I can rejoice in all things.

FEBRUARY
21

Commit your way to the LORD, trust also in Him, and He shall bring it to pass. . . . Rest in the Lord, and wait patiently for Him.

—PSALM 37:5,7

Lord, I take these words of the psalmist as my strategy for living in the pressure of today. Before the problems pile up and the demands of the day hit me, I deliberately take this moment to commit my way to You, to trust in You, to rest in You, and wait patiently for You.

Nothing is more important than being in an honest, open, receptive relationship with You. Everything I need to live as Your disciple comes in fellowship with You. I am awed by the fact that You know and care about me, and I am humbled that You have chosen me to carry out the tasks I will do today. In response, I want to be spiritually fit for my responsibilities. Thus I turn over to Your control my life, my relationships, and all the duties You have entrusted to me. I trust You to guide me; I rest in Your security and strength. I will not run ahead of You nor lag behind, but will walk with You in Your timing and pacing toward Your goals.

May the serenity and peace I feel at this moment sustain me throughout this day. I thank You, in advance, for a great day filled with incredible surprises of sheer joy.

FEBRUARY
22

George Washington's birthday prayer
for the United States of America
exactly as it is preserved in the
chapel at Valley Forge.

Almighty God: We make our earnest prayer that Thou wilt keep the United States in Thy holy protection; that Thou wilt incline the hearts of the citizens to cultivate a spirit of subordination and obedience to the government, and entertain a brotherly affection and love for one another and for their fellow citizens of the United States at large. And finally that Thou wilt most graciously be pleased to dispose us all to do justice, to love mercy, and to demean ourselves with that charity, humility, and pacific temper of mind which were the characteristics of the Divine Author of our blessed religion, and without a humble imitation of whose example in these things, we can never hope to be a happy Nation. Grant our supplication, we beseech Thee, through Jesus Christ our Lord.

FEBRUARY
23

*Through the Lord's mercies we are not con-
sumed, because His compassions fail not. They
are new every morning; great is Your faithfulness.*

— LAMENTATIONS 3:22-23

Almighty God, whose mercies are new every
morning and whose presence sustains me through the day,
I seek to glorify You in all that I do and say.

You provide me with strength for the day, guidance
for my decisions, vision for the way, courage in adversity,
unfailing empathy, and unlimited love. You have
promised to never leave nor forsake me, and You have
said You will never require more of me than You enable
me to accomplish.

I want to dedicate this day to discerning and doing
Your will. I give You my mind; think Your thoughts in it.
I give You my heart; express Your love and encouragement
through it. And I give You my voice; speak Your truth
through it.

Thank You, dear God, for Your continual faithfulness to me. May Your attribute become my attitude.
When this day is done, my hope is that I will have been
faithful.

FEBRUARY
24

The LORD your God in your midst, the Mighty One, will save; He will rejoice over you with gladness, He will quiet you in His love, He will rejoice over you with singing.

— ZEPHANIAH 3:17

Dear God, thank You for Your constant presence in My life. I am humbled when I consider that the Sovereign of the universe cares enough to rejoice over me and quiet me with His love.

I also marvel at Your provision for me. Because Your strength is unlimited, my inner well never has to be empty. Your strength is artesian, constantly surging up to exactly what I need in every moment. You give me supernatural wisdom that supersedes my knowledge. You provide emotional equipoise when I am under pressure. You engender resoluteness in my will and vision when my responsibilities become demanding.

Father quiet my heart with Your unqualified, indefatigable love. Provide me with confidence, security, and peace. Enable me to have absolute trust in Your faithfulness. You make me stable and secure. Nothing can separate me from Your love in Christ. Whatever I go through today will be used to deepen my relationship with You and help me grow in Your grace.

February
25

Oh, give thanks to the LORD! Call upon His name; make known His deeds among the peoples.

—PSALM 105:1

Gracious Lord, You have created me to know, love, and serve You. Thanksgiving is the memory of my heart. You have shown me that gratitude is the parent of all other virtues. Without gratitude my life misses the greatness You intended and remains proud, self-centered, and small. Thanksgiving is the thermostat of my soul, opening me to the inflow of Your Spirit and the realization of even greater blessings.

I begin this day with a gratitude attitude: for the gift of life, intellect, emotion, will, strength, fortitude, and courage. I am privileged to live in this free land so richly blessed by You.

But I also thank You for the problems that make me more dependent on You for Your guidance and strength. When I have turned to You in the past, You have given me the skills I needed. Thank You, Lord, for taking me where I am with all my human weaknesses, and using me for Your glory. You pour out Your wisdom and vision when with humility I call out to You for help. I am profoundly grateful, Lord!

FEBRUARY
26

Call upon Me in the day of trouble; I will deliver you. — PSALM 50:15

Sovereign Lord, my help in all the triumphs and defeats of life, and all the changes and challenges of each day, You are my Lord in all seasons and for all reasons. I can come to You when life makes me glad or sad. There is no place or circumstance beyond Your control.

Wherever I go, You are there waiting for me. You are already at work with people before I encounter them. You prepare solutions for life's complexities and are ready to help me resolve conflicts even before I ask You. And so, I claim Your promise given through Jeremiah, "Call to Me, and I will answer you, and show you great and mighty things, which you do not know" (Jeremiah 33:3).

Lord, I want to do my work this day in such a way that it will be an expression of my love for You. May my only goal be to please You in what I say and accomplish. And thank You for giving me Your strength to endure and Your courage to triumph in tasks great and small . . . done for the good of all.

Trust in the LORD with all your heart, and lean not on your own understanding; in all your ways acknowledge Him, and He shall direct your paths.

— PROVERBS 3:5-6

Dear God, my Creator, Sustainer, and Strength, You have given me the gift of life, blessed me with this new day, and given me work to do for Your glory. May three words—admit, submit, and commit—be the equation of excellence in my work today.

Father, I admit my need of Your insight and inspiration. You never intended that I should depend only on my own intellect and understanding. I humbly place my total dependence on Your power to maximize the use of the talents You have entrusted to me.

Sovereign of my life, I submit to You the specific challenges and opportunities before me. I accept Your absolute reign and rule in my mind. Guide me, Lord, and thank You for the peace of mind I have when I submit my needs to You.

Source of my courage, I unreservedly commit to You my life and the decisions to be made today. I relinquish my control and intentionally ask You to take charge.

Thank You, Lord, that Your grace and mercy are such that I can never ask too much.

FEBRUARY
28

Rejoice always, pray without ceasing, in every-thing give thanks; for this is the will of God in Christ Jesus for you.

— 1 THESSALONIANS 5:16-18

Gracious Father, whose presence and power is revealed to the heart that longs for Your guidance, to the mind that humbly seeks Your truth . . . I ask that this time of prayer be an authentic experience of communion with You that issues into an inspiring conversation with You throughout the day.

I seek to live in Your presence continually, to think of You consistently, and to trust You constantly. I urgently need Your wisdom for the work that's before me today. I have discovered this comes only in a reliant prayer relationship with You. You've taught me that prayer enlarges my mind and heart so that they can be channels for the flow of Your Spirit.

As I move through this day, may I see each problem, perplexity, or person as an opportunity to practice Your presence and accept Your perspective and patience. I don't want to forget You, but if I do, interrupt my thoughts and bring me back into an awareness that You are waiting to bless me and equip me for the tasks that lay ahead. Thus, may my work be my worship this day.

FEBRUARY
29
〜✦〜

*God be merciful to us and bless us, and cause
[Your] face to shine upon us. That Your way
may be known on earth, Your salvation among
all nations.*

— PSALM 67:1-2

Almighty God, in the quiet of this magnificent
moment of conversation with You I dedicate this day; I
want to live it to Your glory.

I praise You that it is Your desire to give Your presence and blessings to those who ask You. You give
strength and power to Your people when we seek You
above anything else. You guide the humble and teach
them Your way. Help me to humble myself as I begin this
day so that no self-serving agenda or self-aggrandizing attitude will block Your blessings to me or to other people
through me. Speak to me so that I may speak with both
the tenor of Your truth and the tone of Your grace.

Make me maximum by Your Spirit for the demanding responsibilities and relationships of this day. I
say with the psalmist, "Let all those rejoice who put their
trust in You; let them shout for joy, because You defend
them; let those also who love Your name be joyful in You"
(Psalm 5:11).

MARCH
1

Hear my cry, O God; attend to my prayer.

—PSALM 61:1

Dear God, this prayer began with You. You have given me the desire to pray. Guide me as I move through the steps of prayer as conversation with you.

I praise You Lord for Yourself, and my adoration is for the way You have allowed me to know You through Your Son, Jesus Christ my Lord.

Hear my confession of anything that stands between You and me or between me and any other person. Guide my confession from the depth of my heart. Forgive my sins of omission and commission. Thank You for the assurance of pardon through the cross of Calvary.

Guide my reflection about the needs of family, friends, people in special need, the sick, and those in authority. Especially, I intercede for _____.

I surrender all my concerns and worries, hopes and hurts, problems and perplexities, fears and frustrations. Particularly, I pray for _____.

Now I commit this day to You. Help me make the most of it. I trust You to show me the way. Empower me with Your strength. My motto for today stirs my courage: "You are my light and my salvation; whom shall I fear? You are the strength of my life; of whom shall I be afraid?" (Psalm 27:1, adapted). In Jesus' name. Amen.

MARCH
2

*For it is the God who commanded light to shine
out of darkness who has shone in our hearts to
give the light of the knowledge of the glory of
God in the face of Jesus Christ.*

— 2 CORINTHIANS 4:6

God, of grace and glory, thank You for the rest of
the night and the fresh energy to begin a new day. As the
brightness breaks through the clouds of the morning sky,
illuminate my heart with Your own darkness-dispelling
presence. Drive away the clouds of doubt that question
Your faithfulness in trying circumstances and the clouds of
fear that make me cautious when I need to be courageous.

I know I can make a pretty small package when I get
all wrapped up in myself. Set me free from self-concern so
that I may focus on others. Renew my assurance that I am
loved and forgiven by You so that I may be a communicator of Your grace to the people around me. Remind me
that grace is kept only if it is given away. All You have
taught me on the mountaintops of victory or the valleys
of trials has been to help me say to others, "I know what
you're going through—I've been there!" Help me see life
as a school of grace equipping me for a ministry of sharing.

Thank You, Lord, for what I will learn today that will
enable me to help someone who will need just what I've
discovered.

MARCH
3

*Let each of us please his neighbor for his good,
leading to edification.*

—ROMANS 15:2

Gracious God, I ask You to help me keep my priorities straight. You have created me to love people and use things. It's easy, however, to reverse that order—to love things and use people. Or even worse, to sometimes use people as if they were things.

Help me to not lose a sense of the sacredness of the people around me. Often I become insensitive to people's needs and use them as means to accomplish my ends. Open my eyes so that I can see those who are in need of help, and open my heart and make me willing to help.

In this quiet moment, I picture the people of my life. Dilate into sharp focus the face of each of them. Help me truly to see him or her. Now place in my mind loving thoughts about what I could do today to lift burdens, express empathy, or inspire courage. I dedicate myself to the specific words and actions You guide. Don't let me forget. Give me the will to put my prayers into action . . . through Christ, who taught us to do what love demands.

MARCH
4

God has spoken once, twice I have heard this:
that power belongs to God. Also to You, O
LORD, *belongs mercy.*
— PSALM 62:11-12

Lord of all life, I thank You that You are concerned about every area of my life. I receive great assurance from knowing that no problem I face is too big for You, and no detail is too small to escape Your attention. I know I can ask for Your wisdom in my most momentous deliberations and receive Your guidance in the most mundane decisions.

Before I press on with the demands of today, I need to open my mind to You. I say with the psalmist, "Truly my soul silently waits for God" (Psalm 62:1). So often I rush off in all directions before I know what You want me to be and do. Sometimes the communication lines with You get jammed by my flow of words to You without listening to what You have to say to me. Prayer becomes like a telephone conversation in which I hang up on You before You have a chance to respond to the needs and questions I have spread out before you.

Today, Lord, I want to keep the line open and really listen to You. Give me the patience to wait for Your creative insight about how to solve problems and guidance for helping the people of my life.

MARCH
5

*Behold, now is the accepted time; behold, now
is the day of salvation.*
— 2 CORINTHIANS 6:2

Gracious God, You have been faithful to help me when I ask for Your guidance and strength. May I be as quick to praise You for what You have done for me in the past as I am to ask You to bless me in the future. You have been on time and in time in Your interventions.

Thank You, Lord, for Your providential care in my everyday needs. And help me never to take for granted the goodness You so generously pour out upon me.

Lord of the now, I express my excitement over the gift You give me completely to live in each moment today. Thank You for settling the past with forgiveness and the future with assurance. In this quiet moment I realize how delighted I am to be alive. I want to use each moment to savor the gift of life.

You are never finished with me; You will use all that happens to reveal more of Your grace and glory. Help me to live today to the fullest!

MARCH
6

The LORD bless you and keep you; the LORD
make His face shine upon you, and be gracious
to you; the LORD lift up His countenance upon
you, and give you peace.

—NUMBERS 6:24-26

Holy God, help me to be ever mindful of Your presence in every moment of this day. May I practice Your presence by opening my mind to think Your thoughts. Make this be a day filled with surprises in which You intervene with solutions to my problems, and, with superlative strength that replenishes my limited human endurance. Fill me with expectancy of what You will do in and through me today.

I claim Isaiah's promise, "You will keep him in perfect peace whose mind is stayed on You" (Isaiah 26:3). Stay my mind on You so I may know Your lasting peace of mind and soul. You know how easily I can become distracted; often hours will pass without thought of You or Your will in my work. In those times, invade my mind and remind me You are in charge and I am here to serve and please You.

Lord, keep my mind riveted on You throughout this day so that I might draw from Your unlimited wisdom for all that I say and do. May I have in me the mind of Christ, in whose name I pray.

MARCH
7

Be anxious for nothing, but in everything by prayer and supplication, with thanksgiving, let your requests be made known to God; and the peace of God, which surpasses all understanding, will guard your hearts and minds through Christ Jesus.

—PHILIPPIANS 4:6-7

Gracious God, the day stretches out before me filled with more to do than it seems possible to accomplish. The rigors of responsibilities and the pressures of people weigh heavily upon me. I humbly confess that in the midst of the needs before me, my greatest need is to renew my relationship with You with an unreserved commitment of my life to You.

Thank You for the confidence I can know when I commit to You my worries and fears; I am grateful for and appreciate Your amazing grace and abundant guidance.

In this quiet moment, I want to renew my commitment to You as my Lord and Savior, my strength and courage, my guide and inspiration. I commit all my relationships to You; help me to communicate Your hope and encouragement to the people around me. And I commit my work to You; help me to fulfill my responsibilities with a diligence and excellence that glorifies You.

MARCH
8

Be still, and know that I am God; I will be exalted among the nations, I will be exalted in the earth!

— PSALM 46:10

Holy God, Your call to prayer startles me. Be still? In a world like this? I fear I've become addicted to the blaring of the television, the noise pollution inflicted by the screeching sounds of society, the angry voices of argumentative people. Talk is cheap. I often contribute to its devaluation by talking before I know what I want to say.

Be still? You know how much I need to experience an inner stillness filled with Your peace. Remind me again, Lord, that the Hebrew words of this challenge to be still translate into the idea of letting go . . . leaving off . . . letting up. I want to do that consistently throughout this day. Loosen my tight grip on everything and everyone. I open the floodgates of my mind and heart so I can receive Your serenity.

Lord, I do want to know You and exalt You. My deepest desire is to know what You desire; my lasting pleasure is to please You. Be exalted in my life. I will be still, but please, Lord, don't be still. Speak to me through the thoughts You now instigate in my receptive, attentive mind.

MARCH
9

If anyone is in Christ, he is a new creation; old things have passed away; behold, all things have become new.

— 2 CORINTHIANS 5:17

Gracious God of new beginnings, who makes all things new and fills me with newness of life, I thank You for the fresh start You have given me in this day.

Forgive me for my past failures and sins. Help me to claim Your love and forgiveness through Christ and the cross. Give me the freedom to forgive myself and really believe that there is no condemnation for those who are in Christ. Thank You for a fresh start today.

I trust You, Lord, to guide and provide. Give me viable hope and vibrant expectancy as I confront the problems and issues before me. I need You, Father, for my own strength, ability, and experience are inadequate.

Give me a vision of what I could be and do if, in total trust to You, I receive Your wisdom, knowledge, insight, and inspiration. Fill me with Your Spirit and help me to remain steadfast as I seek to do Your will in every opportunity placed before me. Through Christ who died that I might be a new creation.

MARCH
10

*I am Your servant; give me understanding, that
I may know Your testimonies.*
— PSALM 119:125

Blessed God, You have elected me to glorify You
through the calling You have given me. Help me to remain focused on my role as a servant—one who can lift
up and encourage others by serving them. I know my sole
purpose is to accept Your absolute Lordship over my life
and give myself totally to the work of each day.

Give me the enthusiasm that comes from knowing
that I am exactly where You need me in Your sovereign
plan for my life.

Lord, help me to humble myself and always be
ready to ask how I may serve. I know that happiness
comes not from having things and getting recognition,
but from carrying out Your will in my work and relationships. Help me to delight in the great paradox of life as
You designed it to be: The more I give myself away, the
more I can receive of Your love.

In the Name of Him who came not to be served but
to serve, and to give His life that I might live—now and
forever.

MARCH
11

Where can I flee from Your presence? . . . If I take the wings of the morning, and dwell in the uttermost parts of the sea, even there Your hand shall lead me.

—PSALM 139:7,9-10

Almighty God, I thank You today for Your omnipresence and omniscience. It is a comfort and a challenge to realize that You are not only everywhere but You also know everything. There is no place I can go to escape You, but also, there is no place devoid of Your potential grace and guidance.

Father, You know what I am faced with today. Thank You for the comforting truth that I am not alone; You are always with me. And because You know the difficulties that are before me, You can give what I need to be faithful to You and to live out my convictions. In this assurance I commit to You whatever is causing me anxiety or frustration.

Grant me Your vision and Your power, Lord. Think, speak, and act through me. You provide the day; You show the way; Your love and patience in me display. May I know Paul's assurance as I press on to the challenges of this day: "The Lord stood with me and strengthened me" (2 Timothy 4:17).

MARCH
12

*O Lord, You are my God. I will exalt You, I
will praise Your name, for You have done
wonderful things; Your counsels of old are
faithfulness and truth.*

— Isaiah 25:1

Almighty God, whose mercies are new every
morning, I praise You for Your faithfulness. You are the
same yesterday, today, and forever. Thank You for the
strength, security, and serenity You provide in the midst of
the strain and stress of each day.

For this day, Lord, refresh my body and renew my
mind. Give me light when my vision is dim, courage
when I need to be bold, decisiveness when I am tempted
to equivocate, and fresh hope when others are discouraged. Help me to listen to You so that my decisions are
guided by how I perceive You would want me to decide.
Make me an attentive listener to what You have to say
about how I should live. And help me to reach out to
others to affirm that I care . . . with a care that You first
showed to me.

I prayerfully commit this day, Lord, to emulating
Your faithfulness in the work that You have given me to
do. In the name of Christ, who promised light in darkness,
peace in turmoil, hope in discouragement, and joy in the
ups and downs of life.

March
13

The LORD is my strength and my shield; my heart trusted in Him, and I am helped; therefore my heart greatly rejoices.

— PSALM 28:7

Father, thank You for the joy I experience when I receive Your unqualified grace and unlimited goodness. Your joy is so much more than mere happiness that is dependent on circumstances and the attitudes of others. When I allow You to fill me with Your love, an artesian joy floods my mind and heart.

With Your joy, I can face difficulties, deal with impossible situations, and endure the most frustrating problems. You are the source of my strength for the tasks of this day, wisdom for the decisions before me, and encouragement for the challenges ahead of me. You know what I need before I ask You, and You guide me in the way of Your will for me.

May the joy I experience with You radiate on my face and be expressed in my attitudes. This is the day You have made, and I will rejoice and be glad in it! Today I will open my heart to receive the joy of Jesus, in whose name I pray.

MARCH
14

Be strong and of good courage; do not be afraid, nor be dismayed, for the LORD your God is with you wherever you go.

— JOSHUA 1:9

Gracious God, I praise You for the wondrous gift of life and the privilege of living this day to the fullest. You are for me and not against me, and seek to liberate me from anything that would debilitate me in living and working with freedom and joy, peace and productivity.

Thank You for setting me free from any burdens of worry and anxiety so I can remain focused on the challenges and decisions I face today. Thank You that You will give me exactly what I need to serve You with excellence each hour. I claim Your promises to give me strength that endures, peace in the pressures, light for the way, wisdom for the choices, and love for those whom I meet today.

Today I will face my problems, unwrap them and seek Your wisdom to understand their component parts, spread them out before You, and thank You in advance for what You will do. I will follow Your orders for what You reveal I am to do and then stand by to watch Your miracles. Through Christ, through whom all things are possible.

MARCH
15

Listen . . .

— ACTS 13:16

Today my prayer is to listen to the Lord's fear-dispelling words to me. "Fear not, I am with you. I will never leave nor forsake you. You are Mine for eternity. Seek to please only Me, and you'll have nothing and no one to fear. Face your fears, retrace them to their root in your soul, displace them with My indwelling presence, and erase them with an assurance of My forgiving love. Love yourself as I love you. I have healed your frightening memories.

"My love casts out fear. You don't have to worry about being inadequate ever again. I am your strength, wisdom, and courage. When others reject you, be sure of My unqualified love for you.

"Let go of your own control and humbly trust Me to guide you each step of the way. You have the gift of imagination to picture and live My best for your life. Don't spend your life worrying about sickness and death—live your life to the fullest now. You don't need fear to manipulate people any more. You are free to motivate them with love. And be sure of this—the 'good work' I have begun in you will be completed. You have nothing to fear. I love you!"

MARCH
16

*The LORD searches all hearts, and understands
every intent of the thoughts.*

— 1 CHRONICLES 28:9

Almighty God, from whom no secrets are hidden,
I come to You humbly and with a longing to be in a right
relationship with You. If there is anything between us that
needs Your forgiveness and cleansing, I confess it to You
now. If there is any broken relationship with others that
needs healing, I ask for Your reconciling power. If I have
done or said anything that has hurt or maliciously distressed others, help me make restitution. And if there is
any area of my responsibilities in which I have resisted
Your will and guidance, I open myself to Your Spirit anew.

Father, You have shown me time and again how crucial it is for me to be an open, receptive channel for the
flow of Your power. I commit to You all that I have and
am so that I will think Your thoughts and realize Your
plans for my life.

Accept me as I am in my deep need of You, and
help me to be all that You intend me to be for Your glory
today.

MARCH
17

I arise today, through God's might to uphold me, God's wisdom to guide me, God's eye to look before me, God's ear to hear me, God's hand to guard me, God's way to lie before me and God's shield to protect me.

— SAINT PATRICK

Gracious Father, I thank You that You know my needs before I ask for Your help, but have ordained that in the asking I would find release from the anxiety of carrying the burdens of life on my shoulders. Help me to remember that You are the instigator of prayer. It begins with You, moves into my heart, and then returns to You in petitions You have refined and guided me to ask.

I never cease to be astonished that You have chosen to do Your work through me. Remind me throughout this day to yield myself in prayer so that my mind is directed by Your guidance for the matters I face. I say with the psalmist, "You are my rock and my fortress; therefore, for Your name's sake, lead me and guide me" (Psalm 31:3). With those words I see prayer in a whole new perspective: It's the method by which You brief me on Your plans and bless me with Your power.

May this whole day be filled with magnificent moments of turning to You so that for Your purposes, I may receive vision to do that which is most pleasing to You.

MARCH
18

~~~

[Praying the Scriptures in the first-person singular is a wonderful way to personalize them. Paul's prayer for the Ephesians in his epistle to them (3:14-21) becomes a powerful prayer for us to pray for ourselves.]

For this reason I bow my knees to the Father of our Lord Jesus Christ, from whom the whole family in heaven and earth is named, that He would grant me, according to the riches of His glory, to be strengthened with might through His Spirit in the inner man, that Christ may dwell in my heart through faith; that I, being rooted and grounded in love, may be able to comprehend with all the saints what is the width and length and depth and height—to know the love of Christ, which passes knowledge; that I may be filled with all the fullness of God.

Now to Him who is able to do exceedingly abundantly above all that I ask or think, according to the power that works in me, to Him be glory in the church by Christ Jesus throughout all ages, world without end. Amen.

MARCH
19

Your ears shall hear a word behind you, saying,
"This is the way, walk in it."

—ISAIAH 30:21

Gracious Lord God, I claim Your promise given through the prophet Isaiah and dedicate this day to walking humbly with You. I commit my mind and heart to listening attentively to You. Speak to me so that what I speak may be an echo of Your voice, which has sounded in the depths of my soul. Grant me the willingness of a mind tuned to the frequency of Your Spirit's guidance. Free me of any thoughts that may have not been refined by carefully listening to You. I ask these things so that all through this day I may heed Your words: "This is the way, walk in it."

Lord, I look ahead to the work of this day in the assurance that You are in control and that You can accomplish Your plans through me if I will just trust You. I admit my total dependence on You to give me strength and courage. With that in mind, I ask that You bless me and keep me, make Your face shine upon me, lift up Your countenance before me, and grant me Your peace.

Put off the old man with his deeds, and . . . put
on the new man who is renewed in knowledge
according to the image of Him who created
him.

— COLOSSIANS 3:9-10

Sovereign Lord of my life, I thank You for Your
scriptural reminders of my need to repent—to return to
my real self for an honest inventory, and to return to You
with a humble and contrite heart.

Forgive my sins of omission: the words and deeds
You called me to do and I neglected. Forgive also my sins
of commission: the times I turned away from Your clear
and specific guidance, and when I knowingly rebelled
against Your management of my life and Your desire for
righteousness.

Show me myself in my relationships. Convict me
about any selfishness, self-glorification, or self-serving attitudes that are holding up Your progress in my life and in
my associations. Help me to write out on a piece of paper
what they are and then, as an offering to You, burn the
paper in affirmation that I want to be different. Then help
me write out what I would do if I knew I could not fail in
serving You and others.

Arouse me, Lord, and call me to spiritual renewal.
Awaken me to my accountability to You for all that I do
in my life. Thank You for Your atoning grace . . . and for
the opportunity for a new beginning. In the name of
Christ, who makes all things new.

MARCH
21

Whatever you do in word or deed, do all in the name of the Lord Jesus, giving thanks to God the Father through Him.
— COLOSSIANS 3:17

Lord Jesus Christ, I pray that my work today will be an expression of my faith. It's with that thought in mind that I renew my commitment to excellence in all that I do. Help me to see my duties as opportunities to glorify You and carry out Your will.

Grant me this day a profound sense of Your peace—a true peace that comes from complete trust in You and dependence on Your guidance. Free me of anything that would distract or disturb me as I give myself to the tasks and challenges of today—all of which I know You have entrusted to me for Your purposes.

Today I want to live my life as an expression of Your love rather than as an effort to earn or deserve Your love. I have tried about everything to prove my worth. Nothing satisfies. I am weary of doing the right thing because of guilt and not grace. Thank You for the limitless power of Your love, which sets me free from a "guilted cage" to fly and soar to new heights of joyous praise today.

MARCH
22

The joy of the LORD is your strength.

—NEHEMIAH 8:10

Lord God, I thank You for the energy-releasing power of Your Spirit. Life's challenges and difficulties so often are able to cut trenches in the heart. These can be riverbeds for the flow of discouragement or joy. In this moment of prayer, I ask that Your joy overflow the banks of my heart.

Nehemiah expressed this assurance when the Israelites were faced with the arduous task of rebuilding Jerusalem's walls after the exile. He told them, "The joy of the LORD is your strength." Only You, Lord, could give the Israelites what they needed to persist and endure.

The same is true for me in my work today. I don't always find joy in my work; sometimes it is demanding and exasperating. But I can bring *Your* joy to my work—a joy that lasts, a joy that bursts forth from Your love, forgiveness, and hope.

Thank You, Lord, for making Yourself available to me as a source of never-ending joy. Fill me with all joy and peace in believing, that I may abound in hope by the power of the Holy Spirit (Romans 15:13).

MARCH
23

Should we feel at times disheartened and discouraged, a simple movement of the heart toward God will renew our powers. Whatever He may demand of us, He will give us at the moment the strength and courage that we need.

— FRANCOIS DE FENELON

O God, my help in ages past, free me to be open to Your gift of hope for years to come. Particularly I pray for a lively hopefulness for today.

Grant that I may not allow my experience of You in the past to make me think You are predictable or limited in what You can do today.

Help me not to become so familiar with Your customary daily blessings that I lose a sense of expectancy for Your special interventions in the challenges of this day. Today I will expect great things from You and will attempt great things for You.

Thank You that a clear vision of what You can do with my needs and the problems around me, multiplied by total trust in You, will equal a great day. Your work, done in Your way, will never lack Your resources. I can't wait to see what You will do today. I press on with excitement in the power of Jesus.

MARCH
24

Love your enemies, do good, and lend, hoping for nothing in return; and your reward will be great, and you will be sons of the Highest. For He is kind to the unthankful and evil. Therefore be merciful, just as your Father also is merciful.

—LUKE 6:35-36

Almighty God, ultimate Judge of all, free me from the tendency to think less of others when they do not agree with me. Help me to not question their character nor quietly condemn them when they don't measure up to my ideals. And remind me that I am not justified in refusing to pray for people simply because I'm not in agreement with them. I realize it's easy for me self-righteously to neglect in my prayers the very people who most need Your blessing.

Give me Samuel's heart; he said, "Far be it from me that I should sin against the LORD in ceasing to pray for you" (1 Samuel 12:23). Remind me that You alone have the power to change the minds and hearts of people if I am faithful to pray for them. Make me an intercessor for all those whom You have placed on my heart—including those whom I may have previously condemned with my judgments. I pray this in the name of Jesus, who, with Moses and the prophets, taught that we should do to others what we would want them to do to us.

MARCH
25

Our Father in heaven, hallowed be Your name.
Your kingdom come. Your will be done on earth
as it is in heaven.
— MATTHEW 6:9-10

God, give me the desire to do what I already know of Your will, so that I may know more of it and make it my will. I want to be a positive, open, receptive person who willingly receives Your guidance for each new challenge. You have shown me that discovery of Your will comes from consistent communion with You. And I also know that such communion is vital for helping me to prepare for all the big decisions ahead of me in the future.

I recognize that today's obedience results in tomorrow's guidance. Action is the nerve center of my spiritual life. Motivate me to do what You have called me to do in the mundane details of life so that I will be ready to do Your will when momentous opportunities arise. Keep my soul fit with the consistent practice of Your presence. And may prayer throughout the day be as natural as breathing.

I am filled with awe and wonder . . . gratitude and praise . . . that You who are Creator of the universe and Sovereign Lord of all nations would use me to carry out Your will in my small realm of influence. Through Christ, through whom I am reconciled with You forever and recommissioned to serve You daily.

MARCH
26

With me it is a very small thing that I should be judged by you or by a human court. In fact, I do not even judge myself. . . . He who judges me is the Lord. . . . Each one's praise will come from God.

— 1 CORINTHIANS 4:3-5

Help me, O Lord, to have no other gods before me. I say I trust in You, but there are times when my worries and fears expose me to the idols of my heart. Sometimes I find myself preoccupied with what other people think about me; I become more concerned with maintaining my popularity than my spiritual pulse.

Father, help me to abide by the true measurement of humility: not to stoop until I am smaller than myself, but to stand at my real height and compare myself to the greatness You intend for me to achieve.

Stretch my soul today until it is enlarged enough to contain the gift of Your Spirit. Then sound in my soul Your renewed call to serve You with concern for only what *You* think of my performance. Free me from the need for people's approval so that I may more freely give myself away for the needs of others.

In the Name of Christ, who gives me the courage to receive judgment on my life and accept the forgiveness He offers through the cross.

MARCH
27

*O LORD, You are our Father; we are the clay,
and You our potter; and all we are the work of
Your hand.*

— ISAIAH 64:8

Gracious Lord, the divine Potter of my life, my days
are in Your hands. Shape the clay as You have planned.
May the day work out exactly as You have arranged it for
Your glory and my growth. I say with the psalmist, "I delight to do Your will, O my God, and Your law is within
my heart" (Psalm 40:8).

Now, at the beginning of this day, I commit to You
the challenges and decisions before me. I desire to glorify
You, so show me what You desire. With inspired intentionality, I put my relationship with You first and make
my primary goal what is best for Your kingdom.

I pray the words of the familiar hymn as the clay of
my life is placed on Your potting wheel and Your hand
shapes me into the person You intended me to be:

Have thine own way, Lord!
Thou art the potter, I am the clay!
Mold me and make me after Thy will
While I am waiting, yielded and still.

Hymn, "Have Thine Own Way, Lord!"
George C. Stebbins

MARCH
28

I am persuaded that neither death nor life, nor angels nor principalities nor powers, nor things present nor things to come, nor height nor depth, nor any other created thing, shall be able to separate us from the love of God which is in Christ Jesus our Lord.

—ROMANS 8:38-39

Almighty God, You have said that nothing can separate Your children from You. That is both a source of comfort and challenge. I am comforted by Your constant love, forgiveness, and care. And I am challenged by my accountability to You. I am reminded of the scripture that says, "To whom much is given, from him much will be required" (Luke 12:48).

You are the righteous Judge of my words and decisions; help me to seek Your will in all that I do. You have said, "Let him who glories glory in this, that he understands and knows Me, that I am the LORD, exercising lovingkindness, judgment, and righteousness in the earth. For in these I delight" (Jeremiah 9:24). I want to do what delights You. Help me to repent of the pride of ever thinking that I can live my life without Your priorities of righteousness, purity, and truth.

I now commit myself to living this day to Your glory, totally dependent on Your presence and Your power through Jesus Christ my Lord.

MARCH
29

Amazing grace, how sweet the sound
That saved a wretch like me!
I once was lost, but now am found
was blind, but now I see.

—JOHN NEWTON

Almighty God, I praise You for Your amazing grace. Your unlimited love casts out fear, Your unqualified forgiveness heals my memories, Your undeserved faithfulness gives me courage, Your unfailing guidance gives me clear direction, Your presence banishes my anxieties.

You know my needs before I ask You, and Your Spirit gives me the boldness to ask for what You are ready to give.

You enable me to discern the needs of others so I can be a servant. Your love for me frees me to love, forgive, uplift, and encourage the people around me.

I commit this day to be one in which I take the initiative to communicate Your grace to others. Lead on, gracious God; I am ready for a great day filled with Your grace.

MARCH
30

Who has directed the Spirit of the LORD, or as His counselor has taught Him? With whom did He take counsel, and who instructed Him, and taught Him in the path of justice? Who taught Him knowledge, and showed Him the way of understanding?

— ISAIAH 40:13-14

Gracious Father, I humbly fall on the knees of my heart as I answer Isaiah's questions. You alone are the ultimate source of wisdom, knowledge, and guidance.

Forgive me when I use prayer to try to manipulate Your will. Prayer is not a way for me to instruct You, make demands, or barter for blessings.

I confess my total dependence on You not only for every breath I breathe, but also for every ingenious thought I think. You are the author of my vision and the instigator of my creativity.

So I begin this day with thanksgiving that You have chosen me to serve You. All my talents, education, and experiences have been entrusted to me by You. The need before me brings forth the expression of the supernatural gifts You have given to me.

Thank You in advance, Lord, for Your provision of exactly what I will need to serve You this day. I trust You completely, in Jesus' name.

MARCH
31

Rejoice in every good thing which the LORD your God has given to you.

— DEUTERONOMY 26:11

Gracious Father, this is a day for rejoicing over the manifold good things You have given me. Help me to take nothing and no one for granted. As I move through this day, I want to savor the sheer wonder of being alive. Thank You for giving me the ability to think, understand, and receive Your guidance. And I praise You for the people You have placed in my life. Help me to appreciate the never-to-be-repeated miracle of each personality.

I am grateful as well for the challenges I have before me, which compel me to depend on You more. Thank You, too, for the opportunities that are beyond my ability to fulfill so that I might be forced to trust You for wisdom and strength. I rejoice over Your daily interventions to help me; I even rejoice in my problems, for they allow You to show me Your power to provide solutions. Rather than pray, "Get me out of this," help me to pray, "Lord what do You want me to get out of this?" Then free me to rejoice in the privilege of new discoveries.

In all things, great and small, I rejoice in You, gracious Lord of all! Through the indwelling presence and inspiring power of Christ my Savior and Lord.

APRIL

1

As He was now drawing near the descent of the Mount of Olives, the whole multitude of the disciples began to rejoice and praise God with a loud voice ... saying, "Blessed is the King who comes in the name of the Lord!"

—LUKE 19:37-38

Blessed Christ, as on this day I keep the special memory of your entry into Jerusalem, so grant that now and ever You may triumph in my heart to give me courage to enter into the spiritual, moral, and interpersonal Jerusalems that I face each day. I confess I would rather retreat to the quiet of the plains of Galilee than turn my face to Jerusalem. Often I want an easy religion of familiar phrases and hymns, rather than be challenged to face reality as it is and live out my faith in difficult situations, with impossible people and in trying decisions.

Yet I do not want to pray for an easier life, but rather, that You would enable me to be a stronger person. I do not want to pray for tasks equal to my power, but for power equal to my tasks!

May the knowledge of Your forgiveness and love free all the creative strength and power of Your Spirit within me so that I may know Your will and do it in every area of my life.

APRIL
2

*I heard the voice of the LORD, saying, "Whom
shall I send, and who will go for Us?"*

—Isaiah 6:8

Sovereign Lord, may I hear Your passionate, persistent call sounding in my soul as I begin this day: "Whom shall I send?" Everything within me responds with a renewed commitment: "Here am I! Send me."

Help me, Father, to see my work as my divine calling, my mission. Whatever I am called to do today, I want to do my very best for Your glory. My desire is not just to do different things, but to do the same old things differently: with freedom, joy, and excellence.

Give me new delight for matters of drudgery, new patience for people who are difficult, new zest for unfinished details. Be my lifeline in the pressures of deadlines, my rejuvenation in routines, and my endurance whenever I feel exhausted.

May I spend more time talking to You about my life's concerns than I do talking with others about these concerns. And may my communion with You give me deep convictions . . . and the courage to defend them.

Spirit of the living God, fall afresh on me, so that I may serve with fresh dedication today.

APRIL
3

Being found in appearance as a man, He humbled Himself and became obedient to the point of death, even the death of the cross.

—PHILIPPIANS 2:8

Holy Lord God, I stand in awe today as I realize the immense impact of the incarnation. You have gone to the uttermost to love and forgive me. Thank You for the blood of the cross and the assurance that nothing can ever separate me from You because of the once-for-all-time sacrifice of Your only begotten Son.

It is shocking to realize that if I had been the only person alive on the day Christ went to the cross, He would have had to suffer for me, for my sins, for my reconciliation.

What can I do in response? What can I say? Nothing but this: I love You, dear Father, because You first loved me. I say with Isaac Watts,

Were the whole realm of nature mine,
That were a present far too small;
Love so amazing, so divine,
Demands my soul, my life, my all.

APRIL
4

Down beneath the shame and loss
Sinks the plummet of the cross
Never yet abyss was found
Deeper than His love could sound.
                                    —ANONYMOUS

Father, I want to stand at the foot of the cross today and contemplate all that You did for me through Christ's death. I need to get my thinking straight and my feelings sorted out. I'm stunned again as I meditate on the magnitude of what happened during those six hours, and the magnetic power it has for me. The truth of Colossians 1:19-20 captures my thoughts and liberates my feelings. "For it pleased You, Father, that in Christ all the fullness should dwell and by Him reconcile all things to Yourself, by Him, whether things on earth or things in heaven, having made peace through the blood of the cross." Awesome!

Thank You that there was a cross in Your heart before there was a cross on Calvary. You knew what humankind would do with the freedom of will You gave. Rebellion and sin. Pride and self-centeredness. And yet, You sent Christ to reconcile the world to Yourself. That becomes very personal now for me as I realize He died for me. I was saved from the power of sin and death, and daily I am forgiven through the love of the cross.

Now, in this quiet moment, I feel Your nourishing, encouraging, healing love. You have brought me back to complete harmony with You. I could never atone for myself. The cosmic atonement of the cross is my personal assurance that comes from knowing that, in spite of everything, I am loved and forgiven.

It is finished!

—JOHN 19:30

Blessed Savior, because You said, "It is finished!" I need never say, "I'm finished!" Your finished work of redemption means that I can never be finished, defeated, or conquered by sin, fear, or anxiety. Your finished work of salvation on the cross has accomplished forgiveness and deliverance from my sin, reconciliation to the Father, the fulfillment of His judgment, the revelation of His grace, the manifestation of His glory. And wonder of wonders, I have been given the gift of faith to know that You have finished my exoneration and set me free from the power of sin, Satan, and death.

Now it dawns on me that there is another way I need not say, "I'm finished" because of Your finished work on Calvary. My work is never finished because You finished my redemption. I'll never be finished with my calling to share the good news of Your love and forgiveness. Today, I want to pour out myself in practical caring and concern for the people You have put on my agenda today. Help me to communicate what You mean to me. I long to be a firsthand witness to the real meaning of Your cross and resurrection.

In this quiet moment, may Your cross and resurrection be recapitulated in my mind and heart. I long to die to pride and self-centeredness and be resurrected to the new, eternal person You created me to become. Make me an Easter person whose person-to-person encounter with You is expressed by undeniable joy!

APRIL
6

Worthy is the Lamb who was slain to receive power and riches and wisdom, and strength and honor and glory and blessing!

—REVELATION 5:12

Reigning Lord Jesus, my crucified Savior and risen King, I bless and praise You. All that is within me glorifies Your name. I love You Lord for dying for my sins. I claim that through Your shed blood I have been forgiven. Now show me anything I need to confess so I can claim freedom from guilt. Especially, I ask for Your power to liberate me from any repetitive thoughts, habit patterns, or attitudes that keep me from living at full potential for Your glory. Particularly I surrender_____.

Thank You Lord for setting me free to soar today. I ask for a fresh anointing of Your joy so that I may bring gladness into the dull, gray drabness in which so many people live.

Give me a vibrant expectation for how You will intervene in the challenges I face today. I commit myself to seek and do Your will in each moment. But Lord, You know I often blunder ahead without asking for Your guidance. So keep my mind stayed on You and my heart open to You. Because You conquered at Calvary, rose from the dead on Easter, and live to lead Your people to triumph, I can face today's problems and tomorrow's possibilities.

Today I will answer the question—who would be convinced that You are alive and mighty to help those who trust You because of the way I live today?

An Affirmation of Faith Prayer
on Easter

I believe in Jesus Christ as my Savior.

He died on the cross for my sins to set me free of guilt and condemnation. I know that I am loved and forgiven. Old memories of failures and mistakes have been healed forever.

I believe in Christ as my Lord.

He rose from the dead and reigns as my victorious conqueror over death. He liberates me from the fear of death and all lesser fears that may have kept me from living with freedom and joy. I don't have to take life alone.

I believe in Christ as indwelling power.

He has promised to abide in me and I in Him. I invite Him to live in my mind, to think His thoughts through me, to take charge of my will, to guide me to do His will, and to control my emotions to love through me.

I accept the awesome wonder that I am an Easter miracle.

By grace, I have been resurrected from the graves of self-centeredness, worry, and anxiety to live for others. Therefore, I commit my whole life to Christ and will seek to be His faithful and obedient disciple in all my relationships and responsibilities. For me to live is Christ! I am truly alive, now and forever. Hallelujah and Amen!

APRIL
8

LORD, what is man, that You take knowledge of him? Or the son of man, that You are mindful of him?

—PSALM 144:3

I praise You, dear God; You are the same yesterday, today, and forever! Your love is constant and never changes. You have promised never to leave nor forsake me. My confidence is in You and not myself, for I am prone to waver, to fall, and need Your help.

I come to You in prayer not trusting in my goodness, but solely in Your grace. You are my joy when I am down, my strength when I am weak, my courage when I vacillate. You are my security in a world of change and turmoil. Even when I forget You in the rush of life, You never forget me. I know that if I ever feel distant from You, it's because I moved, not You. Thank You for Your faithfulness.

Filled with wonder, love, and gratitude, I commit this day to live for You and by the indwelling power of Your Spirit. Control my mind and give me discernment. Fill me with Your sensitivity to people and their needs, and give me empathy in caring for the troubled souls around me. Give me a boldness to take a stand for what You have revealed as being right and just.

Thank You for the privilege of living this day to the fullest!

APRIL
9

Day by day, dear Lord, of Thee
three things I pray:
To see Thee more clearly,
To love Thee more dearly,
To follow Thee more nearly.

—RICHARD OF CHICHESTER

This is my longing for this new day, dear God. Help me to see You in the beauty of the world around me, in the never-to-be-repeated miracles of Your grace, in the people of my life, and in Your providential care in timely interventions to help me in the circumstances of life. Yes, Lord, I do want to see You more clearly.

I love You not just for what You do for me, but most of all, for who You are. Your lovingkindness, mercy, and faithfulness are my stability in a world of change. You are my help when I am helpless, my hope when I am tired in body and troubled in mind. Yes, Lord, I do want to love You more dearly.

I hear Your summons to follow You sounding in my soul. I commit myself to walk humbly with You through this day. May I neither run ahead of You nor lag behind, but keep pace with You. Help me to know what You desire, and give me the strength to do what love requires. Yes, Lord, I do want to follow You more nearly.

APRIL
10

The heavens declare the glory of God; and the firmament shows His handiwork. Day unto day utters speech.

—PSALM 19:1-2

Almighty God, Sovereign of the universe and Lord of my life, by the revolution of the earth around the sun, You have brought forth a new day. Just as You have made the sun rise, You have made me what I am; just as I cannot take credit for the sunrise, I dare not take pride in what I have made of my life. I can, however, be humbly grateful. To fail to glorify You for either the new day or the miracle You have made of my life over the years would be blasphemy. Help me to praise You both for this new day and the privilege of living life to the fullest. All that I have and am is your gift. This day will be like no other day past or to come. Help me cherish each moment and each hour.

You, who are everlasting Mercy, give me a tender heart toward all those for whom the morning sunrise brings less joy than it does to me, those for whom the beginning of a new day does not bring rejoicing, but anxiety, suffering, or trouble. Free me to do all I can for all whom I can to communicate Your care. As I seek to make this a great day for others I will discover the practical love You want to communicate through my words and actions, deliberations and decisions. I repeat my motto: "This is the day You have made and I will rejoice and be glad in You. Through my Lord and Savior, Jesus Christ."

APRIL

11

*He gives power to the weak, and to those who
have no might He increases strength.*
—Isaiah 40:29

Gracious God, thank You for Your love that never
gives up on me. Help me to discover the power of resting
in You and receiving assurance and encouragement of
Your amazing grace.

Here I am at the beginning of another day; You
know my needs and are prepared to meet those needs with
exactly the right gift of Your Spirit. You are present, impinging with inspiration to lift my spirit, hovering with
hope to press me onward.

All through this day there will be magnificent moments when I overcome the temptation of trying to make
it on my own strength, and instead, yield to the inflow of
Your wisdom, insight, vision, and guidance.

My soul, Lord, is meant to be a container and
transmitter of Your power. I thank You, in advance, for a
stunning day in which I am blessed by being carried by
Your presence ... rather than being bogged down by
trying to carry my own problems.

APRIL
12

[I pray] that they all may be one, as You, Father, are in Me, and I in You; that they also may be one in Us, that the world may believe that You sent Me.

—JOHN 17:20-21

Almighty Father, I know that Your desire is for all Your children to be one in mind and heart. Take charge of the control center of my brain, and think Your thoughts through me, and send to my nervous system the pure signals of Your peace, power, and patience. Give me a mind that is responsive to Your guidance.

Take charge also of my tongue, so that I may speak the truth with clarity, without rancor and anger. May my conversations with others always be an effort to reach agreement rather than simply to win an argument. Help me to think of others in the church as fellow disciples; make me a channel of Your grace to others. And may I respond to Your nudges to communicate affirmation and encouragement to those around me.

May I be intent, Lord, on marching to the cadence of Your drumbeat so that I may walk hand-in-hand with others who hear the drumbeat of Your guidance. Here is my life; invade me with Your calming Spirit, strengthen me with Your powerful presence, and imbue me with Your gift of faith to trust You to bring unity in the diversity present among Your children.

APRIL
13

*Who is so great a God as our God? You are the
God who does wonders; You have declared
Your strength among the peoples.*

—PSALM 77:13-14

Almighty God, thank You for the gift of vibrant
confidence based on vital convictions. I am confident in
Your unlimited power; therefore, at no time am I ever
helpless or hapless. My confidence is rooted in Your commandments; therefore, I am strengthened by Your absolutes that give me enduring values. My courage is based
on the assurance of Your ever-present, guiding Spirit;
therefore, I will not fear. My hope is rooted in trust in
Your reliability; therefore, I will not be anxious. Your interventions in trying times in the past have made me an
experienced optimist for the future; therefore, I will not
spend my energy in useless worry.

You, Lord, have called me to glorify You in the work
I do today. Therefore, I give You my best for this day's responsibilities. You have guided me through difficult times
in the past; therefore, I ask for Your direction in the crucial decisions of today.

Thank You, Sovereign Father, for the courage that
flows from my unshakable confidence in You . . . and You
alone.

APRIL
14

See then that you walk circumspectly, not as fools but as wise, redeeming the time, because the days are evil.

—EPHESIANS 5:15-16

Lord of all life, thank You for the gift of time. You have given me the hours of this day to work for Your glory by serving those around me. Remind me that there is enough time in any one day to do what You want me to accomplish. Release me from that rushed feeling when I overload Your agenda for me with things which You may not have intended for me to crowd into today. Help me, in every matter, to live on Your timing.

Grant me serenity when I feel irritated by trifling annoyances, by temporary frustrations, by little things to which I must give time and attention. May I do what the moment demands, always with a heart of readiness. Also, give me the courage to carve out time for quiet thought and creative planning to focus my attention on the big things I must take care of in my life.

Before I move ahead into today's routine, help me to be silent, wait on You, and receive Your guidance. And may the people I serve and those with whom I work sense that in the midst of pressure and the rough and tumble of life, I have had my mind replenished by listening to You.

APRIL
15

The heavens are Yours, the earth also is Yours;
the world and all its fullness, You have founded
them.

—PSALM 89:11

Almighty God, You have all authority in heaven and on earth. You are the sovereign Lord of my life; in all that I think, say, and do, I want to submit to Your authority.

Help me to see my every task today as an opportunity to serve You. May I commit my every action to You so that You may use it as You wish. Make this a productive day not for my own sake, but for Your glory's sake.

In everything, Lord, give me a positive attitude that exudes hope. In each difficult impasse, help me to seek Your guidance. Draw me closer to You so that I might think Your thoughts, speak Your words, carry out Your actions. May my one desire, above all, be to live as a servant fit for Your use.

Thank You for allowing me that privilege.

APRIL
16

I will remember the works of the LORD; surely I will remember Your wonders of old. I will also meditate on all Your work and talk of Your deeds.

—PSALM 77:11-12

Almighty God, my Creator, Sustainer, and loving heavenly Father, thank You for this moment of profound communication with You. I come to You just as I am . . . with my hurts and hopes, fears and frustrations, problems and perplexities. I also come to You with great memories of how You have helped me so faithfully when I trusted You in the past.

Now, in the peace of Your presence, I sense a fresh touch of Your Spirit. With a receptive mind and a heart wide open, I receive the inspiration and love You give so generously. Make me secure in Your grace, and confident in Your goodness. I need Your power to carry the responsibilities that are upon me today.

Humbly I now ask for divine inspiration in the decisions of this day. Because I am here to please You in all that I do, my hope is that at the end of this day I will hear Your voice sounding in my soul, "Well done, good and faithful servant."

APRIL
17

Knowledge we ask not
Knowledge Thou has lent
But Lord, the will
There lies our bitter need
Give us to build above the deep intent
The deed; the deed!

—JOHN DRINKWATER

Dear Lord, help me to put into action what I believe. You have made faith and works inseparable. Application of my convictions—which are based upon Your holy Scriptures—is my challenge.

You have made faith and works inseparable. Strengthen my will so that I can follow through on what I know You have guided me to say and do in my relationships and responsibilities. Forgive my passive resistance when it comes simply to obeying Your orders. I try to keep my control by what I neglect. In this quiet moment, I reflect on situations in which I know perfectly well what You want. Often, I settle for less than the best because I put off until some distant future what should be done today. I think of people whom I need to forgive, of others I need to encourage, and still others I need to help in practical ways.

You have called me to serve You. The question lingers: "What would I do if I truly loved You with all my heart?"

If we walk in the light as He is in the light, we have fellowship with one another.

—1 JOHN 1:7

Lord Jesus, You are the light of my life. You promised that if I follow You I will not walk in darkness but have the light of life. In Your light I can see the truth, live the truth, and speak the truth.

Master, I want to have Your light penetrate into my relationships. You have shown me that nothing debilitates deep relationships more than pretense. When I pretend to be adequate, a stiffness and strain results in my communication with others. They are forced to pretend with me. I forget that walking in the light shows me who I really am, not just in my weakness but also in my security in You.

Remind me that the key to great relationships is vulnerability, letting people know the growing, sometimes failing, but loved and forgiven person inside my skin. Help me laugh at myself and then laugh with others about the frailties and fallibilities we all share. May I loosen up so I can listen up to the needs people express. Free me from the defenses of superiority and superficiality. Make me real and authentic. May the warmth of Your love melt my icy judgmentalism. When I walk in Your light I can see others as You see them. Lord, thank You for leading me out of loneliness to the privilege of loving and being loved.

The things which are impossible with men are possible with God.

—LUKE 18:27

Lord of all life, lots of people I will meet today seldom read the Bible. Many of them don't pray often. Still others just don't observe Your beauty in the world around them. I will spend my day with these people who don't seem to know much about You. All this is on my mind as I start this day. Help me to live in such a way that people will want to know the reason for the joy I know because of Your love for me. I realize my life is the only Bible some will read today and my attitudes will be the only evidence of what You can do for them if they too trusted You. Make me aware of the image of a Christian I project today.

You will give me many opportunities with people today. Make me a radiant Christian who lights up the grayness of life most people experience. May the happiness I have because of You lift the spirits of people around me. In the negativeness, make me an affirmer; in the grimness, help me share hope; in the boredom, may I infuse the excitement for living You have given me.

I can't wait to see what You are going to do through me to make this a great day for others.

April

20

These things I have spoken to you, that in Me you may have peace.

—John 16:33

Oh God, You have promised to keep me in perfect peace if I allow You to stay my mind on You.

That is the peace I need today. The conflict and tension present in my life threaten to rob me of a calm and restful mind and heart. It is so easy to catch the emotional virus of frustration and exasperation. Help me to remember that Your peace is a healing antidote that can survive in any circumstance.

Provider of Peace, give me the peace of a cleansed and committed heart, a free and forgiving heart, a caring and compassionate heart. May Your deep peace flow into me, calming my impatience and flowing from me to others claiming Your inspiration.

I ask this in the name of the Prince of Peace, who whispers in my soul, "Peace I leave with you, My peace I give to you; not as the world gives do I give to you. Let not your heart be troubled, neither let it be afraid" (John 14:27).

"The mountains shall depart and the hills be removed, but My kindness shall not depart from you, nor shall My covenant of peace be removed," says the LORD, who has mercy on you.

—ISAIAH 54:10

Almighty God, I praise You for Your faithfulness. You sustain me, watch over me, and infuse me with Your wisdom and strength. Above all, You have given me life eternal through Your Son, and I know there is nothing that can separate me from Your love.

I praise You for Your willingness to send the Light of the world to dispel the darkness that once held me captive. Your indefatigable love is incredible. You never give up on me; You persistently pursue me, offering me the way of peace to replace the way of perversity. You offer Your good will to replace my grim willfulness. In spite of everything I do to break Your heart, You remain steadfast with me.

Help me to be as kind to others as You have been to me. To express the same respect and tolerance for the struggles of others as You have expressed in helping to turn my struggles into stepping stones. To understand others as You have understood me.

Thank You again, Lord, for Your great faithfulness.

Precious Lord, take my hand
Lead me on, help me stand;
I am tired, I am weak, I am worn;
Through the storm, through the night
Lead me on to the light.

—THOMAS A. DORSEY

Lord, You have all authority in heaven and on earth. I submit my life to Your authority. Fill my mind with clear convictions that You are in charge of my life and those about whom I am concerned. I surrender myself and them to You.

Now Lord, may this commitment result in a new, positive attitude that exudes joy and hope about what You are going to do today and in the future. I leave the results completely in Your hands. My need is not to get control of my life, but to commit my life to Your control. You know what You are doing, and will only what is best for me.

There is nothing that can happen that You can't use to deepen my relationship with You. So when success comes, help me to be amazed at the way it will develop an attitude of gratitude. When difficulties arise, help me immediately turn to You and receive from You an attitude of fortitude.

All this makes me very excited about the day ahead. I place my hand in Yours and ask You to lead me. It will be a great day if I don't pull away and run off in my own direction. Here's the day; show the way. Here's my hand; help me stand.

APRIL
23

O LORD, my strength and my fortress.

—JEREMIAH 16:19

Lord, I need Your help. I am feeling the strain of stress. My body is agitated by worry and fear. I confess to You my inability to handle it alone.

I surrender my mind to You; take charge of my thoughts. Think Your thoughts through me so that I might respond to my circumstances with peace and patience. I don't want to have a divided mind fragmented from Your control.

Forgive my angers rooted in petulant self-will. Make me a channel, a riverbed, of Your love to others suffering as much stress as I. Help me act on the inspiration You give me rather than stifling Your guidance.

I dedicate my tongue to You so that it will become an instrument of healing. Make me a communicator of love and encouragement as I cheer others on to their best.

Help me to know and do Your will. I commit my schedule to You. Slow me down before I break down. Set me free of the tyranny of acquisitiveness and security in things. I thank You in advance for giving me strength to conquer stress.

APRIL
24

Humble yourselves in the sight of the Lord, and He will lift you up.

—JAMES 4:10

Lord, I need to talk to You about the stress I often feel because of envious competition. I long to be the unique person You created me to be and not anyone else. Forgive me when I envy the gifts, talents, and success of others rather than praise You for all You have given to me. Sometimes I covet the opportunities and skills of others when they seem to exceed my own. I admit that I miss becoming the distinctively different person You have in mind. The limiting formula results: my comparisons with others, multiplied by combative competition, equals the stress of envy.

You do not play favorites or pit people against one another. You are for me and not against me. Your will is that I be the miracle You planned for me to be. Help me set my goals to accomplish Your will for me. I confess that I've been so busy competing with others that I've taken my eyes off You. When You take up residence in my heart the dominant desire is to please You.

You have promised that if I humble myself in Your sight, You will lift me up. I know You will multiply my potential beyond my wildest expectations. So I press on with a liberating formula: an honest recognition of the assets You have given me, multiplied by Your indwelling power, will equal greater excellence without stress today.

APRIL
25

Seek the LORD and His strength; seek His face evermore. Remember His marvelous works which He has done, His wonders, and the judgments of His mouth.

—PSALM 105:4-5

Heavenly Father, I praise You for dividing my life into days. Each morning You give me the opportunity to prepare for a new beginning. You open Your forgiving heart, and offer me a fresh start. With freedom from the past, I can know a hope in You that will last.

Lord, go before me today to show me the way and grant me the courage to endure. If ever I needed Your wisdom and guidance, it is now. I stand on the threshold of a day loaded down with unresolved issues and decisions. I ask for a special anointing of Your sustaining power, that I might bear my responsibilities with diligence and without fear.

I now commit to You this day and all of the challenges and opportunities within it. May I always be aware of Your Spirit impinging on my mind; may I listen to Your voice before I speak ... and speak with echoes of Your tone, tenor, and truth.

APRIL
26

To God our Savior, who alone be glory and majesty, dominion and power, both now and forever.

—JUDE 25

Almighty God, Lord of my life and Sovereign of this world, I humbly confess my need for Your supernatural power. Thank You that You do not tailor my opportunities to my abilities, but rather, that You give me wisdom, strength, and vision to match life's challenges.

Help me to surrender the pride of thinking that I can make it on my own resources. I realize I am totally dependent on You. I could not think a thought, speak a word, or carry out an action without Your constant and consistent blessing.

You, Lord, are the source of all that I am and have. I praise You for the talents, education, and experience You have given me. But I know that You alone can provide the insight, innovation, and inspiration I so urgently need for facing life's problems.

You have told me there is no limit to what You will do to empower me when I trust You completely and give You the glory. I commit this day, then, to glorifying You in all that I say and do.

APRIL
27

*As far as the east is from the west, so far has
He removed our transgressions from us.*

—PSALM 103:12

Almighty Father, the one great need in my life is
for a profound spiritual awakening. Stir my somnolent
soul wide awake to experience Your presence. I praise You
that You have created me to know, love, and serve You,
and that You've placed a longing within me for a deep relationship with You. And I am astonished that even before I ask, You offer Your forgiveness. In spite of
everything I have said or done, You draw me closer to
Your heart and offer me fresh grace.

Thank you, dear God, for Your intervention in
every area of my life. May I use this time of respite now to
turn the issues of this day over to You. I want to be as
quick to thank You for Your provision as I am to ask for
Your help. Knowing that Your involvement in my life is a
constant enables me to face the struggles of this day with
renewed confidence.

I ask You now for the infilling of Your Spirit into my
mind so that I may think Your thoughts, discover Your solutions, and act on Your guidance. Thank You for rejuve-
nating me in this time of prayer.

APRIL
28

Come to Me, all you who labor and are heavy laden, and I will give you rest.

—MATTHEW 11:28

Almighty God, I feel awe and wonder that You have chosen me to serve in the place You have given me in life. May I live this day humbly on the knees of my heart, honestly admitting my human inadequacy and gratefully acknowledging Your power.

Today, Lord, dwell in the secret place of my heart to give me inner peace and security. Help me with Your wisdom and strength as I maintain the relationships and responsibilities You have entrusted to me. Remind me of my accountability to You for all that I say and do. Reveal Yourself to me; be the unseen Friend by my side in every changing circumstance. Give me a fresh experience of Your palpable and powerful Spirit. Banish weariness and worry, discouragement and disillusionment. Often today, may I hear Your voice saying, "Come to Me, all you who labor and are heavy laden, and I will give you rest."

Lord, help me to rest in You and receive the incredible resiliency You provide. Thank You in advance for a truly productive day.

APRIL
29

Give to the LORD the glory due His name; bring an offering, and come before Him. Oh, worship the Lord in the beauty of His holiness!

—1 CHRONICLES 16:29

Sovereign God, gracious Father, blessed Redeemer, inspiring Spirit, I worship You for Your faithfulness, lovingkindness, judgment, and mercy. The offering I bring to my worship is myself. Nothing in my hands I bring; simply to Your grace I cling.

I worship You in wonder and winsomeness, joy and gladness, delight and dependence. The blessedness of belonging to You is the beauty of holiness I have to offer in my worship. All that I have and am belongs to You. The life You have given me is Yours, the blessings You've given me are because of Your goodness, and my triumph in the future is assured only as I trust in You alone.

May this whole day be spent in worship of You. I seek to worship You in my work, my talk, and my thoughts. I commit this day to practicing Your presence in the sublime and simple, with people of great and no reputation, and in duties that bring me recognition and those that only You see. To You be the glory!

You, LORD, have made me glad through Your work; I will triumph in the works of Your hands.

—PSALM 92:4

Gracious Father, thank You for the stirrings in my mind and the longings in my heart that are a sure evidence that You are calling me into prayer. Long before I call, You answer by creating the desire to renew my relationship with You. You allow that feeling of emptiness in the pit of my being to alert me to my hunger for fellowship with You.

My thirst for Your truth, my quest for Your solutions to my needs, and my yearning for Your answers to my problems—are all assurances that before I articulated my prayer, You were preparing the answers. It is a magnificent, liberating thought that all through this day when I cry out for Your help, You have already been waiting for me to give up my dogged self-reliance and start drawing on the supernatural strength and superabundant wisdom You are so eager to give me.

Thank You, Lord, for a day filled with serendipities of Your intervention.

MAY
1

*Let nothing be done through selfish ambition or
conceit, but in lowliness of mind let each esteem others better than himself.*

—PHILIPPIANS 2:3

Gracious God, thank You for this moment of prayer
in which I can affirm Your call to seek unity with my sisters and brothers in Christ. Thank You for giving us all
the same calling: to express our love for You by faithfully
serving You and those around us. So often we're inclined—myself included—to spend time focusing on our
differences that we forget the bond of unity that binds us
together.

We are one in our belief in You, the ultimate and
only Sovereign of this world. You are the magnetic and
majestic Lord of us all, who draws us out of pride and self-
centeredness to worship You together. We find each other
as we praise You with one heart and express our gratitude
in one voice.

Help me, Father, to accept the unique role You
have given me in Your kingdom on earth. I thank You for
Your design for all Your people to work together in unity.
Help me not to take for granted that unity, nor to neglect
it. May a fresh burst of praise for Your providential care for
Your church give me a renewed sense of commitment.
Keep me close to You and open to others as I do the sa-
cred tasks You have assigned me . . . in the unity of the
Spirit and the bond of peace.

MAY
2

This hope we have as an anchor of the soul,
both sure and steadfast.

—HEBREWS 6:19

Thank You, dear God, for the anchor of hope in You that I have for the storms of life. When I lower my anchor, I know it will hold solid in the bedrock of Your faithfulness in spite of the billows of adversity and blasts of conflict. I am able to ride out the storms of difficulties and discouragements because I know You will sustain me. I share the psalmist's confidence: "I wait for the LORD, my soul waits, and in His word I do hope" (Psalm 130:5).

My hope is not in the supposed reliability of people, the presumed predictability of circumstances, nor the imagined security of human power. My hope is in Your grace and truth. I know You will never leave me nor forsake me.

Keep me anchored today so I won't drift from my commitment to serving You. I claim Your destiny for my life. And throughout this day, may I feel the tug of the anchor and know that I am indeed secure.

MAY
3

Humble yourselves under the mighty hand of God, that He may exalt you in due time.

—1 PETER 5:6

Father, remove any vestige of pride within me as I come into Your presence. All that I am and have is Your infinitely gracious gift to me. I am here by Your planning and for Your purpose. You have made possible any success I have known. Any recognition I have received is a reflection of the abilities You have given me. You have blessed me with loved ones, friends, and fellow workers who have made possible any accomplishments I have achieved. All my opportunities are a result of Your careful arrangement of circumstances. Again, I affirm that nothing happens without Your permission.

So I commit this day to be one of special gratitude for all Your blessings. May my gratitude spill over with words of affirmation and encouragement to others. Help me make this a "just because" day in which I do special acts of kindness just because of Your love for me and my delight in others. If there is any good word I've been thinking about saying or any act of caring that I've put off doing, may I say and do them today.

Just because of You, Lord, and all that You have done for me . . .

MAY
4

National Day of Prayer
(First Thursday in May)

Almighty God, on this National Day of Prayer, I join with millions across our land in intercession and supplication to You, the Sovereign Lord of the United States of America. As we sound that sacred word Sovereign, may we echo Washington, Jefferson, Madison, and Lincoln, along with other leaders through the years, in declaring that You are our ultimate ruler. We make a new commitment to be one nation under You, God, and we place our trust in You.

You have promised that if Your people will humble themselves, seek Your face and pray, You will answer and heal our land. Lord, as believers in You, we are Your people. You have called us to be salt in any bland neglect of our spiritual heritage and light in the darkness of what contradicts Your vision for our nation. Give us courage to be accountable to You and Your Commandments. We repent of the pride, selfishness, and prejustice that often contradict Your justice and righteousness in our society.

Lord of new beginnings, our nation needs a great spiritual awakening. May this day of prayer be the beginning of that awakening for me and all Americans. We urgently ask that our honesty about the needs of our nation and our humble confession of our spiritual hunger for You may sweep across this nation. Hear the prayers of Your people and continue to bless America. In Your holy name, Amen.

MAY
5

Trust in the LORD with all your heart and lean not on your own understanding; in all your ways acknowledge Him, and He will direct your paths.

—PROVERBS 3:5-6

Sovereign Father, I put my trust in You. I resist the human tendency to lean on my own understanding; I acknowledge my need for Your wisdom in my search for solutions to the problems before me. Direct my path as I give precedence to Your ways and loyalty to Your will over and above anything else.

I lift up my voice in confessing my total dependence on You. I believe that You are the author of my life and destiny. I know that the work You began when You called me to follow You will continue to develop to full fruition. Help me to move forward in keeping with Your vision. It is awesome to realize that You can use me to accomplish Your goals.

Lord, keep me mindful of the eight words of God-centered servanthood: Without You, I can't; without me, You won't. Think Your thoughts through me, speak Your truth through my words, and enable Your best for others through what You lead me to do.

MAY
6

My door was open wide
Then I looked around
If any lack of service might be found,
And sensed God at my side!
He entered, by what secret stair,
I know not, knowing only He was there.

—ANONYMOUS

Lord, You always have a secret stair. You come in ways that I least expect. You are the Lord of circumstances, people, and possibilities that I would never imagine.

When problems mount and I wonder how I am going to make it, You give me a thought that turns out to be the key to unlock the solution. When I stumble upon an answer to a problem, I later find that it was You who guided me at the fork in the road.

Yet the greatest evidence of Your intervention comes from within me. Suddenly in a spiritual dry spell, I can feel the wells of strength begin to fill up again. I am aware of a fresh courage replacing my fear. I am gripped by a new perspective: The only things that matter are that I belong to You, and that You are in charge. You have not given up on me; You have plans for me.

Thank You for the confidence that You will use everything that happens today . . . for Your glory, and for my growth.

The love of God has been poured out in our hearts by the Holy Spirit who was given to us.

—ROMANS 5:5

Dear God, thank You for revealing the quality of Your love, which You seek to reproduce in my relationships with others. You have told me that . . .

> Love suffers long and is kind; love does not envy; love does not parade itself, is not puffed up; does not behave rudely, does not seek its own, is not provoked, thinks no evil; does not rejoice in iniquity, but rejoices in the truth; bears all things, believes all things, hopes all things, endures all things. Love never fails (1 Corinthians 13:4-8).

Father, may I experience this quality of love in my relationship with You so I will be able to love others with the same giving and forgiving, indefatigable and inexhaustible love.

Give me tough love for troublesome, thick-skinned people and tender love for overly sensitive, thin-skinned people. Today, help me to be as kind, accepting, and patient to others as You have been to me.

MAY
8

I have been crucified with Christ; it is no longer I who live, but Christ lives in me; and the life which I now live in the flesh I live by faith in the Son of God, who loved me and gave Himself for me.

—GALATIANS 2:20

Lord, Your patience with me is a source of amazement and contrition. You accept me as I am, but You never leave me there. Thank You for implanting Christ's nature within me so that I can joyously anticipate that You will make me like Christ in my disposition, temperament, and attitudes.

You know, too, that I do not want to sin. Thank You for forgiving any temporary aberrations in my life. Enable me to accept Your forgiveness and move on to growing up in Christ.

In this time of conversation with You, I consciously confess my dominant desire to love and obey You. I know that nothing can separate me from You now. It may seem that I have let go of You at times; thank You for never letting go of me.

Thank You that You are always more ready to help me than I am ready to ask.

MAY
9

He who has My commandments and keeps
them, it is he who loves Me.

—JOHN 14:23

Gracious Father, Almighty Sovereign and loving Lord of my life, I come to You with a heart of gratitude. I thank You for the privilege of living a life that has been blessed bountifully. It's with awe and wonder that I realize anew that Your dealings in my life are a providential demonstration of Your superabundant grace and lovingkindness.

May my response to Your love be spelled out in an unwavering commitment to serve You. Enable me to grasp the greatness of the blessing of being Your child. May I never lose my enthusiasm for seeking opportunities to use my abilities and talents for Your glory. Help me to make the best use of the gifts You have given me by keeping my priorities straight.

In this quiet moment, may I experience a fresh touch of Your affirmation for the calling You have given for me to fulfill. Again, I am grateful for the privileges You have entrusted into my hands. May my appreciation overflow into praise that makes known to others Your goodness.

MAY
10

Behold, I am making all things new.

—REVELATION 21:5

Oh God, the Lord of new beginnings, the Savior who gives me a fresh start—You have promised that You will make all things new.

Father, recreate me within so that I will sense again the excitement of being a partner with You in bringing Your very best to those around me. Banish the boredom of doing the same things the same old way. Give me that wonderful conviction that You have chosen me to have a strategic place in Your plans for this world. I want to attempt great things for You, and expect great power from You.

Lord, grant me a revived enthusiasm, renewed gusto, and regenerated hope. Make me resilient with newness as I seek to influence this world to conform more to Your purpose and plan.

Fill my heart with Your presence and my mind with Your supernatural power to discern and do Your will. Help me to listen to Your voice consistently, and to speak Your truth courageously.

MAY
11

Cause me to hear Your lovingkindness in the morning, for in You do I trust; cause me to know the way in which I should walk, for I lift up my soul to You.

—PSALM 143:8

Dear God, I respond now to Your invitation to enjoy a moment of conversation with You. I praise You for who You are: my Creator, Sustainer, and loving heavenly Father. It is awesome to me that You have chosen, called, and commissioned me to be Your blessed child.

Forgive me when I resist the greatness You desire for me and refuse Your guidance. I thank You for the times I did trust You and, as a result, received Your blessings of wisdom, strength, and determination.

You have called me to place into Your capable hands the trials and tribulations within me and about me. Help me to turn my cares over to You, and to rest in the assurance that Your solutions are greater than my problems. Give me a clear head and a trusting heart as I press onward on the path You have marked before me.

I now commit myself anew to You, and I reorder my priorities so as to place Your noble purposes before my self-serving plans. With confidence, I thank You in advance for Your guidance today.

MAY
12

*Create in me a clean heart, O God, and renew
a steadfast spirit within me.*

—PSALM 51:10

Almighty God and gracious Father, thank You for showing me that the heart of the matter is always the heart. You have opened Your heart to me and blessed me with Your lovingkindness and tender mercy. In grateful response, I offer You my heart in a renewed commitment to care about what concerns You. Touch my heart with compassion motivated by Your love; press my heart next to the pulse-beat of Your heart so that Your love might overflow from me into the lives of others.

Particularly, Lord, open my heart to those in my community who have been debilitated by misfortune, denigrated by adversities, defeated by failures, and dehumanized by poverty. Help me to feel the wrench of hunger, the loneliness of being forgotten, the anguish of being homeless.

Yet I know that You do Your work through people who share Your heart. I accept Your calling to join You in the restoration of broken people to spiritual wholeness and creative productivity.

Show me what You want me to do in the winnable war against human suffering in my community.

MAY
13

Speak, for Your servant hears.

—1 Samuel 3:10

Gracious Father, I thank You for all the faculties You have entrusted to me, but today I praise You especially for the gift of hearing.

Help me never to take for granted the amazing process by which sounds are registered on my eardrums, and carried through the audio nerve to my cerebral cortex to be translated into thoughts of recognition, comprehension, and response. Through this wonderful gift I can hear the spring songs of birds returned, majestic music of a sonata, a loved one's words of love and hope, and the truths of Your own Word in the Bible as they are read or proclaimed from across the reaches of time. But most importantly, You have given me a listening heart to hear what You say to me through the guidance of Your Holy Spirit.

I now dedicate my physical and spiritual hearing systems to listening more attentively to You and others. Forgive me when I become so preoccupied with what I want to say that I do not listen. Often I don't hear You or others because I have prejudged what will be said. And there are times when I am so intent on doing my own will that I fail to consult You and listen for Your whisper in my soul.

Today, Lord, I say with Samuel, "Speak, for Your servant hears."

You are my rock and my fortress; therefore, for Your name's sake, lead me and guide me. . . . for You are my strength, into Your hand I commit my spirit.

—PSALM 31:3-5

Gracious Father, thank You that Your power is given in direct proportion to the pressures and perplexities I face. I am given great courage and confidence as I am reminded that You give more strength as my burdens increase, and You entrust me with more wisdom as my problems test my endurance. I am cheered and comforted to know that You will never leave nor forsake me. Your love has no end, and Your patience has no breaking point.

Today I want to affirm what You have taught me: that You have called me to supernatural servanthood empowered by Your spiritual gifts of wisdom, knowledge, discernment, and vision. You lovingly press me beyond my dependence on erudition and experience alone. Thank You for giving me challenges that help to recover my humility and opportunities that force me to the knees of my heart.

Help me, Lord, to move forward with my responsibilities by being attentive to You and obedient in following Your guidance. Give me that sure sense of Your presence and the sublime satisfaction of knowing and doing Your will.

MAY
15

In the day of my trouble I will call upon You,
for You will answer me.

—PSALM 86:7

Almighty God, You have chosen to dwell in the mind that is completely open to You and the heart that is unreservedly responsive to You. Thank You that my longing is to come to You because You have called and chosen me. I'm grateful that even before I pour forth my problems and concerns to You, You already have prepared to impart to me the wisdom and direction that will guide me on the right path.

Because You are all-wise and all-sufficient, You have solutions and provisions ready to unfold and implement in my moment of need. Keep my mind riveted upon You, Lord, and my will responsive to Your direction. Replenish my strength, renew my hope, and refresh me with Your grace.

May I seek Your best in everything that You have entrusted for me to do today.

MAY
16

I love the LORD, *because He has heard my voice and my supplications. Because He has inclined His ear to me, therefore I will call upon Him as long as I live.*

—PSALM 116:1-2

Gracious Father, I am irresistibly drawn into Your presence by the magnetism of Your love. Though You know all my faults, You still offer forgiveness. You know all my needs, and offer more than sufficient strength. You know my responsibilities, and assure me of Your intervening help. You know the decisions I must make, and promise me that if I will seek Your guidance, You will show me the way.

As I begin this new day, give me a renewed vision of the high calling You have given me in life. I am deeply moved that You have called me to serve You by bringing Your grace to my relationships and Your justice to my society. May all that I do, then, be done for Your glory. Remind me that excellence is achieved only when I seek to please You above all else.

May today's work be an expression of my worship to You, and may it proclaim to others Your greatness and Your power.

MAY
17

All things are yours . . . the world or life or death, or things present or things to come—all are yours. And you are Christ's and Christ is God's. — 1 CORINTHIANS 3:22-23

Gracious Lord, I begin the work of this day with awe and wonder. You have chosen and called Your people—including me—to know, love, and serve You. With that calling You have given me intellect, talent, and ability, and You have been faithful to open doors of opportunity, learning, and experience. You have shown me that You are ready and willing to equip me with supernatural power through the anointing of my mind with the gifts of Your Spirit: wisdom, knowledge, discernment, and vision of Your priorities and plans.

When I ask You for wisdom, You reveal Your truth and give me insight on how to apply it to specific decisions before me. I say with the psalmist, "In the day when I cried out, You answered me, and made me bold with strength in my soul" (Psalm 138:3).

I thank You that in a time of restless relativism and easy equivocation, You call me to live out Your absolutes: honesty, integrity, moral purity, complete accountability for the gift of life. Help me to move forward this day with conviction and courage, using to the fullest the gifts and blessings You have entrusted to me. Through Christ my Lord and Savior.

MAY
18

*I delight to do Your will, O my God, and Your
law is within my heart.*

—PSALM 40:8

Gracious Lord, You know what is ahead today for
me. Crucial issues await my attention. Unmade decisions
demand my concentration. And I know that the choices
I make will affect me and others around me.

It's with that in mind that I say with the psalmist,
"Show me Your ways, O LORD; teach me Your paths. Lead
me in Your truth and teach me, for You are the God of my
salvation; on You I wait all the day" (Psalm 25:4-5).

May I prepare for the decisive decisions of this day
by opening my mind to the inflow of Your Spirit. I confess
that I need Your divine wisdom to shine the light of discernment in the dimness of my limited understanding.

I praise You, Lord, that I can face the rest of this day
with the inner peace of knowing that You will answer this
prayer for guidance.

MAY
19

Oh, give thanks to the LORD, for He is good!
For His mercy endures forever.

—PSALM 107:1

Almighty God, I praise You for this new day in which I can glorify You in the crucial work You have called me to do. Through Your goodness, I can say with enthusiasm, "Good morning, Lord!" rather than with exasperation, "Good Lord, what a morning!"

Thank You for giving me expectation and excitement for what You have planned for me today. Help me to sense Your presence in the magnificent as well as the mundane. Give me a deep sense of self-esteem rooted in Your love so that I may exude confidence and courage as I grasp the opportunities and grapple with the problems I will confront.

Make me sensitive, Lord, to the needs of the people whom I meet today. May they feel Your love and acceptance flowing through me to them. Guide my thinking so that I may be creative in my expressions of encouragement and enthusiasm.

I humbly acknowledge that all that I have and am is a gift of Your grace. I now commit myself to service that reflects my gratitude for Your lovingkindness.

MAY
20

Those who wait on the LORD shall renew their strength; they shall mount up with wings like eagles, they shall run and not be weary, they shall walk and not faint.

—ISAIAH 40:31

Heavenly Father, You created me to soar, to mount up with wings like eagles. I realize that it's not just my aptitude, but my attitudes that determine my altitude. My attitudes are the outward expression of the convictions congealed in my character.

Help me to express a positive attitude based on a conviction that You are in control and are working out Your purposes. I want to experience Your love so profoundly that my attitude will exude vibrant joy. May Your peace invade my heart so my attitude will reflect an inner serenity and calm confidence. I long to have the servant attitude of affirmation of others, of a willingness to listen to their needs and of a desire to put my caring into practical acts of kindness.

Lord, if there is any false pride that makes me arrogant, any selfishness that makes me insensitive, any fear that makes me unnecessarily cautious, any insecurity that makes me cowardly, forgive me and give me the courage to receive Your transforming power in my heart. I ask this so that my attitude to others may exemplify Your attitude of grace toward me.

MAY
21

*Teach us to number our days, that we may gain
a heart of wisdom.*

—PSALM 90:12

Almighty God, as I take on my responsibilities today, give me a renewed sense of the shortness of time and the length of eternity. Help me to live this day to the fullest, as if it were my last day. May I never take for granted the gift of life or the privilege of serving You by giving my best to the tasks and challenges I will face today.

Help me to fast-forward the videotape of my life to my own dying. In the full assurance of Christ's victory over death and the gift of eternal life, I accept Your release from any panic over sickness or dying. Death will be a transition in living.

With fear of death and worry over the future behind me I feel a new freedom to love more fully today. Heaven has begun. Now I can add life to my years and care-free years to my life.

MAY
22

The LORD God formed man of the dust of the ground, and breathed into his nostrils the breath of life; and man became a living being.

—GENESIS 2:7

Almighty Father, I am dependent on You for everything. There is nothing I could do in this day or in my life without Your moment-by-moment provision. I place my finger on my pulse, and thank You for the gift of life. I breathe in, saying, "Bless the Lord, O my soul," and breathe out saying, "And all that is within me, bless His holy name."

I list all that is mine from Your loving provision: I praise You for food, my physical body, the people in my life, the opportunities and challenges of today. I want to make this a day for constant and consistent conversation with You, in which I repeatedly say thank You, Lord, for the abundant mercies that You give me in a never-ending flow of goodness.

I know that a thankful heart is not just the greatest virtue, but the parent of all virtues and the source of transformation of my attitudes. Every virtue devoid of thankfulness is maimed and limps along the spiritual road.

With everything that is within me, Lord, I thank You. May this be a day for constant thanksgiving for the privilege of life.

He who abides in Me, and I in him, bears much fruit; for without Me you can do nothing.

—JOHN 15:5

Blessed Lord Jesus, whose love never lets me go, whose mercy never ends, whose strength is always available, whose guidance shows me the way, whose Spirit provides me supernatural power, whose presence is my courage, whose joy invades my gloom, whose peace calms my pressured heart, whose light illuminates my path, whose goodness provides the wondrous gifts of loved ones and family and friends, whose will has brought me to the awesome tasks of today, and whose calling lifts me above self-centeredness to other-centered servanthood...I dedicate all that I have and am to serve You today with unreserved faithfulness and unfailing loyalty.

Just as You arranged circumstances to bring me to willingness to receive You as my Lord and Savior, so too, You use all of life to help me grow in Your grace.

You are with me today watching over all that happens to me. You go before me to guide each step of the way. You are beside me as my companion and friend, and You are behind me to gently prod me when I lag behind with caution or reluctance.

Most of all, Christ, be in my mind to help me understand the purpose of what happens to and around me; moment by moment, use all of the events of life to strengthen in me Your nature and character. Thank You, Lord!

MAY
24

Ask, and it will be given to you; seek, and you will find; knock, and it will be opened to you. For everyone who asks receives, and he who seeks finds, and to him who knocks it will be opened.

—MATTHEW 7:7

Almighty God, infinite, eternal, full of love and compassion . . . I praise You for laying upon my heart the need to seek You in prayer. Yet I need not search for You, because You have already found me. I need not worry that You will not listen, for You already are impinging on my heart. My anxiety lest You be unresponsive to my concerns is unfounded, for You know my need and plan my provision even before I ask.

Awe and wonder grip me as I consider that You are all-knowing, all-loving, all-wise, all-powerful. I openly confess my human inadequacy and my need for You to infuse me with the strength, understanding, and compassion needed for this day.

I thus yield my mind to think, and then communicate, Your thoughts. I yield my attitudes so that I might work effectively with those who differ with me. And I yield the work I must do today that Your will might be carried out through me. I commit to You the care of loved ones and friends who need Your physical healing and physical strength. Especially_____.

MAY
25

"Let not the wise man glory in his wisdom, let not the mighty man glory in his might, nor let the rich man glory in his riches; but let him who glories glory in this, that he understands and knows Me, that I am the LORD, exercising lovingkindness, judgment, and righteousness in the earth. For in these I delight," says the LORD.

—JEREMIAH 9:23-24

Lord, I thank You for this decisive declaration proclaimed through Your prophet Jeremiah. Thank You for this reminder that there is no limit to the power You are ready to release in those who seek to know You and long to emulate Your own attributes of grace, justice, and righteousness.

I thank You also that I can look to You for the supernatural gifts of wisdom, discernment, knowledge, and vision . . . that I need not rely on my own resources, which fall far short of what is needed to live life as You want it lived. Give me the courage and commitment to seek to know and do Your will, and be faithful and obedient to Your guidance.

I ask this that I might be used mightily by You in the advancement of Your kingdom—that through my life, others would see gloriously displayed Your grace and goodness and want to know You. Particularly I pray for

_____ .

MAY
26

Be kindly affectionate to one another with brotherly love, in honor giving preference to one another.

—ROMANS 12:10

Dear Father, help me to have the perspective that all people are precious to You. Grant me all through this day a discernment that seeks to communicate loving affirmation and concern for those whom I meet. Help me to express gratitude for the qualities within the people around me, and not merely the things they do. Create within me a sensitivity that responds to the voices of those who are encumbered with worries or heartaches, and prompt me to make time to listen to them.

Gracious Lord, may I live all this day with an awareness that Your presence dwells within me. Make my heart's desire be to do every task for Your glory. Remind me that the thoughts, feelings, and attitudes within me are open to Your scrutiny. Help me to live in such a way that I'm mindful of Your watchful eyes.

I commit myself now to working for You with excellence so that at the close of this day, I will have the assurance of knowing I did my best for You.

MAY
27

This is love, not that we loved God, but that He loved us and sent His Son to be the propitiation for our sins.

—1 JOHN 4:10

Almighty God, by Your grace, You guided me that I might experience the wondrous gift of salvation offered through Your Son's completed work on the cross. I praise You for that initial intervention in my life and your consistent interventions since. I thank You that You are my sole source of confidence and fulfillment.

As I begin the work of this day I commit my life to You anew. I thank You for the privilege of what You have given for me to do. I open my mind to Your guidance as I move forward in my responsibilities, and I ask that You might give me Your perspective on the problems I face and Your power to solve them.

As I engage myself in each task, enable me so that I might work effectively with efficiency. And when I am finished, may my work be such that what I have done is pleasing to You. I commit to You the challenges of this day, especially_____.

MAY
28

*I will sing of Your power; yes, I will sing aloud
of Your mercy in the morning.*

—PSALM 59:16

Almighty God, Sovereign of my life, I praise You for Your amazing grace. Your unlimited love casts out fear, Your unqualified forgiveness heals my heart, Your undeserved faithfulness gives me courage, Your unfailing guidance gives me clear direction, and Your constant presence banishes my anxieties.

You know my needs, Lord, before I ask You, and Your Spirit gives me the boldness to ask for what You are ready to give. You give me discernment of the needs of others so that I can be a servant. Your love frees me to love, forgive, uplift, and encourage those around me.

I now commit this day to be one in which I initiate opportunities to communicate with others about Your grace. Thus I open myself to the infilling and leading of Your Spirit. Lead on, gracious Father; I am ready for a great day filled with grace.

MAY
29

Come and see the works of God; He is awesome in His doing toward the sons of men.

—PSALM 66:5

Dear God, today I want to let go of my hurting memories of the past. I accept Your forgiveness and want to forgive everything and everyone in the past—including myself.

Thank You that You deliberately forget my failures, but never forget me. You tell me what not to remember and why. "Do not remember the former things, nor consider the things of old. Behold, I will do a new thing, now it shall spring forth; shall you not know it?" (Isaiah 43:18-19).

Lord, I forget the past by remembering You. I remember that You are willing to forget my sins and failures. I confess them specifically. At Your command, I move through the prison of my memories, leading out each captive memory for display before You. You have said, "I, even I, am He who blots out Your transgressions for My own sake; and I will not remember Your sins. . . . state your case that you may be acquitted" (Isaiah 43:25-26).

In response I bring all my hurting memories into the court of Your presence. I'm astounded: As I finish my condemnatory judgment on myself, I hear Your voice sound in my soul, "I forgot that long ago; now you are free to forget it."

MAY
30

O God, my heart is steadfast; I will sing and give praise, even with my glory.

—PSALM 108:1

Gracious God, whose dwelling place is the heart that longs for Your presence and the mind that humbly seeks Your truth, I eagerly ask for Your guidance for the work of this day. I confess anything that would hinder the flow of Your Spirit in and through me. In my personal life, heal any broken or strained relationships that threaten to drain my creative energies. Lift my burdens, and resolve my worries. Then give me a fresh experience of Your amazing grace which can set me free to live with freedom and joy.

Now, Lord, I am ready to work with great confidence fortified by a steady supply of Your strength. Give me the courage to do what I already know of Your will, so that I may know more of it for the specific challenges of this day...

My dominant desire today, Lord, is for Your best in the unfolding adventure of my life.

The LORD is my light and salvation;
Whom shall I fear?
The Lord is the strength of my life;
Of whom shall I be afraid?

—PSALM 27:1

Lord, I really need to answer the psalmist's questions. In this quiet moment, I need Your help to overcome the impact of rejections I have felt in the past. And knowing the pain of rejection, I want to express Your love to those who suffer from the anguish of rejection.

Like the psalmist, I need the perspective of Your illuminating light so I can see things as they really are. Why am I so troubled by people's actions? Why do rebuffs disturb me so much? Could it be that what people think of me is more important than what You think? Do I need people's acceptance more than Yours?

You are my salvation, the source of my deliverance. Graciously, You heal my hurts and set me free. In Your presence I feel the strength of Your Spirit giving me protection and victory.

Savior, You have broken the cycle of rejection and retaliation. You call me to love my enemies, bless those who curse me, and do good to those who spitefully use and persecute me (Matthew 5:43-44). Who can live that quality of love? No one, except by Your power. And now I'm ready for the day: What has happened to me is for what You want to do and say through me to those who feel misunderstood or misused. The only final cure for the frowning face of rejection is Your smiling face of love and acceptance.

JUNE
1

Every day I will bless You, and I will praise Your name forever and ever. Great is the LORD, and greatly to be praised; and His greatness is unsearchable.

—PSALM 145:2-3

Almighty God, You have promised, "As your days, so shall your strength be" (Deuteronomy 33:25). I praise You that You know what is ahead of me today and will provide me with exactly what I need in each hour and in each circumstance. I relax in the knowledge that You neither will be surprised by what evolves, nor incapable of sustaining me in any eventualities.

Thank You, in advance, for giving me the strength I'll need for this day. Therefore, I resist the temptation to be anxious or worry over whether I will have what it takes. Instead, I will receive what You have offered: wisdom for my decisions, love for my relationships, hope for my discouraging experiences, replenishing energy for my tired times, and renewed vision for my down moments.

I dedicate this day to You, Lord. Protect me from the pride that supposes I can make it on my own, and the vanity that presumes I can take care of my needs. Help me to walk more closely with You in a way that enables others to see the wondrous work You can do in a life fully submitted to You.

JUNE
2

Settle it in your hearts not to meditate before-hand on what you will answer; for I will give you a mouth and wisdom which all your adver-saries will not be able to contradict or resist.

—LUKE 21:14-15

Blessed Lord Jesus, Your words to Your disciples help me press on growing in the confidence I received from yesterday's prayer. I'm startled by Your admonition not to meditate beforehand on what I will say when my faith is tested. This prompts me to think about how I sometimes go over and over what I will say to combative people or in contentious situations. I'm also reminded by how much time I spend preparing what I will say in arguments with others. Instead of prayer, I sometimes play out the whole scene on the screen of my mind, creating the acrimonious dialogue as I think it will develop.

Now it dawns on me that if I spent as much time preparing my mind and heart with Your thought and attitude conditioning in prayer, I could go into the day knowing You will give me what to say in each crisis or challenge. If my mind is submerged in Your Spirit, my words will be saturated with Your love, truth and wisdom.

Lord, I commit to You the specific situations and relationships in which I don't know what's best to say or how to say it. I look forward to the wisdom You will give and the courage to share it with love.

JUNE
3

*Give ear to my words, O Lord, consider my
meditation. Give heed to the voice of my cry,
My King and my God. For to You I will pray.*
—PSALM 5:1-2

Almighty God, I thank You for this moment of
quiet in which I can reaffirm who I am, whose I am, and
why I am here. Once again I commit myself to You as Sovereign Lord of my life. My ultimate goal is to please and
serve You, knowing that You have called me to be a servant who glorifies You by seeking to know and do Your
will.

With that in mind, I spread out before You the specific tasks and decisions that must be taken care of today.
I claim Your presence and Your direction in every matter;
guide my thinking and my actions. May all that emerges
from me be consistent with how Your Word calls me to
live.

Help me to draw on the supernatural resources of
Your indwelling Holy Spirit. Grant me divine wisdom,
penetrating discernment, and courageous vision.

And when the day ends, may my deepest joys be
that I received Your best for me and worked for Your best
in the lives of others.

JUNE
4

Come and find the quiet center
In the crowded life we lead,
Find the room for hope to enter,
Find the frame where we are freed;
Clear the chaos and the clutter,
Clear our eyes, that we may see
All the things that really matter
Be at peace and simply be.

— "COME FIND THE QUIET CENTER"
SHIRLEY ERENA MURRAY*

Father, thank You for this sacred moment of prayer. I come to You just as I am and receive from You the strength to do what You want me to do. I trust You to guide me throughout this day. Keep me calm in the quiet center of my life so that I may be serene in the swirling stresses of life. And fill me with the perfect peace that comes from staying my mind on You.

You have promised that, "In returning and rest you shall be saved; in quietness and confidence shall be your strength" (Isaiah 30:15). As I return to You in repentance, I sense Your forgiving love and calming assurance. A profound restfulness replaces the restlessness in my soul. And now, quietness. A sublime inner calm in my soul. I relax in Your everlasting arms. Tension drains from my body. There is nothing I need to do or say. I am safe. Your indwelling Spirit has filled my inner being. This quiet moment has given me confidence and strength. I'm ready for the day!

* Words © 1992 by Hope Publishing Co., Carol Stream, IL 60188. All rights reserved. Used by permission.

JUNE
5

Judge not, that you be not judged. For with what judgment you judge, you will be judged; and with the same measure you use, it will be measured back to you.

—MATTHEW 7:1-2

Dear God, ultimate Judge of all, free me from the condemnatory judgments that elevate myself and put others down when they do not agree with me. Help me not to think that my disagreement justifies my lack of prayer for them. I know my inclination to self-righteously neglect the very people who most need Your blessing.

Help me take seriously Paul's incisive word, "Therefore you are inexcusable, O man, whoever you are who judge, for in whatever you judge another you condemn yourself; for you who judge practice the same things" (Romans 2:1).

Awaken me, Lord, to the danger that results from neglect of prayer for my adversaries. Make me an intercessor for all those You have placed on my heart—even those whom I have previously castigated with my judgments. I accept that You are the only Judge; "Judgment is Mine, says the Lord." I pray this in the name of Jesus, who taught, "Judge not, and you shall not be judged. Condemn not, and you shall not be condemned. Forgive, and you will be forgiven" (Luke 6:37).

JUNE
6

Cast your burden on the LORD, and He shall sustain you.

—PSALM 55:22

Gracious Father, I respond to this uplifting promise with gratitude; as You know, I have some burdens on my heart. Among them are the burdens of my failures. In the quiet I hear You say, "You are forgiven; peace be with you." I also carry the burden of worry over my family and friends. Yet You remind me that You love the people about whom I am concerned, and so I am to turn my anxieties about them over to You.

In my work I am burdened by the unfinished and the unresolved. Help me to do the very best I can each day and leave the results to You. Then there are the burdens of my daily needs; I hear Your whisper in my soul, "I will never leave you nor forsake you."

Father, whatever other burdens I carry right now, I ask You to lift them by Your grace and provide for them out of Your boundless resources. Then help me to lift the burdens of others by being as encouraging to them as You have been to me.

JUNE

7

Whatever things are true, whatever things are noble, whatever things are just, whatever things are pure, whatever things are lovely, whatever things are of good report, if there is any virtue and if there is anything praise-worthy—meditate on these things.

—PHILIPPIANS 4:8

Sovereign Lord, You have given me a mind so that I can think magnificently about You. I contemplate Your majesty, power, goodness, truth, faithfulness, and grace. Everything within me responds to praise You for the wonderful way You care for me and provide for my needs.

Today, I commit my thoughts to You. I accept the admonition of Scripture: "Do not be conformed to this world, but be transformed by the renewing of your minds that you may prove what is that good and acceptable and perfect will of God" (Romans 12:2). Consciously I seek to serve You by allowing You to deepen my understanding. Help me to base my thinking on Your truth, values, and priorities.

Lord, may I come to know You so well that Your will is made clear for each decision. Be on my mind, in my mind, and in control of my mind . . . and may my response be to love You with all my mind.

JUNE
8

Grace, mercy and peace will be with you from God the Father and from the Lord Jesus Christ.

—2 JOHN 3

"I focus on the Lord and not the problems. Then I can deal with the problems holding the strong hand of Jesus."

—MOTHER TERESA OF CALCUTTA

Dear Lord of the future, I praise You that You know what You are doing with my tomorrows. I confidently anticipate each new day and expectantly await the discovery of Your grace, mercy, and peace in all my unresolved problems and potentials. I believe that everything that happens to me will be used for Your plan and purpose. Thank You for healing my concerns about the future.

Break the bind of my "future jitters" and give me the gift of future faith, the kind that sets me free from obsessive worry about what might happen. The bigger the problem, the more of Your abiding presence and power I will receive. Equal to the strain of any of tomorrow's problems will be the strength You will give me. You will never give me more than You and I can face together. I intend to stop missing the joy of today by fretting about the future. Help me, Lord!

JUNE
9

*Trust in Him at all times, you people; pour out
your heart before Him; God is a refuge for us.*

—PSALM 62:8

Lord, I need Your help. I am feeling the strain of
stress. My body is agitated by worry and fear. I confess to
You my inability to handle it alone. I surrender my mind
to You. Think Your thoughts through me and send into
my nervous system the pure signals of Your peace, power,
and patience. I don't want to have a divided mind fragmented from Your control.

Forgive my angers rooted in petulant self-will. Make
me a riverbed for the flow of Your love to others suffering
as much stress as I. Take charge of my tongue so that it
becomes an instrument of healing. Make me a communicator of love and forgiveness as I cheer others on to their
best. Help me act on the inspiration You give me rather
than stifling Your guidance. I commit my schedule to You,
Lord; help me know and do Your will. Slow me down
before I break down. Set me free from the tyranny of
acquisitiveness, seeking my security in things rather than
in my relationship with You.

I long to be the person You created me to be, and not
anyone else. Forgive me when I take my signals of success
from others and not You. Most of all, Lord, help me to
catch the drumbeat of Your guidance and live by Your
timing. Here is my life—invade it, fill it, transform it.
And I thank You in advance for the healing of my life and
for giving me the strength to conquer stress.

JUNE
10

With God nothing will be impossible.

—Luke 1:37

Gracious Lord, I begin this day with disturbing questions that won't go away. What would I do and say today if I truly loved You with all my heart? How would I deal with my present challenges if I put You and the welfare of others above all else? What do You want me to do to move forward?

You have taught me, "If you have faith as a mustard seed, you will say to this mountain, 'Move from here to there' and it will move; and nothing will be impossible for you."

Is Your promise applicable to me in my current circumstances? Will You give me the power to remove mountainous problems and issues if I have faith in You—even as small as a mustard seed? I dare to claim that You will.

Guide me, Lord, to Your solutions for my present concerns. I place my faith in You, for I know that nothing is impossible for You. Help me, Lord; I need You.

JUNE
11

May my meditation be sweet to Him; I will be glad in the LORD.

—PSALM 104:34

Almighty God, I thank You for the gift of imagination You have entrusted to me. With my imagination, You have enabled me to form, hold, and achieve images of what You can make possible. Coupled with the gifts of hope and expectation, You help me to imagine Your best for my life and those around me.

Now at the beginning of this day, I thank You for Your presence with me right now here in this room. Knowing that I am accountable to You for every thought that I think and word that I speak, I contemplate how I should act and react under the guidance of Your Spirit. I hold the image of how You want me to relate to loved ones, friends, and others, and I sense the civility and the greatness of character You want from me. Help me to express to others the same kindness, graciousness, and respect that I have received from You.

So renew my dedication to You, Lord. In loyalty to You, I commit myself to working for Your glory and the good of those whom I have the opportunity to serve.

JUNE
12

Every good gift and perfect gift is from above, and comes down from the Father.

—JAMES 1:17

Lord of all life, I thank You for surrounding me with outward evidences that remind me of Your unceasing blessings. You have given me loved ones and friends, provided me shelter and sustenance, endowed me with talents and abilities, and given me the privilege of living in a creation that is infinitely inspiring and refreshing.

My heart is moved as I consider the abundance with which You have expressed Your lovingkindness. May my response of gratitude be evident in my commitment to be a diligent steward of the people, provisions, and possibilities You have entrusted to me.

I acknowledge, Lord, that You truly have been generous with me. I praise You for the work to which You have called me. May I experience this day a fresh strength and vision as I renew my dependence upon Your Spirit's promptings to guide me in the way You would have me to go.

JUNE
13

We urge you, brethren . . . that you also aspire to lead a quiet life, to mind your own business, and to work with your own hands.

—1 THESSALONIANS 4:10-11

Glorious God, I thank You for the change that takes place in my attitudes when I remember that my calling is to glorify You in my work. May my desire be to work with excellence so that You might be pleased. Help me to be mindful that no matter what it is I do, I am responsible not only to those for whom I work but ultimately to You. Help me to realize how privileged I am to be able to work, earn a wage, and provide for my needs. Thank You for the dignity of work.

So I press on today with enthusiasm, remembering that You have gifted me with the attitudes and abilities to fulfill my responsibilities. Whatever I do, in word or deed, I do it to praise You.

In this way, I will bring meaning to my work rather than trying to make my work the meaning of my life. You are the real meaning of my life. Help me to live out my faith in my work rather than putting my faith in my work as the source of my security. You are the Lord of my life and not my job. The result is that I can do my job with greater excellence and give You the glory!

JUNE
14

Flag Day

God, who gave us life, gave us liberty. Can the liberties of a nation be secure when we have removed a conviction that these liberties are the gift of God?

—THOMAS JEFFERSON
Inscribed on his Memorial

Almighty God, Sovereign of the United States, I thank You for outward symbols of profound meaning that remind me of Your blessings. The sight of the flag stirs my patriotism and dedication. It reminds me of Your providential care through the years of the blessed history of America. I am moved deeply by the privilege of living in this land.

Today, on Flag Day, I repledge my own allegiance to You and my country. I commit myself to the unfolding drama of the American dream. The words of Thomas Jefferson remind me that the liberties I enjoy are Your gift. I am deeply concerned that this conviction is ignored by many Americans in an increasingly secularized society. There is a dangerous drift from historic belief that this is one nation under You, the ultimate Sovereign of our land.

I accept Your call for a great spiritual awakening in our nation. May it begin with me. Make me salt in the bland neglect of our spiritual heritage and light in the darkness of the lack of righteousness in our culture. May a new spirit of gratitude to You as the author of liberty sweep across this land and save us from becoming a godless nation.

JUNE
15

The LORD is my strength and my shield; my heart trusted in Him, and I am helped; therefore my heart greatly rejoices, and with my song I will praise Him.

—PSALM 28:7

Almighty God, source of all that I have and am, forgive me for taking Your blessings for granted. I go to sleep at night fully confident that I will awake each morning, but often I fail to praise You for the wonder of being alive. Too frequently I rush into the day on my high horse and ride off in all directions without thanking You for filling the day to overflowing with Your goodness. Too often I presumptuously assume that I am in control of my life, other people, and my circumstances.

Yet I know that everything accomplished seemingly on my own is really the result of what You plan for me out of sheer grace. You are the One who gives me the strength to attempt and achieve, and I am too quick to take the credit.

As I walk through this day, may I remember that life is a privilege to be lived to the fullest in serving with humble gratitude. Remind me that I could not breathe a breath, think a thought, nor work creatively without Your permission and Your power.

Now I am ready for a day of opportunities and challenges!

JUNE
16

Whoever has this world's goods, and sees his brother in need, and shuts up his heart from him, how does the love of God abide in him? My little children, let us not love in word or tongue, but in deed and in truth.

—1 JOHN 3:17-18

Lord God of love, I thank You for communicating to me the urgency of loving others. You created me so that I could not be fulfilled without Your love and the love You inspire in me for other people. Help me to know what it means to lay down my life for loved ones, friends, and even strangers. Then motivate me to action, so that when this day ends, I will be able to feel the excitement of praise for the ways You have loved through me.

So I accept the challenge—*Carpe Diem:* Seize the Day! I commit it to be a day of accepting with enthusiasm the opportunities to serve others whom You send my way. My question to others, spoken or implied, will be, "How may I serve you?"

May the expression on my face be receptive and unguarded. Remind me that it takes more energy to frown than to smile. May I radiate the warmth of acceptance of, and delight in, others. Then when I discover needs I can meet, help me act. Today is a day for generosity!

JUNE
17

I will bless the LORD who has given me counsel. . . . I have set the LORD always before me; because He is at my right hand I shall not be moved.

—PSALM 16:7-8

Almighty God, Sovereign of this universe, I begin this day with an acute sense of my accountability to You. I claim Solomon's promise, "In all your ways acknowledge Him, and He shall direct your paths" (Proverbs 3:6). In response, I say with the psalmist, "Let the words of my mouth and the meditation of my heart be acceptable in Your sight, O LORD" (Psalm 19:14).

Help me to remember that every thought I think and every word I speak is open to Your scrutiny. With that in mind, I commit this day to loving You with my mind and honoring You with my words.

Guide me, Lord, in every matter that comes before me today. Help me to think as You do and see as You do by blessing me with Your gifts of wisdom and vision. Remind me to draw upon Your sufficient and supernatural strength. And quiet the concerns of my heart by granting me the profound inner peace that results from trusting You completely.

JUNE
18

In this is love, not that we loved God, but that He loved us and sent His Son to be the propitiation for our sins.

—1 JOHN 4:10

Lord, my prayer is that I may allow the Holy Spirit to fill my heart with the pulsating, surging, exuberant vitality of the gift of love. With boldness I ask that You will teach me to love myself as much as You do. I know that when that happens, my self-condemnatory heart will be healed, and I can get on with the true business of life—loving others.

You have shown me that will require quality time with the people You have called me to love. Make me sensitive. Help me to listen intently so I can discover what's really going on inside them. Make me concerned about their hopes and fears. Give me empathy to feel what they are feeling. Show me opportunities to do practical things that will communicate my caring.

Most of all, give me an astute awareness of the right time to talk about Your love. Help me be vulnerable to share how Your love has healed and transformed me. Enable me to be personal. Remind me of experiences of Your unqualified love that will relate directly to the precise needs I've discovered in a person by listening. Thank You for setting me free to live a truly significant life for others.

JUNE
19

[Jesus said,] "Father, glorify Your name."
Then a voice came from heaven, saying, "I
have both glorified it and will glorify it again."

—JOHN 12:28

Gracious Father, it is Your nature to go beyond what You've done before. Whatever I've experienced of Your glory, it is small in comparison to the revelation of Your glory You have prepared for me. There's always an element of surprise in my relationship with You. You give me fresh knowledge when I foolishly think I know it all. What I have learned is only a fraction of what You have stored up for me.

As I look ahead to the challenges facing me today, I say, "Father, glorify Your name." Your response is to remind me of my own spiritual pilgrimage and how You met me at every fork of the road with clear guidance and fresh grace. I beheld Your glory. Now I hear You saying that what I have discovered before is minuscule in comparison to the mighty acts You will do. I hear You, Lord: "I have glorified my name in your life and will glorify it again." Excitement and expectation fill my heart. You are not finished with me; the adventure has barely begun!

Lord, You are able to do miracles in people and problems. Fill my mind with vision and my heart with hope so that I can believe that all things are possible with You. I hold particular people before You and commit specific needs to You. There's no limit to what You can and will do to manifest Your glory. What a difference thinking positively about Your power has made for my attitude to this new day!

JUNE
20

*One thing I do, forgetting those things which
are behind and reaching forward to those things
which are ahead, I press toward the goal for the
prize of the upward calling of God in Christ
Jesus.*

—PHILIPPIANS 3:13-14

Gracious Father, help me not to lose my sense of humor. Free me to laugh at myself when I do the wrong thing at the right time or the right thing at an inappropriate time.

Sometimes I say things that, upon later reflection, make me cringe. Or, I'll take myself too seriously and become tense. Little issues can become so crucial to me that I miss the big issues confronting me. And often I'll worry about what others think of me. Relieve me, Lord, of my assumed importance, and help me realize that others most often are consumed with their own concerns.

Forgive me for all the energy I have wasted on checking my own popularity pulse. Make me secure in Your love so I can lighten up, and then, listen up to what You want me to do about what really matters.

Make me care-free, but never careless. Remind me that by worrying I cannot add a single cubit to my stature...and that by seeking first Your kingdom, I can expend my energy on the things that are truly important.

JUNE
21

*The eyes of the LORD run to and fro throughout
the whole earth, to show Himself strong on behalf of those whose heart is loyal to Him.*

—2 CHRONICLES 16:9

Almighty God, I long to be loyal to You. I am deeply
moved by the reminder that my loyalty can bring joy to
You, that You are in search of men and women whose commitment to You is expressed in consistency.

As I reflect on that, I realize that everything I know
about loyalty, I've learned from You. You are faithful and
true. Your love never changes; You never give up on me;
You never waver in life's battles; You never leave me.

In response, I want to be known as a person who belongs to You and believes in You. The desire of my heart
is to love and serve You first and foremost. May I never
shrink from the question, "Who is on the Lord's side?" I
want people to know where I stand in my relationship
with You, Your moral absolutes, and Your ethical standards. In my relationships, I want loyalty to be the foun-
dation of my character. That's possible only as I live in a
steady flow of Your faithfulness.

Show Yourself strong in my life today. Give me boldness and courage when my faith is tested. When I'm
tempted to remain silent about my commitment to You,
when issues of righteousness and justice demand my witness, and when I am called to sacrificial service in living the
commandment to love—then, in those crises, make me
strong with the staying power of Your Spirit.

JUNE
22

Commit your way to the LORD, trust also in Him. . . . Rest in the LORD, and wait patiently for Him.

—PSALM 37:5,7

Lord, as I begin a new day, I take these four vital verbs of the psalmist as my strategy for living in the pressure of what's ahead of me. Before the problems of the day pile up, I will deliberately stop to commit my way to You, to trust in You, to rest in You, and wait patiently for You.

I realize that nothing is more important than being in an honest, open, receptive relationship with You. Everything I need to be faithful and obedient comes in fellowship with You. I am stunned by the fact that You know and care about me, and that You have chosen to bless others through what I say and do.

In response, I want to be spiritually fit for the responsibilities You have given me. So I turn over to Your control my personal life, my relationships, and my duties. I trust You to guide me and provide me with security and strength. Help me to not run ahead of You or lag behind, but to walk with You in Your timing and pacing toward Your goals.

JUNE
23

*Give unto the LORD, O you mighty ones, give
unto the LORD glory and strength. Give unto
the LORD the glory due His name; worship the
LORD in the beauty of holiness.*

—PSALM 29:1

Almighty God, I begin this day with adoration expressed in great affirmations:

- You are the Creator, Sustainer, Redeemer of all
- You are the Sovereign of this world
- By Your providence, You have blessed me
- You have called me to serve You
- I am here by Your appointment
- You are the source of the wisdom I need
- You will guide my decisions

So this is a day for joy, optimism, and courage. Set me free of all negative thinking about myself and my circumstances. I know that nothing is impossible for You!

You are working in my mind to give inspiration and in my body to give strength. Your Spirit is working in the people with whom I talk, in the situations I will confront, and in the problems I will face.

Fill me with Your Spirit so that if I am jostled, only Your love, patience, encouragement, and hope will spill over onto others.

JUNE
24

Cast your burden on the LORD, and He shall sustain you.

—PSALM 55:22

Gracious Father, through the Lord Jesus Christ You have set me free, yet on many days I don't feel free. So often I let myself become tied down by feelings of guilt, bound up by frustrating anxieties, uptight over problems, incarcerated by people's criticisms or negative opinions, and pressured by fears of the future.

In all that, I feel within me a longing to be free. Truly free. Free to enjoy life, myself, and others. Free to give and receive love, forgiveness, and acceptance. Free me to pull out all the stops and live with boldness and courage.

You have shown me that a new burst of personal freedom comes only from knowing You, trusting You, and committing to Your care the burdens I carry. Untie me when I get tied up in knots; unbind me when I get bound up in myself; unleash me when I hold back; I want to serve You by serving others.

Free me, Lord, from self-concern . . . and help me to give myself away to loved ones, friends, and those whom I meet during the course of this day.

JUNE
25

In quietness and confidence shall be our strength.

—ISAIAH 30:15

Almighty God, for this brief moment I retreat into my inner world, that wonderful place where I find Your strength. Here, I escape from the noise of demanding voices and pressured conversations. With You, there is no need to impress, there are no thoughts to defend, there are no feelings to hide.

In Your presence, I can simply be. You love me in spite of my mistakes and give me a new beginning each day. I thank You that I can depend on Your guidance in all that is ahead of me.

Suddenly I realize that this quiet moment—in which I have placed my trust in You—has refreshed me. I am replenished with new hope. Now I can return to my outer world with greater determination to keep my priorities straight.

Today, Lord, is a magnificent opportunity to serve You by giving my very best. Thank you for allowing me this privilege.

JUNE
26

Seek first the kingdom of God and His righteousness, and all these things shall be added to you.

—MATTHEW 6:33

Gracious Father, thank You for this time of prayer in which my mind and heart can be enlarged to receive Your Spirit. You are the answer to my deepest need. More than any secondary gift You can give, I long for the primary grace of Yourself offered in profound love and acceptance. I have learned that when I abide in Your presence and am receptive to Your guidance, You inspire my mind with insight and wisdom, my heart with resiliency and courage, and my body with vigor and vitality.

Lord, before I begin this day, I commit all my worries to You. I entrust to You my concerns over the people I will meet and the circumstances I will encounter. My desire is to give myself to the work of this day with freedom and joy. Give me strength when I become tired, fresh vision when my well becomes dry, and enthusiastic hope when others become disappointed.

Thank You, Father, for the constancy of Your care and love.

JUNE
27

For I am the LORD, I do not change.

—MALACHI 3:6

Dear God, with whom there is no variableness or shadow of turning, more steadfast than the stars and more reliable than the rising and setting of the sun, I thank You for Your changelessness. You are the same yesterday, today, and forever. You are my one fixed stability in the midst of changing circumstances.

Your faithfulness, Lord, is my peace. It is a source of comfort and courage that You know exactly what is ahead of me. Go before me to show the way. Here is my mind; inspire it with Your wisdom. Here is my will; infuse it with desire to follow Your guidance. Here is my heart; infill it with Your love.

I realize, Father, that there is enough time today to do what You desire . . . so grant me freedom from the tyranny of the urgent. You have been so patient with me; help me to be patient with those around me.

I commit this day to You, and thank You for Your power and presence.

JUNE
28

Seek the LORD and His strength; seek His face evermore. Remember His marvelous works which He has done.

—PSALM 105:4-5

Gracious God, thank You for Your faithfulness. You bless me beyond my expectations, and give me what I need—on time, and in time. Today, my prayer is for a much better memory of how You have heard and answered my petitions in the past.

Lord, I commit this quiet moment to recounting my blessings. I thank You for the gift of life, for my relationship with You, for Your grace and forgiveness, for my family and friends, for the privilege of work to do well, for problems and perplexities that force me to trust You more, and for the assurance that You can use even the dark threads of difficulties in weaving the tapestry of my life.

Knowing how You delight to bless a thankful person, I thank You in advance for Your strength and care today. Thank You not just for what You do, but for who You are—my blessed God and loving Father.

JUNE
29

Happy is he who has the God of Jacob for his help, whose hope is in the LORD his God, who made heaven and earth, the sea, and all that is in them.

—PSALM 146:5-6

Holy Father, who transformed a clever manipulating Jacob and renamed him Israel, meaning "God strives," I thank You that You are the person-smith of my life, hammering out the character You want for me.

Gracious God, show me enough of my real self to expose my false pride and enough of Your grace to overcome my self-sufficiency. When I am tempted, fortify me with Your strength. Give me keen intellect to listen for Your voice in every difficulty. Be with me on the mountain peaks of success to remind me that You are the source of my talents and gifts. Also, be with me also in the deep valleys of discouragement to help me receive Your courage to press on.

You are my light, Lord. I was not meant to walk in darkness or fear or uncertainty. I trust You to use all the victories and defeats of life to bring me closer to You.

May the serenity and peace I feel in this time of prayer sustain me throughout this day. I thank You in advance for a great day filled with incredible surprises of sheer joy!

JUNE
30

"Behold, the days are coming," says the Lord GOD, "That I will send a famine on the land, not a famine of bread, nor a thirst for water, but of hearing the words of the LORD."
—AMOS 8:11

Almighty God, and Lord of creation, in Your presence I fall on the knees of my heart with praise and adoration. It is with awe and wonder that I behold Your signature in the natural world and the sheer majesty of Your creation of human life. You have given humankind minds to think Your thoughts, emotions to express Your love, wills to discern and do Your will, and bodies intricately made to reflect Your glory. I particularly thank You for the ability of hearing not just sounds from the world around me but Your voice within me.

Thank You for prayer in which You speak through thoughts You form in my mind and impress on my heart. Help me to listen to You intently. May I never become so resistant to what You have to say that You would send a famine of hearing of Your words. I want to keep the ears of my mind and heart open. Speak Lord, now in the sacred silence or receptive prayer.

Help me put into action what You instruct me to do. I know that simply hearing without action will result in spiritual dullness. I will take seriously Christ's words, "Not everyone who says to Me, 'Lord, Lord,' shall enter the kingdom of heaven, but he who does the will of My Father in heaven" (Matthew 7:21). Today I will listen and act!

JULY
1

In God I have put my trust; I will not fear.

—PSALM 56:4

Gracious God, knowledge of You is my purpose and passion. It is also my greatest need and most urgent desire. I really want to know You . . . not just as Creator and Sustainer of the universe, but as my Father and Friend.

I confess that often, my lack of knowledge of You is the cause of my insecurity, inconsistency, and insufficiency. It also accounts for the vacillation in my prayers.

I commit this day, Lord, to seeking to know You better. I want to open my true self to You; I want to be real, honest, and vulnerable with You; I invite You to invade every aspect of my life. Show me Your will and give me the strength and courage to follow Your guidance. Help me to dedicate myself to making the knowledge of You my first priority. Show me Your grace and goodness, Your righteousness and power.

I place my total trust in You and will live by faith in You today. Be the unseen but undeniable presence in every moment of this day.

JULY
2

*The LORD is gracious and full of compassion,
slow to anger and great in mercy.
The LORD is good to all, and His tender mercies are over all His works.*

—PSALM 145:8-9

Gracious God, You give me so much more than I deserve in blessings, and withhold what I deserve for my lack of faithfulness and obedience. I praise You for Your lovingkindness and mercy. With a fresh realization of Your unqualified grace to me, I recognize my need to be to the people of my life what You have been to me.

Help me to give mercy as I have received it so generously from You. I think of people who need my forgiveness, another chance, encouragement, and affirmation. At times I punish others with my purgatorial pouts, leaving them to wonder about what they can do to regain my approval. Instead, Father, help me to be an agent of reconciliation and renewal. May grace overcome my grudges and joy diffuse my judgments.

Indeed, may this be a day of new beginnings, in which I take the initiative to reach out to others in genuine friendship.

July
3

Seek the peace of the city where I have caused you to be . . . and pray to the LORD for it; for in its peace you will have peace.
—JEREMIAH 29:7

Dear God, You care profoundly about my city. Its problems are on Your heart. Now in this time of prayer I sense You are placing these problems on my heart and on my agenda. As I read today's verse from Jeremiah that You spoke to the people of Israel in exile, I sensed that it was a personal word to me about my involvement in my city. You have placed me where I live so You could use me to help solve the problems. Help me to see citizenship as prayer in action. Enable me to focus on the particular need You have assigned to me. I can't do everything, but I can do something. I want to be on the forefront of the battle for social justice, out in the trenches in the war on poverty. You have put the lost, lonely, and disadvantaged on my heart, but show me the particular people and places You want to invest me. I'm willing and ready. Help me get busy with Your unfinished agenda for the poor, homeless, illiterate, addicted, and those victimized by violence.

I wonder if everyone in my city lived out his or her faith as a citizen the way I do, what kind of city would it be? Often I leave the burden of responsibility on other people's shoulders and then criticize them for what they do or leave undone.

Lord, wake me up to my responsibilities!

JULY
4

Blessed is the nation whose God is the LORD.
—PSALM 33:12

Almighty God, Sovereign of this nation, Lord of my life and Author of the liberties I enjoy as a citizen, may this Independence Day really be a "Dependence Day" for me and my fellow Americans. I want this day to be more than a Fourth of July of picnics, firecrackers, and parades. As I celebrate the birth of this nation, I want to reaffirm the vision for America You planted in the founding fathers and mothers, and the unique role You have given this nation as a demonstration of democracy.

Today, when I say the words "One nation under God" in the Pledge of Allegiance, may it be a fresh commitment to work for righteousness and justice for everyone in every part of society. There is so much in America that contradicts our declaration of dependence on You. I confess that often I reflect our secularized society that gives little thought to You. Then I think of Washington on his knees, of Franklin asking for prayer when the Constitutional Convention was deadlocked, and of Lincoln praying for wisdom in the dark night of the nation's divided soul. You have answered the prayers of Your people all through our history. Today I pray for a spiritual awakening.

Guide the President, Vice President, members of Congress, and the Justices of the Supreme Court. May America be great because she is good. God bless America!

JULY
5

Oh, that men would give thanks to the LORD for His goodness, and for His wonderful works to the children of men! For He satisfies the longing soul, and fills the hungry soul with goodness.

PSALM 107:8-9

Gracious God, I begin this day praying with the psalmist, "Teach me to do Your will, for You are my God; Your Spirit is good" (Psalm 143:10). In a world of people with mixed motives and forces of evil seeking to distract me, I thank You that I can know You are good. It is wonderful to know that You will my good, and seek to help me know what is good for my loved ones. You are constantly working things together for my good and arranging circumstances for what is ultimately best for me. You know what will help me grow in Your grace and what will make me mature spiritually.

Today, I want to be filled so full of Your goodness that I will know how to discern Your good for my decisions. Help me to be an instrument of Your good, who abides by Your standards of righteousness. Help me to confront any mediocrity that may keep me from Your good vision for my life and the lives of those around me.

I commit myself to fight the good fight for ethical and social goodness. Give me strength and courage to take a stand based on Your absolutes.

JULY
6

Let patience have its perfect work, that you may be perfect and entire, wanting nothing.

—JAMES 1:4

Almighty God, Creator and Sovereign of all, slow me down, for I am moving too fast. Sometimes I do not realize Your blessings until they are past. Frequently I jet along at high speed to my destination only to end up circling in a holding pattern. Life also has its own holding patterns, which require me to wait. Yet I am not very good at waiting; I usually want my desires met yesterday. Help me to trust in *Your* timing; You are always on time.

Today, help me to enjoy life as it unfolds—to live to the fullest in each hour, and to relish the sheer wonder of Your grace and goodness. Open my eyes so that I may see Your glory in the people and opportunities You give me. Unstop the ears of my heart so that I may hear Your guidance. Release my will from the bondage of my selfish attitudes so that I can act on what You have called me to do. And replenish my physical strength so that I can have resiliency for each challenge.

If life dishes out to me a holding pattern today, may I use it wisely . . . to remember where I have been by Your grace, and where I am going under Your guidance.

JULY
7

In you, O LORD I put my trust.... incline Your ear to me, and save me. Be my strong habitation, to which I may resort continually.

—PSALM 71:1-3

Gracious Father, my heart is filled with gratitude. I am thankful that You have chosen to be my God and chosen me to know You. Your love embraces me and gives me security; Your joy uplifts me and gives me resiliency; Your peace floods my heart and gives me serenity; Your Spirit fills me and gives me strength.

I truly believe that Your loving hand is upon my life; help me to be sensitive to every guiding nudge of direction. Keep me from making up my mind and then asking for Your approval. Keep me from acting as if I have Your answers to all questions. Keep me humble in my search for my application of Your truth to the matters that face me. Free me from condemnatory judgments, and save me from the exhaustion and frustration of rushing up self-chosen paths without Your guidance.

Give me insight to see Your path for my life, and the patience and endurance to walk in it with my hand firmly in Yours.

JULY
8

The patient in spirit is better than the proud in spirit.

—ECCLESIASTES 7:8

Almighty God, You created me to praise You. Forgive me for the pride that too frequently takes the place of praise in my heart. So often, I want to be adequate in my own strength, to be loved by You because of my self-generated goodness, and to be admired by people because of my superior performance. Yet pride pollutes everything: it stunts my spiritual growth, creates tensions in my relationships, and makes me a person who is difficult for You to bless. Most important of all, my pride separates me from You, dear Father. When pride reigns, life becomes bland, truth becomes relative, and values become debased. I lose that inner confidence of convictions rooted in the Bible and Your revealed truth.

Now in this quiet moment, I praise You for breaking the bubble of illusion that, with my own cleverness and cunning, I can solve life's problems. Help me recover my sense of humor so I can laugh at myself for ever thinking I could make it on my own. I humble myself before You. Fill me with Your Spirit. Now, with my mind planted on the Rock of Ages, I have the power to face the ambiguities of today with the absolutes of Your truth and guidance.

JULY
9

*Yes, the L*ORD *will give what is good.*

—PSALM 85:12

Gracious God, thank You for the serendipities You arrange—those unusual surprises in usual circumstances. You delight to surprise me with interventions and inspiration I do not expect. In a timely way, You guide my thoughts with wisdom and insight that I could not have discovered on my own. You help me untie knotty problems and I am amazed, wondering why I had not thought of the solutions You provide. You use people to help me, bolster my esteem, and to communicate Your love in remarkable ways. You have given me a life full of surprises!

Now as I begin a new day, I want to live expectantly, open for what You will do or give. I am so thankful for Your goodness. May that give me a positive attitude toward what is ahead today. Banish my grimness with Your grace.

Dear God, it's great to be alive and have the privilege of serving You. I report in for the duties of the day with delight!

JULY
10

Beloved, do not believe every spirit, but test the spirits, whether they are of God.

—1 JOHN 4:1

Lord, life and the people around me present me with a mixed bag of challenges and opportunities. Thank You for showing me that love is not sentimental or stupid. There are many good things that may not be Your best for me, and even more bad things that may look good yet could scuttle my ship.

I trust You, abiding Lord, to give me the gift of testing the spirits. I want to trust You completely and to love people sufficiently so as not to bless what comes from either ego or evil. Show me how, dear Lord, today!

I pray for the gift of discernment. Maximize every faculty You have given me to show me Your will and way. Help me think clearly. Guide my thoughts to conclusions that will move me forward in Your plan for me. Control my feelings so that I may trust my inner heart to alert me to potential problems. Take charge of my will and create in me a desire to obey the guidance You give me.

Give me a profound love for people that has integrity. Help me take seriously people's suffering as well as their sin, so I can be both one who honestly confronts and humbly comforts others.

*Let all those who seek You rejoice and be glad
in You; and let those who love your salvation
say continually, "Let God be magnified!"*

—PSALM 70:4

Almighty Father, this is a new day! Vanish all the
gloom and darkness of worry and fear. Set me free to
praise and worship You in joy and gladness. May I neither
gloat over yesterday's successes nor be grim over yesterday's defeats. Help me make a fresh start and give myself fully to the challenges and opportunities of this day.

Grant me a vibrant enthusiasm so that I can accept
each responsibility with affirmation. I know that life is an
accumulation of days lived fully for Your glory or wasted
on anxious care. Fill my mind with Your Spirit so that I
can think creatively; transform my attitudes so I may reflect Your patience and peace; brighten my countenance
so that I will radiate Your joy; infuse strength into my
body so that I will have resiliency for the pressures of
whatever the day will bring.

I look ahead with anticipation to the opportunities
before me today...and my deepest longing is that I will
not miss Your best for me.

JULY
12

*Let us not grow weary while doing good, for in
due season we shall reap if we do not lose heart.
Therefore, as we have opportunity, let us do
good to all, especially to those who are of the
household of faith.*

—GALATIANS 6:9-10

Gracious God, Sovereign of my life, You have
blessed me with the opportunity to be a vital part of Your
blessing to other people. I commit this day to being sensitive to the needs of others around me. Show me the
people who are in need of encouragement or affirmation.
Give me exactly what I should say to give them a lift. Free
me of preoccupation with myself and my own needs. Help
me to remember that people will care about what I know
when they know I care about them. May my countenance, words, and actions communicate my caring.

Make me a good listener, Lord, and enable me to
hear what people are expressing beneath what they are
saying. Most of all, remind me of the power of intercessory
prayer. May I claim Your best for people as I pray for
them . . . including those with whom I disagree. Help me
to see them not as enemies but as individuals who will
help sharpen my edge. Lift me above petty attitudes or
petulant gossip. Rather, fill me with Your presence, and
my heart with Your magnanimous attitude toward others.

JULY
13

Nevertheless I have this against you, that you have left your first love.

—REVELATION 2:4

Gracious, loving Father, You have taught me to give thanks for all things, to dread nothing but the loss of closeness with You, and to cast all my cares on You. Set me free from timorous timidity when it comes to living the absolutes of Your commandments and speaking with the authority of Your truth. All around me I see much evidence of moral confusion. People talk a great deal about values, but have lost their grip on Your standards.

Help me to be one who lives honestly, with integrity, and trustworthily. I want to be an authentic person rather than a studied caricature of character. Free me from capricious dissimulations, from covered duality, from covert duplicity. Instead of manipulating others with power games, help me motivate them with love. Grant me the passion I had when I first heard Your call to commit my life to You, the idealism I had when I first understood the greatness of Your cause, and the inspiration I knew when Your Spirit was my only source of strength.

May this be a day for recapturing my first love for You and my first priority of glorifying You through all that I do.

JULY
14

Your Father knows the things you have need of before you ask Him.

—MATTHEW 6:8

Almighty God, long ago the prophet Isaiah asked some penetrating questions:

> Who has measured the waters in the hollow of his hand, measured heaven with a span and calculated the dust of the earth in a measure? Weighed the mountains in scales and the hills in a balance? Who has directed the Spirit of the LORD, or as His counselor has taught Him? With whom did He take counsel, and who instructed Him, and taught Him in the path of justice? Who taught Him knowledge, and showed Him the way of understanding? (Isaiah 40:12-14).

Those questions expose the shallowness of my understanding of prayer. So often I come to You in prayer as if it were my responsibility to brief You on all my needs. And then there are times when I try to get You to bless plans about which I never consulted You.

Father, You created prayer for me to be with You, to know You, to have my character emulate Your character, and to be filled with Your Spirit. I humble myself now, and open myself completely to receive Your marching orders and follow You. Not my will, but Yours be done.

It is God who arms me with strength, and makes my way perfect.

—PSALM 18:32

Gracious Father, make me maximum for the demanding responsibilities and relationships of this day. I say with the psalmist, "The LORD is my strength and my shield; my heart trusted in Him, and I am helped; therefore my heart greatly rejoices" (Psalm 28:7).

My day is filled with challenges and decisions that will test my knowledge and experience. I dare not trust in my own understanding. In this moment of solitude, fill my inner well with Your Spirit. My greatest desire is to live today for Your glory and by Your grace.

I praise You that it is Your desire to give good gifts to those who ask You. You give strength and courage when we seek You above everything else. You guide the humble and teach them Your way. I open my mind now to receive Your inspiration; astound me with new insights and fresh ideas that I would not conceive without Your blessing.

Thank You that when I truly seek You and desire to do Your will, You will guide me in what to ask. For I know that when I ask what You guide, then You will provide.

The First Beatitude

Blessed are the poor in spirit, for theirs is the kingdom of heaven.

—MATTHEW 5:3

Lord Jesus Christ, today I claim that I am a blessed person—chosen, cherished, and called by You to experience the lasting joy of true greatness according to Your measurements. You have shown me that to be poor in spirit is to be humble. Help me not be less than I am, but to confess my need for Your help to be all that You have destined for me to be and do. I admit my insufficiency and inadequacy, while humbly putting my trust in You. Today I seek to know and do Your will and grow through what You reveal in and around me.

And at the end of the day, help me take a creative inventory: Was I humble in spirit? Did I live on the growing edge? Was I quick to admit my need for You? Have I grown today through what I have thought and experienced? Did pride or my need to be adequate get in the way of what You wanted to teach me?

Now Lord, I commit to You all of my unresolved problems and unfinished tasks. Knowing that I am a citizen of the kingdom of heaven under Your rule, I thank You in advance for what You will do in my life today.

JULY
17

The Second Beatitude

Blessed are those who mourn, for they shall be comforted.

—Matthew 5:4

Sovereign Lord, I begin this day knowing that greatness is living in daylight compartments. It is keeping short accounts with You, with myself, and with others. Help me never to carry over to the next day unconfessed sins I have committed, unforgiven hurts done to me by others, and unhealed resentments about what life has dished out to me.

Therefore, today Lord, I receive Your grace and will live as a forgiven and forgiving, empathetically caring person. Help me to mourn over what breaks Your heart. I pray that I will be quick to seek Your forgiveness for my failures and will not carry the burden of guilt. Because of Your forgiveness, may I quickly forgive others and seek their forgiveness. And feeling the suffering of the world, I pray that I will become an intentional disciple to bring healing and hope to other people.

Throughout this day, I pray for the comfort of Your presence, forgiveness, encouragement, exhortation, and power. Thank You for Your comfort when I feel deeply the pain and suffering of others. May I be a comfort to them today.

July
18

The Third Beatitude

Blessed are the meek, for they shall inherit the earth.

—Matthew 5:5

Gracious Lord Jesus, You have taught me the true meaning of meekness. It is not weakness; in fact, it requires strength and determination. I think of the Hebrew word *anaw*, used to describe a person who is moldable, who out of love and obedience, openly accepts the providence and guidance of the Father. Then I think of the Greek word *praus,* used for an animal that is leadable by the bit and reins of its master. Now I remember Psalm thirty-seven's vivid description of a meek person: doesn't fret, takes delight in the Lord, commits his way to Him, is willing to wait for guidance, and follows orders. Today I want to experience Your kind of meekness. Fill me with Your Spirit; make me like Yourself. I commit this day to discover and do what You desire. Enable me to be an open, leadable, responsive disciple today.

With Your quality of meekness, may I inherit the limitless spiritual wealth You have for me. I claim that I am a "joint heir" with You (Romans 8:17). In Your name I accept the spiritual riches You have stored up for me. May I draw on the grace, peace, joy, strength, wisdom, and courage You offer me. Help me also claim every situation, relationship, and opportunity as part of the inheritance in which You will manifest Your presence and power today.

The Fourth Beatitude

Blessed are those who hunger and thirst for righteousness, for they shall be filled.

—MATTHEW 5:6

Dear Father, I thank You for the gift of grace given through Your Son, Jesus Christ. I commit today to be a day of righteous living. My dominant desire today, above all else, will be to seek first Your kingdom and Your righteousness in my decisions, ethics, and morality. I will hunger and thirst for righteousness today.

Fill me with a consuming passion to be in a right relationship with You and reconciled with others. Not only do I desire Your righteousness as my passion, but also with other people and their needs. Any person who does not know Your love and any area of injustice in society will become a part of Your agenda for me.

In this quiet moment, I pray for a sense of Your assurance for receiving the gift of a hunger and thirst for Your righteousness. I affirm that I want to do right because I am righteous through Your love and forgiveness. Thank You, Lord, for making each day a fresh opportunity to hunger and thirst for righteousness.

The Fifth Beatitude

Blessed are the merciful, for they shall obtain mercy.

—MATTHEW 5:7

Lord of mercy, thank You for recalling me to the greatness of being merciful. Help me to know what it means to lay down my life for the people around me. Then motivate me to action, so that when this day ends, I will be able to know that Your mercy has been expressed through me.

Today I ask for an assurance of Your mercy, which is the basis of trust and confidence, strength and courage, hope and joy. Help me, Lord, to be merciful. As I receive Your mercy, today I will seek to multiply that mercy by being merciful to others.

Remind me of the times when I've experienced Your mercy and the times when I was less than merciful to others. Looking back, what could I have done or said differently that would have been pleasing to You? And what can I do or express today to be a merciful person? My desire, gracious Lord, is to receive grace—Your outgoing love; mercy—Your ingoing love; and peace—Your ongoing serenity. I know that receiving and giving mercy maintains the flow of grace, and peace is the abiding sense of being accepted and loved. I accept Your forgiveness, and commit myself to make a fresh start today.

JULY
21

The Sixth Beatitude

Blessed are the pure in heart, for they shall see God.

—MATTHEW 5:8

Holy God, just as the fluid in my physical eye keeps my eye cleansed, so may Your Holy Spirit cleanse, dilate, and focus the vision of the spiritual eyes of my heart. As I begin this day, I open my heart to be filled with the Holy Spirit. I desire to be pure in heart so that I can see You more clearly and love You more dearly. I know that mixed motives prevent me from seeing You. I long for my heart to be free from the admixtures of pride, selfishness, manipulation, lust for power, jealousy, envy, negative criticism, and resentment. I reaffirm my desire to put You first in my life and make an unreserved commitment that enables me to rivet my attention upon You.

Today, I accept the gifts of the Holy Spirit so that I may live supernaturally. I will gratefully be a channel for the flow of the fruit of the Spirit—love, joy, peace, patience, kindness, goodness, faithfulness, gentleness, and self-control.

I pray that I will see more clearly Your presence in the world, in circumstances, in people, and in the new person You are creating in me. I want to start this day with a pure heart so that I will behold more of the wonder of Your grace and goodness.

JULY
22

The Seventh Beatitude

Blessed are the peacemakers, for they shall be called sons of God.

—MATTHEW 5:9

Blessed Father, I praise You for the peace that comes from You through Christ and the blood He shed on the cross. Your Son came to bring peace and has called me to be a peacemaker. Today in my relationship with You, Father, I want to express my family likeness by manifesting the fruit of the Spirit of peace, and will accept my calling to be a peacemaker.

I pray that I will not sow discord, fan the fires of misunderstanding between people, take sides in petty conflicts, or participate in gossip. Rather, I seek to be a peacemaker and share Your peace with those around me. Help me to try to bring healing of hurts and reconciliation of estrangement and brokenness between people.

My constant prayer to You is, "Lord, make me an instrument of Your peace." Work through me to communicate serenity, tranquility, and joy. Help me be quick to forgive, slow to judge, and resourceful in conflicts. I confess anything that robs me of Your peace so that I can receive anew Your grace and commit on this day to be a peacemaker.

JULY
23

The Eighth Beatitude

Blessed are those who are persecuted for righteousness' sake, for theirs is the kingdom of heaven.

—MATTHEW 5:10

Lord, I pray that my conduct today will be a reflection of my convictions and belief in You. Often, I remain silent when I should take a stand. I confess that I sometimes compromise my convictions and have become a chameleon who blends into the culture around me. Would the people around me know that I belong to You and have put You first in my life? Is the trouble I sometimes face a result of pursuing righteousness, or is it because of my personality quirks, insensitivity, or ego needs?

Today I seek Your guidance for what I am to do and say in each situation and relationship. Out of love for You, I seek to be faithful and obedient. Under Your control and with Your guidance, I want to speak the truth in love and take stands on issues of righteousness.

Help me not to accept popularity at the cost of compromising my convictions. Today I want to soar like an eagle rather than blend like a chameleon. I would rather face trouble for what's right than succeed in what's wrong. If I am misunderstood or rejected or hurt in the battle of faith, hope, and love, I will trust You, Lord, for Your help, healing, and courage.

JULY
24

By one Spirit we were all baptized into one body.... God composed the body, having given greater honor to that part which lacks it, that there should be no schism in the body, but that the members should have the same care for one another.

—1 Corinthians 12:13,24-25

Lord, thank You for making me special. I am nourished in the depths of my heart by the realization that I am special to You.

Help me, Father, to reach out to people in my life who need to feel special to me so that I can help them to know that they are special to You also. I commit this day to being an active, contagious communicator of affirming esteem in those around me. Thanks in advance for Your love for each person I meet. And thank You for making it all possible through the limitless love of the cross.

As I move through this day, I want to claim Your blessings for people. Remind me to greet people warmly, pray for them as I shake their hands, and listen patiently to them. May my "How are you?" never be glib nor perfunctory, but sincere and desirous of an answer. When I learn about needs, give me the courage to do what love demands—even if it's inconvenient.

JULY
25

You shall love the LORD your God with all your heart, with all your soul, and with all your might.

—DEUTERONOMY 6:4

Almighty God, I fall on the knees of my heart with awe and adoration. The psalmist gives wings to my deep longing to tell You how much I love You: "As the deer pants for the water brooks, so pants my soul for You, O God. My soul thirsts for God, for the living God" (Psalm 42:1-2).

As I think magnificently of You, my praise is like a thermostat opening me to the outward flow of my gratitude and an inflow of Your Spirit—an artesian geyser of grace assuring me that I am loved *now*.

Amazed again by Your unqualified love, I confess anything that stands between You and me or between me and any other person.

Most of all, I confess the idols of my heart. So often I think of myself; so easily I try to focus upon both You and my idols of pride, prestige, popularity, and power. Yet Your sovereign demand is that I have no other god before You.

Help me to remember, Lord, that I could not think a thought, speak a word, or take an action without Your permission and power. And so, I surrender my life anew to You.

JULY
26

If God is for us, who can be against us?

—ROMANS 8:31

Gracious God, I begin this day with three liberating convictions: You are on my side, You are by my side, and You are the source of strength inside. Help me to regain the confidence that comes from knowing that You are for me and not against me.

I continue to remain awed at the knowledge that You have created me to know and love You, and have called me to serve You wherever You lead me. You have programmed me for greatness by Your power, so help me to place my trust in You and live fully for You.

I thank You that You are with me, seeking to help me know and do Your will. Guide me today in all that I face. I invite You to take up residence in my mind so that I may see things from Your perspective. And grant me the courage to give You my all. May Your justice, righteousness, integrity, honesty, and truth be the identifiable qualities of my character.

Lord, I commit all that I have and am to glorifying You with all that I do today.

JULY
27

I press on . . .

—PHILIPPIANS 3:13 (NIV)

Almighty God, Lord of progress, I commit this day to be one of growth in every area of my life.

Help me to develop a deeper relationship with You. Free me to give over to Your control areas of my life I have kept closed off from Your guidance and transforming power.

Today, I want to grow intellectually. Guide me to new truths, ideas, and insights I have not known before. I am astounded by how much there is to learn and by how little I know of the broad spectrum of knowledge.

May this be a day to make steps toward more creative, satisfying relationships with people. Free me to do something today that I have been procrastinating. Inspire me to express love and practical caring more freely today.

This is also a day to do my job better than ever before. Lift me out of the ruts of mediocrity. I want to press on to excellence.

Give me an opportunity to take action to help solve some social problem today. Extricate from me that bland tolerance that accepts the false idea that things have to remain as they are.

My steps forward today may be small, but at least they are steps off dead center. Keep me moving, Lord!

I know how to be abased, and I know how to abound. Everywhere and in all things I have learned both to be full and to be hungry, both to abound and to suffer need.

—PHILIPPIANS 4:12

Lord Christ, You have all authority in heaven and on earth. I submit my life to Your authority. Possess my mind with clear convictions that You are in charge of my life and the lives of those about whom I am concerned. I surrender myself and them to You.

Brand in my heart and on my mind the great truth that Paul wrote while he was in prison: "I can do all things through Christ who strengthens me" (Philippians 4:13). Let me have the kind of faith that enabled Paul to run the race that You marked out for him—a race that he ran diligently, no matter what difficulty or suffering befell him.

I confess that so often my happiness is based on having everyone's approval and having everything go well as I had planned. Toughen me up so I'm not so thin-skinned and so easily upset by people's changing moods and their opinions of me. In this time of prayer I place my trust totally on You.

JULY
29

You shall be perfect, just as your Father in heaven is perfect.

—MATTHEW 5:48

Heavenly Father, I come before You wanting to be like Your Son Jesus Christ. Refine my character into the character of Christ so that I may trust in the plans You have for me rather than relying on my own plans. Let me be a recipient of Your courage and strength.

Lord, make me empathetically sensitive to others who endure difficulties so that I can be like Christ to them. May my faith have the ring of reality, the authenticity of truth lived out in the real world. As I walk through this day, may I be able to radiate the true joy of Christ, which is so much more than simply being happy.

In this moment, I have been disquieted by Christ's exhortation that I am to be perfect as You are perfect. How can that be? Then I realize that the word *perfect* in the New Testament, means "complete, mature, accomplishing our purpose." I want You to help me to be prepared for this kind of perfection. I realize I will be fully complete only when I reach heaven, but Lord, may Your miracle of true maturity continue today.

*No temptation has overtaken you except such
as is common to man; but God is faithful, who
will not allow you to be tempted beyond what
you are able, but with the temptation will also
make the way of escape, that you may be able
to bear it.*

—1 CORINTHIANS 10:13

Gracious God, there will be times when I am tempted today. I press on with the day knowing that You will be faithful to the promise I read in today's Scripture: When I am tempted, You will offer me a way of escape. So I claim that I am not a helpless victim of temptations either in my thinking or actions. I firmly believe that You within me are greater than Satan in the world (1 John 4:4). You will help me in the crisis when I'm tempted to deny You or denigrate my calling to glorify You.

You have called me to absolute truth, purity, honesty, and integrity. It's tempting to put a spin on sin. Half-truths, titillating fantasies, dissimulations and inconsistencies can be very tempting. And yet, in each instance You can invade my mind with what is right and give me the courage to say or do what is right.

In my relationships, there is that split second when You give me a choice not to hurt or hassle the people around me. Give me a momentary lockjaw when I'm about to assassinate someone's character with words or manipulate another with fear. Take control, Lord, and give me the strength to choose to take Your way of escape from temptation.

The effective, fervent prayer of a righteous man avails much.

—JAMES 5:16

Dear God, You have called me to the awesome opportunity of intercessory prayer. Today, I want to pray for people You have put on my prayer agenda who are in trouble because of sin in their lives. I know from my own life the pain and anguish my sins have caused me and other people. Out of gratitude and praise for Your forgiveness of me, I want to pray for the people I love.

Lord, before it's too late, open their hearts to Your love. Now in this time of intimate conversation with You, show me how I can be part of Your pursuit of them. Enable me to know what to be and say, when and how I am to incarnate Your love by intervening with comfort or confrontation.

I confess that I don't know how to pray for what is best for people. Guide my thinking so I can word my intercessory prayers and ask for what You want for people about whom I am concerned. You never give up on people; may I never lose hope in what You can do to help, change, or guide them.

Thank You, Father, for showing me a love that knows no limits.

AUGUST
1

❧❧

Be kind to one another, tender-hearted, for-
giving one another, even as God in Christ also
forgave you.

—EPHESIANS 4:32

Holy God of love, You have revealed to me what it means to love in Jesus Christ, my Lord. You have shown me that to love means to will the ultimate good of another. In His life and death I see giving and forgiving, caring and daring love. In my experience of You, I have found that You love me just as I am and in spite of what I have done. Most of all, I know that You are involved with me to enable me to be the person I was created and destined to be. I can trust You because I have found You utterly reliable each time I have trusted my needs and problems to You.

I confess that it's difficult to love others as You have loved me. At times I love things and use people; I wish it could be the other way around! As I pray this silent prayer and consider what Your Word proclaims about relationships, my mind is flooded by the people I have used for my own purposes with too little thought of what was best for them. I am often a burden and not a boost, a load of care and not a lift of concern. Help me to get back into the flow of Your love so that I can be an encouraging enabler of the people You have given me.

In this sacred moment of openness and receptivity, teach me, Lord, how to love!

AUGUST
2

Sanctify them by Your truth. Your word is truth.

—JOHN 17:17

Lord Jesus Christ, the Way, the Truth, and the Life, You are the truth You spoke. You didn't just teach truth, You exemplified it in Your life and ministry. The more I know of You, the more I know of the nature of God and reality. What's more, You reveal what I can become. I am astounded when I consider Your promise, "These things I have done you shall do also" (*see* John 14:12).

Lord, I want to focus my whole life on the truth today. Help me to do truth in all my responsibilities. May the truth of Your love in the incarnation enable me to be an extension of the incarnation in the challenges and demands of the hours of this day.

In this quiet moment, I open myself to the pervading power of Your truth about me and my life. Help me to find deep, healing fellowship with those who share the truth. Give me patience and sensitivity with those who do not know the truth. I want to live the truth so vividly that people will want to know the reason for the hope that is in me. In a world of half-truths and distorted truth, I want to be a person who can speak the truth and live it.

AUGUST
3

Two men went up to the temple to pray, one a Pharisee and the other a tax collector. The Pharisee stood and prayed thus to himself, "God, I thank You that I am not like other men—extortioners, unjust, adulterers, or even as this tax collector. I fast twice a week; I give tithes of all that I possess." . . . everyone who exalts himself will be abased, and he who humbles himself will be exalted."

—LUKE 18:10-12,14

Dear God, You must smile at some bogus prayers that are not really prayers at all. Some prayers, like the prayer of this Pharisee, are really prayers to ourselves. They are confined to the close inner chamber of self-sufficiency, they express pride in self, not praise to You, and they compare our achievements to other people's inadequacies.

Forgive me when my prayers drift into a self-justifying effort to impress You. Pride can so easily twist and distort my prayers. It can trick me into seeing only what I want to see. You have created prayer for me to be totally honest with You.

Help me to learn how to pray like the tax-collector in Jesus' parable. He knew his need and prayed, "God, be merciful to me a sinner!" Give me the authentic humility that asks and answers the crucial questions: What do I have that I was not given? How can I glorify You more? What are the next steps You have for me to take in being a faithful servant?

AUGUST
4

You are My friends if you do whatever I command you.

—JOHN 15:14

Lord Jesus, You are the vine and I am the branch. I cannot respond to the high cost of loving without this quiet moment of enabling connection between You as the vine and me as the branch. The source of the love I need to express is the sap of Your Spirit moving from You, the vine, into me, one of Your branches.

Thank You for this love-connection in which I can listen for Your guidance for what You want me to say and do. What a great promise! I will be given orders for what I am to do to be an expression of Your love to people today. You will make it plain. You have shown me that each time I do what You guide in problematical relationships, I will receive clarity for the next step. You draw me into Your confidence, help me picture what I am to express, and then give me strength to get on with it.

Lord, it is wonderful to be Your friend. I'm amazed at the confidence You place in me. I long to be worthy of that trust today.

What a sublime Friend You are! We share a vision, a hope, a dream together. You guide me each step of the way and pick me up when I stumble. You help me to be true to my calling to be a communicator of Your love.

AUGUST
5

*The LORD bless you and keep you; the LORD
make His face to shine upon you, and be gracious to you; the LORD lift up His countenance
upon you, and give you peace.*

—NUMBERS 6:24-26

Father, I begin this day by claiming this magnificent
fivefold assurance. I ask You to make this a delightful day
filled with the assurance of Your blessing. May I live today
with the creative esteem of knowing You have chosen me
and called me to receive Your love and to serve You. Keep
me safe from danger and the forces of evil. Give me the
helmet of salvation to protect my thinking from any in-
trusion of temptation to pride, resistance to Your guidance, or negative attitudes. Smile on me as Your face,
Your presence, lifts me from fear or frustration.

Thank You for Your grace to overcome the grimness
that sometimes pervades my countenance. Instead, may
my countenance reflect Your joy. May Your peace flow
into me, calming my agitated spirit, conditioning my disposition and controlling all that I say and do.

Help me to say to others, "Have a blessed day," and
to expect nothing less for myself. Help me to experience
the peace of a forgiven, forgiving heart, the peace of a
heart completely open to You, and the peace of a pure
heart filled with Your Spirit. You are the sole source of
perfect peace.

AUGUST
6

You are manifestly an epistle of Christ . . . written not with ink but by the Spirit of the living God, not on tablets of stone but on tablets of flesh, that is, of the heart.

—2 CORINTHIANS 3:3

Lord, who calls all believers into discipleship and all disciples into the ministry of the laity, I accept my calling to be an epistle of Christ with a mixed sense of thanksgiving and trepidation. You want to send a letter of good news to the people around me today, and You plan to send it not on paper or E-mail, but through me personally. Today people will read what it means to know You, to live by grace, to be inspired by supernatural power. They will see how life was meant to be lived: joy, peace, patience, vision, hope.

Or will they? It is a sobering thought to picture myself as the only communication of Your truth they might receive today. It makes me wonder what kind of example I am. Further, I don't really have a choice. If people know I believe in You, they will take their readings about how that faith works in the down-to-earth application in everyday living.

So Lord, before I go further in this day, I ask for a fresh infilling of Your Spirit, a renewed experience of Your love and forgiveness and rejuvenated assurance of Your peace. Do in me what You want others to read in the epistle of my life.

AUGUST
7

*Blessed are those who keep His testimonies,
who seek Him with the whole heart!*

—PSALM 119:2

Gracious God, the deepest longing of my heart is to know You. I echo the yearning of the psalmist when he said, "With my whole heart I have sought You" (Psalm 119:10-11).

Father, help me live today with a sense of accountability to You. So often I live my life on the horizontal level, thinking only of the wins and losses in my human struggles. There are people I want to please and others I want to defeat. Awaken me to the reality that every word I speak and every action I do is open to Your review. Make me sensitive to my sins against You and Your absolutes for faithful living. Help me to have Your Word, Your will and way, be the mandate in the hidden, inner sanctuary of my soul. Give me courage to remove any idols of my heart and be true in my commitment to worship only You. Make me fearless, decisive, and unreserved in my desire to be obedient to what You reveal to me today.

Even as I pray for Your guidance and the will to follow through, I am deeply moved again that You have chosen me to be one through whom You can think Your thoughts. I'm stunned every time I reflect on that. It makes me want to live at full potential today. I'm expectant and very excited about the day ahead!

AUGUST
8

Eye has not seen, nor ear heard, nor have entered into the heart of man the things God has prepared for those who love Him. But God has revealed them to us through His Spirit.

—1 CORINTHIANS 2:9-10

Gracious Father, enlist me in the triumphant fellowship of the inadequate. Help me to live beyond the meager resources of my adequacy and learn that You are totally reliable when I trust You completely. I want to discover the secret of how You constantly lead me into challenges and opportunities that are beyond my energies and experience. I know that in every circumstance You will provide me with exactly what I need.

Looking back, I know that I could not have made it without Your intervention and inspiration. And when I settle back on a comfortable plateau of satisfaction, suddenly You press me on to new levels in the adventure of living. You are a disturber of false peace, the developer of dynamic character, and the ever-present Deliverer when I attempt what I could not do on my own.

May this be a day in which I attempt something humanly impossible and discover that You are able to provide the power to pull it off. Give me a fresh burst of excitement for the duties of this day so that I will be able to serve courageously. Indeed, I will attempt great things for You and expect great things from You!

Be strong and of good courage, do not fear nor be afraid of them; for the LORD your God, He is the One who goes with you. He will not leave you nor forsake you.

—DEUTERONOMY 31:6

Lord, You know better than I do what I am facing today. I need Your courage. I surrender all my hopes and dreams, desires and visions to Your perfect will. I want to do what You want me to do. I've learned that that's the only source of Your gift of courage. Thank You for the challenges of today. I know You will be with me; that's all I need to know.

Moses' words to Joshua ring in my heart. I claim their fear-dispelling power and Your confidence-inspiring presence. Help me make this day one of constant conversation with You. Whisper Your instructions for each relationship and situation. I commit myself to be attentive. Show me Your will and way, Lord. I gratefully remember the times You helped me make it through very difficult circumstances. I can say with Paul, "The Lord stood with me and strengthened me" (2 Timothy 4:17).

Oh God of courage, put steel in my spine, vision in my mind, and hope in my heart. There are things I can't do today without Your power, and there are other things I would not even think of doing because You are present. So give me courage to say yes to what You will and no to what You would not bless.

August
10

Beloved, if God so loved us, we also ought to love one another.

—1 John 4:11

Gracious Lord, You have loved, forgiven, and cared for me. In Your holy presence, all my self-righteousness fades like a candlelight before the rising sun. Awaken me again to the wonder of Your love for me. Bring me again to realize the unqualified grace of Your justification on the cross. May the radiance of Your Spirit invade my heart, vanishing all the gloom and darkness of worry and fear and sin.

Father, set me free to worship You in joy and gladness. The people in my life desperately need Your love. Liberate me with the sure knowledge of Your unfailing love so that I will be able to be free to love unselfishly. Speak to me now so that in wondrous awe I may be energized with new life and throb with new power to do the loving things You will guide me to do today. Make me creative in finding new ways to put love into action. Show me innovative ways to tell people how much they mean to me. Specifically, I pray for those who need affirmation through me, encouragement expressed by me, hope communicated from me. Regretfully, I think of relationships that need to be repaired. Help me to take the first step toward reconciliation today. Guide me as I seek or express forgiveness. I commit this day to abiding in Your presence and abounding with your power.

AUGUST
11

Come to Me, all you who labor and are heavy laden, and I will give you rest. Take My yoke upon you and learn from Me, for I am gentle and lowly in heart, and you will find rest for your souls. For My yoke is easy and My burden is light.

—MATTHEW 11:28-30

Blessed Lord Jesus, Carpenter of Nazareth, source of truth and Lord of my life, today I want to learn from You how to live a full and abundant life. I come to You because of Your gracious invitation, "Come to Me."

Teach me what it means to take Your yoke upon me. I think of the kind of yokes You must have had in your carpenter's shop: two openings, one larger for the strong training ox and the other smaller one for the trainee.

Now I understand what You mean by Your yoke being easy. When I am yoked with You, You carry the load, show the direction, and set the pace. Today I don't want to pull away and rub my neck raw because of willfulness. Help me to do things Your way and in Your timing.

In this quiet moment, I feel Your lifting and pulling power. You have assumed responsibility for the burdens I have been carrying. I experience the rest that comes from relinquishing my control. The strain is gone; the tension is released. Now I can move forward toward Your goals. Show me the way, just for today!

August
12

Holy, holy, holy is the LORD of hosts;
the whole earth is full of His glory!

—Isaiah 6:3

Holy Lord God Almighty, praise and honor be to You; Ruler of the universe, reign in me; Lord of all creation, recreate my heart to love You above all else.

Hear my confession, but help me to get to the deeper sins that cause the surface sins I repetitiously pray about. Guide my confession; confront the idols of my heart. Forgive me, Lord.

In the quietness, I hear Your absolution given through the blood of the cross: "I do not condemn you; go in peace; receive strength to be different; you are free."

Thank You for Your amazing grace. It creates in me the desire to love and glorify You more fully. In You, Lord, I live and move and have my being. Awaken me to Your presence with me in all that I do today. May I do or say nothing that would make me ashamed in Your presence.

Place on my heart the needs of people who need my prayers of intercession and Your answers. Sometimes I wonder Lord: if You know everything, why do You wait to act until I intercede for others? I hear You, Lord: You wait to bless in order to deepen caring relationships between Your children. So guide me in my prayers for _____ and _____ , and provide for their needs.

AUGUST
13

*Multitudes, multitudes in the valley of decision!
. . . the LORD is near in the valley of decision.*

—JOEL 3:14

Lord, I live in the valley of decision most of the time. Decisions must be made. Today I want to pray over the questions You press me to answer before making an important decision:

- Is my ultimate purpose to know and do Your will?

- Which of the alternatives before me will be congruent with this life agenda?

- Can I do it and keep my priorities straight? Does it contradict Your commandments in any way?

- Will it extend Your kingdom rule in my life, relationships, and society?

- If I made that choice, would it glorify You and help me to grow as Your child?

- Will it enable the ultimate good of all concerned; that is, in spite of temporary pain or difficulty, would it finally be creative for everyone involved?

- Can I look back on having made this choice and still feel good about myself?

- Will it cause uncreative stress and anxiety?

- Can I affirm Your presence in every aspect of carrying out this decision?

Speak Lord through the thoughts You give me in answer to these questions.

August
14

For You are my hope, O Lord GOD. . . .

—PSALM 71:5

God of hope, I need Your vibrant optimism. My own optimism is like a tea bag: I never know how strong it is until I get into hot water. It is in these times of frustration or adversity that my optimism is tested. When the process of human efforts grinds slowly and people disturb my pace of progress, my attitudes are given a litmus test. Often my realism too soon turns to resignation; I expect far too little, and receive it. Lord, transform my experienced pessimism into expectant hope. So often I live as if I had to carry the burdens alone. Today I relinquish to You any negative thoughts and receive a fresh infusion of Your hope.

Here are my needs for healing, wholeness and health; here are my emotional conflicts, tensions and fears. The wonder of it all is that You know, care about me, and invite me to come to you for the personal encounter of this quiet moment with You.

Dear God, increase my faith. Give me deeper trust and higher expectancy. I think of specific concerns. Oh, how I need to know that You want to help me with these problems and opportunities. I think of _____ and _____especially. Then my mind goes to people who desperately need You, particularly _____ and _____. May I hear You say, "Be of good cheer; My hope will give you courage. Go in peace."

AUGUST
15

Oh God, our Help in ages past,
Our Hope for years to come . . .
Be Thou our Guide while life shall last,
And our eternal home!

Almighty God, above time and yet with me in the passage of time, You give me enough time each day to do what You want accomplished. Thank You for the minutes and hours of the day ahead. May I feel neither rushed nor restless. Help me to think of them as Your investment in this day's account, there for me to draw on to do what You want me to do on Your timing.

Make me a good steward of the gift of time I have today; may I not squander or sequester it. Free me from the manipulation of time to get my way. May my goal be to do Your will in the order of Your priorities for the good and encouragement of others.

I commit myself to being sensitive to the guidance of Your Spirit in the convictions I express and how I express them. Give me generosity in my attitudes and frugality in my verbiage. Remind me all through today of my accountability to You; fill my life with Your glory and my mind and heart with Your wisdom.

AUGUST
16

Don't copy the behavior and customs of this world, but be a new and different person with a fresh newness in all you do and think.

—ROMANS 12:2 (TLB)

Lord, I want to live in reality. Give me the courage to see things as they are. Help me be totally honest with myself so I can open myself completely to Your transforming power. May I not be overly consumed in other people's opinions. Set me free from being swayed by compliments or swamped by criticism.

At the same time, give me eyes to see the people around me as they truly are in their humanity and in their need for Your love. Forgive my projected wish dreams for people that set up expectations and create tension. Often I want people to act and react according to my ideas of what they should be or accomplish. Then You know how easy it is for me to fall into the trap of negative criticism or manipulation.

When it comes to circumstances and situations around me, give me a balanced combination of realism and vision. I tire of the fake and the false. I'm fatigued by the pretense that polishes problems and evades Your judgment. The spin runs thin; the damage control delays absolute honesty. Distinctions between the real and the false are blurred. Thank You for this time of prayer in which I can be real with You, and bring healing and hope in my relationships and responsibilities today.

AUGUST
17

Sanctify yourselves, for tomorrow the Lord will do wonders among you.

—JOSHUA 3:5

Holy God, You have called me to holy living. You have shown me that to be holy is to belong first and foremost to You. My only claim to this awesome word *holy* is that You have chosen and called me to be Your person.

With that in mind, I accept for myself Your promise to the people of Israel on the banks of the Jordan, about to cross over and claim the Promised Land. I picture them there. You promised to roll back the waters when the priests carrying the Ark would dare to put their feet in the water. What You wanted to do for them required their cooperation, trust, and courage.

The same is true for me today. You want to make the future a friend with each tomorrow filled with Your blessings. And yet, You patiently wait for me to claim my status as Your person, and consecrate myself completely to You. I put myself inside the skin of one of those priests as he shouldered the Ark and moved toward the overflowing river. It wasn't until the priests were up to their necks in the river that You caused the river to recede so all the people could pass through. You were faithful to Your promise.

Lord, give me the courage to trust You knowing You will be on time with Your intervention to give me exactly what I need.

AUGUST
18

Mary took a pound of very costly oil of spike-nard, anointed the feet of Jesus, and wiped His feet with her hair. And the house was filled with the fragrance of the oil.

—JOHN 12:3

Blessed Lord Jesus, as Mary broke open the cruse and poured out the oil on You, anointing You in love and gratitude, so this prayer is a breaking open and pouring out of myself in response for all You mean to me. When I think of all You have done for me, I wonder how I can put my gratitude into words. I love You, Lord. Thank You for Your life, message, death, resurrection, and reigning presence in my life. Particularly, I praise You for the way You have answered my prayers for strength and courage.

In this quiet moment I remember that You not only welcome our expressions of love to You, but desire us to be broken open and poured out to the people You call us to care for in Your name. I think of the people who need my love and affirmation today. Why am I so stingy, Lord? Why do I control with the approval I withhold? Why do I use busyness as an excuse?

Savior, You have chosen to do a crucial part of Your ministry of healing and hope through me. If I remain uncaring or insensitive, others will not receive the encouragement You want to give them through me. Today I want to do to others what I would do to You. Thank You for the privilege of serving You by caring for others.

AUGUST
19

Moses returned to the LORD and said, "Oh, these people have sinned a great sin, and have made for themselves a god of gold! Yet now, if You will forgive their sin—but if not, I pray, blot me out of Your book which You have written."

—EXODUS 32:31-32

Holy God, Moses' broken sentence out of a broken heart over the people's sin makes me think of times I wish I could have taken the burden of guilt for people's failures and suffer Your judgment on their behalf. Your response to Moses reminds me that You're not impressed with self-oblation. You have called me to be a communicator of Your atonement rather than try to atone for others.

On this side of Calvary, it is wonderful for me to know that You have provided Christ's shed blood as atonement for sin. My task is not to repeat the atonement by my self-justifying efforts but to accept the atonement and share the good news that You forgive.

Today, I want to be specific in my prayers of intercession for those I know who are estranged from You because of unconfessed sin. Also, I pray for those whose resistance to Your grace has become so habitual that they no longer are sensitive to Your judgment. Father, help me to share the good news of Your unqualified love that will not ever forsake. You are the initiator of the desire to repent and return to You; create that desire in the people for whom I pray.

August
20

Be not dismayed, for I am Your God.

Dear God, every so often, it happens. It's this sense of distance from You. A feeling of separation. There's a longing for Your love, the flow of Your joy, the assurance of Your guidance, but something is wrong.

Occasionally, the real problem is a rift in my heart. It's difficult for me to admit, but there are times when I entertain disturbing questions. How could You, a good God, allow bad things to happen? When these things afflict me personally or those I love, the rift becomes all the more poignant. For a time, I even wonder if You are listening to my prayers.

Today, I feel Your reach across the rift. You allow me to get in touch with it, confess it, and heal it. Now I know that when I feel a distance it is not You, but I who moved. When I have a quarrel with how You managed things, You help me trust You more deeply. You are working Your purposes out in spite of the evil in the world and the meanness of some people. You can bring good even out of evil and turn difficult people to praise You. Forgive me when my vision is limited.

The cross is Your reach across the rift. You come to me with grace and hope. It's not my job to run the universe. I want to allow You to be God today. I smile. Did I have a choice? You are in charge and You know what You are doing!

AUGUST
21

This is the day which the LORD has made; we will rejoice and be glad in it.

—PSALM 118:24-25

Dear Father, the best that can happen today is that I will experience deep fellowship with You and enjoy You. The worst that can happen is that I might become so busy or distracted by life's demands that I would miss this privilege of friendship with You. This puts into perspective my secondary goals for today or the glitches in my plans that might occur.

This is the day You have made. I will rejoice and be glad in You, not just in another day. You alone are the source of the joy of any day. You have taught me that the secret of a truly great day is that You will show the way. You have plans for me today. I don't want to miss them. So make me sensitive to the surprises You send my way.

So often I act as if I can contrive a great day by careful planning alone. I load up the day with what I think is crucial. Then the tyranny of the urgent controls my day. I forget that You are with me and want to have a moment-by-moment dialogue with me throughout the day.

So today, help me plan the day with Your guidance so there is time for brief respites to rest in You and claim Your strength and wisdom.

AUGUST
22

Likewise the Spirit also helps in our weaknesses. For we do not know what we should pray for as we ought.

—ROMANS 8:26

Holy Spirit, thank You for Your help when I felt weak and didn't know how to pray. You gave me hopefulness when I recognized my helplessness. You have taught me that it is precisely at this point that You can begin Your work. Only when I acknowledge that I cannot help myself do You come alongside to help me. You take up where I give up. My limitation is my best qualification.

Thank You for taking my feeble, faltering petitions and articulating them to express my deepest needs and Your greatest hopes for me. You get to the depth of me and sound what's best to the heights of heaven. You know the Father's will for me and have assumed responsibility for helping me pray for those things that are within His plan for me, the people I intercede for, and the problems and concerns on my mind. You supply the wisdom and faith to pray creatively and boldly. You are my Counselor.

I praise You for the way You are at work in me right now. I sense Your inspiration. My extremity is Your opportunity. Now in the silence of this moment, speak to me through my thinking brain. I'm listening. Then loose my tongue to ask for what You have prompted me to ask. Thank You for helping me in my weakness.

AUGUST
23

Forgetting those things which are behind. . . .

—Philippians 3:13

Holy Spirit, my Counselor, I come to You to ask that You help me overcome the memory of failures I cannot forget and successes I fear I cannot top. Thank You for enabling me to take my "yesterdays" to the cross. You remind me of all that Christ has done for me. That's Your assignment and I'm grateful. Now in this time of honest confession, lead me to a deeper understanding of the real cause of my repetitive behavior that results in guilt. Shine Your light into the hidden corridors of my mind. You want to set me free of the sorrows, injuries, losses, and mistakes of all my yesterdays.

At the same time, expose the false confidence in the successes of the past, which are crippling my expectancy. Help me succeed my old self and break old records of achievement. Free me to expect great power from You and attempt great things as a disciple of Christ. Your plan is to fashion me in Christlikeness. The thought of that takes my breath away. Good thing; now I can ask You to breathe into me the breath of Your power.

You work in me to help me to participate in the wondrous activity of the Trinity. You enable me to share the Son's communion with the Father; You bring me into union with the Son; You make me a part of the glory circle. The Father glorifies the Son, the Son glorifies You, and You give me words to praise Father, Son, and Holy Spirit. Hallelujah!

AUGUST
24

Oh, that I had wings like a dove! For then I would fly away and be at rest.

—PSALM 55:6

Holy Spirit, there are times I share the psalmist's desire to escape responsibility. Along with most people, there are moments, even days, when I'd like to get away from problems and challenges, difficult people, the troubles of the city, and the seemingly impossible situations life dishes out. I bring this turbulent feeling to You, my Counselor. You know how to work with people who sometimes want to leave the post of duty or have been AWOL from discipleship.

Remind me that You don't train escape artists. You develop courageous people who are faithful and consistent. You do not provide easy escapes from reality.

So here I am: the same old person in the same old circumstances. Give me new eyes to see what You want done; give me new enthusiasm for the ordinary circumstances; change my bland, bored attitude to an attitude of expectancy; fill me with love for people who frustrate me; and help me see that my dogged doldrums are simply self-pity.

As a new person filled with Your joy and hope, I'm ready to mount up with wings like eagles and soar in the jet stream right where I am.

August
25

Repay no one evil for evil. Have regard for good things in the sight of all men. . . . Do not be overcome by evil, but overcome evil with good.

—ROMANS 12:17,21

Gracious God, in Christ and the cross You have broken the syndrome of hurt, resentment, and retaliation. When humankind deserved damnation, You gave grace. I have received that grace in unlimited abundance. Now I have the power not to nurse resentment or seek to retaliate. As You did not insist on getting even, set me free of the urge to get even with people who have hurt me.

Forgive me for the different ways I package my retaliation: the pout, harmful gossip, benign neglect, or outright *quid pro quo* punishment. When I do that, I'm the loser in the end. I send the boomerang and it always returns to my own soul. Help me to love myself as loved by You so that I will not inflict this pain on myself.

In each relationship in which I'm tempted to retaliate there is a good I can return instead of evil. Help me discern what is that good thing I can do or say today. Then give me courage to follow through. You know me: I'm better at thinking about what needs to be done than I am at putting it into action. Today's a day to break the syndrome of hurt, resentment, and retaliation—for goodness' sake!

AUGUST
26

To Him who loved us and washed us from our sins in His own blood, and has made us kings and priests to His God and Father, to Him be glory and dominion forever and ever. Amen.

—REVELATION 1:5-6

Lord Jesus Christ, my Savior, this verse gives me a magnificent beginning for my day. It is exactly what I need: to know I'm loved, forgiven, and appointed to serve in the realm of responsibility You have given me. That gets me moving in a positive, dynamic way.

Thank You for Your unqualified, unchanging, unlimited love. It is not mushy or sentimental. Your love for the Father and for humankind brought You to the cross. There You met my aching need for a Savior to forgive my sins. Your life, Your blood, was shed as a sacrifice for my sins. Today, I can live as a loved and forgiven person. The burden of guilt has been lifted.

You have called me to royal responsibility as leader of the people where I live and work. Change my image from one who is under the control of circumstances to the image of one who is to act under Your control. As one called to the priesthood of all believers, help me think of myself as one who goes to the Father in Your name on behalf of others and brings to them His blessing in the love, joy, and encouragement I express. It is going to be a wonderful day!

August
27

You who still the noise . . .

—Psalm 65:7

Dear Father, my life is polluted with noise. The blaring sounds of a noisy society bombard my ears and agitate my soul. The television set is seldom turned off. I turn on my car radio at the same time I turn the ignition key. Music is piped into everywhere I go, from the grocery where I shop to the gym where I exercise. On the streets, horns blare, tires screech, and tempers flare. Meanwhile, people around me talk constantly trying to find out what they want to say in the welter of words. It's so easy to lose the art of being quiet.

Even in this quiet moment, I'm not very quiet. My mind is racing, my nervous system is on red alert and I'm like a sprinter waiting for the starter's gun to go off. Calm me down, Lord, so I can work creatively today. I'm prone to listen to the discordant, incriminating voices within me shouting their guilt-producing reminders of things undone.

Lord, I hear Your voice over the crashing waves, saying, "Peace, be still." I want the miracle of that stillness and accept it as Your gift. I breathe out the tension and breathe in the breath of Your Spirit. In this time of prayer speak to me the whisper of Your love and assurance, grace, and guidance. Get me ready for a day in which I can be still inside while living in a noisy world.

AUGUST
28

Whoever exalts himself will be abased, and he who humbles himself will be exalted.

—MATTHEW 23:12

Dear Christ, forgive my pride. So often, it takes the place of praise in my heart. I desire to be adequate on my own strength, to be loved by You because of my achievement, and admired by people because of my superior performance. I've learned that pride pollutes everything it touches. It keeps me from growing spiritually, creates tension in my relationships, and makes me a person difficult for You to bless. It causes a sense of separation from You.

Today, I want to face spiritual pride as the root of this fake sense of religious superiority. It keeps me from humbly admitting my need for Your power. If I think I can justify myself before You by my good works, I also can imagine I am sufficient for the challenges ahead of me. Whenever I become self-righteous, the ears of my heart become unresponsive to the daily call to discipleship.

Forgive me for any times I have exalted myself. Heal the insecurity in me that prompts me to tout my talents and triumphs rather than exalting You and encouraging others. Set me free of the bane of self-righteousness and fill my heart with the blessing of Your grace.

AUGUST
29

Whoever humbles himself as this little child is the greatest in the kingdom of heaven.

—MATTHEW 18:4

Lord Jesus, I picture You calling the child out of the crowd gathered around You. I see him scamper up onto Your lap. In that unselfconscious response from the child, You taught what You want from Your followers . . . from me . . . today.

The humility of a child? I don't often think of children as humble. Did You mean that the child was not encumbered with inhibitions, reserve, and the debilitating caution people acquire as they become adults?

Lord, I want to recover the enthusiasm, delight, and wonderment of being a child. Give me again the lilt of a child's laughter, the freedom to have fun, the expression of excitement about life, the childlike expectancy.

It is a relief for me to think of humility not as some negative groveling but as the freedom to praise You, the joy of trusting You, and the delight of enjoying You.

Children clasp their hands in mine and skip along with spontaneous happiness. I want to do the same thing in my walk with You today. I admit my need for Your strong hand to uphold and guide me. It's so good to be with You. I feel safe and secure.

AUGUST
30

Let no corrupt communication proceed out of your mouth, but what is good for necessary edification, that it may impart grace.

—EPHESIANS 4:29

Lord, today I need Your help to deal with misunderstandings with people. I try to say what I mean and mean what I say. And yet, there are times when communication breaks down. I want people to judge me by what I perceive are my intentions, while so often I judge people on their actions. Give me courage to be an initiator of reconciliation with those I've misunderstood or those I feel have misunderstood me. Make me a better listener as well as communicator. Provide me with x-ray insight into what causes the things people do and say. And knowing the pain of being misunderstood, make me more understanding.

At the same time, I want my character and personality to be shaped by You. Help me to grow secure in convictions that are biblical, and give me a conscience that is sensitive to Your truth and the courage to live what I believe. With this quality of confidence, may I take the lead in seeking the resolution of misunderstandings with people. Because I am right with You, I give up my need always to be right. Make me flexible in non-essentials and graciously firm about essentials. I don't have to win every argument or triumph in every ego-skirmish. Mold my attitude and guide my words today.

AUGUST
31

Greet Priscilla and Aquila, my fellow workers in Christ Jesus, who risked their own necks for my life.

—ROMANS 16:3-4

Gracious Lord Christ, You have called me Your friend and appointed me to be a faithful friend to others. Today I thank You for the true friends You have given me. What would I do without them? Forgive me when I take them for granted. On this summer day, help me reach out to those special friends with "Thanks for being you!" gratitude and enthusiasm.

Paul's words about Priscilla and Aquila bring to mind the people who have "risked their own necks" for me through the years. I think of people who were there in times of need. They never gave up on me. Knowing both my weaknesses and strengths, they have never stopped praying. I can be myself with them without pretense or strain. Like You, they are for me and not against me. They cheer in life's victories and empathize in life's difficulties.

All this leads me to wonder who in my life needs me to risk my neck for him or her. Jog my memory of friends I've promised to pray for and help. Bring to mind particular friends who need a phone call, a letter, or friends I may have hurt or who have hurt me. May this be a day for healing and reconciliation. You are a Friend who never goes away. What kind of friend am I?

SEPTEMBER
1

The things which you learned and received and heard and saw in me, these do, and the God of peace will be with you.

—PHILIPPIANS 4:9

Dear God, these words of Paul to the Philippians seem audacious at first reading. He actually was confident that the things he taught and lived when he was with them had given them the secret of how to experience and express Your peace. As I reflect on that, I begin to wonder what the people around me are learning about true peace from me. Does Your peace really rule in my heart? Is there anything between You and me, Father, that robs me of Your peace?

These questions lead me to ask for a deeper experience of Your peace. May my inner peace show in my countenance. Help me be a source of peace rather than acrimonious discord. Keep me from agitating arguments, hostile conflict, and contention. Show me the impact in others of my moods for good or grimness. Remind me that I am accountable to You for how much of Your peace flows through me to the people in my life. Make me a peacemaker. Use me to bring reconciliation between people who are separated by hurting memories or current conflict. Will anyone see, feel, understand Your peace from me? If not today, when?

SEPTEMBER
2

Do not lie to one another, since you have put off the old man with his deeds, and have put on the new man who is renewed in knowledge according to the image of Him who created him.

—COLOSSIANS 3:9-10

Lord God of truth, who calls me to absolute honesty in everything I say, I renew my commitment to tell the truth. It's so easy to shade the truth, spin the facts, and withhold information. In a world where people no longer even expect to hear the truth, or what's worse, see the need consistently to speak it, make me a straight arrow who hits the target of truth.

In this quiet moment of prayer with You, Father, I confess any untruth I have spoken or implied. Help me be a person on whom others always can depend for unswerving honesty. Especially keep me from those little white lies that later on need big black lies to cover them up. As I pray this prayer I realize that my renewed pledge to speak, live, and stand for truth brings an immense release inside. There is a wonderful freedom that comes from an integrity that is not for sale at any price.

Today, help me to look people in the eye and speak truth with no equivocation. May the reliability of my word earn me the right to express words about Your love, forgiveness, and faithfulness. Make me sensitive to the power of words to communicate comfort and encouragement.

SEPTEMBER
3

I thank my God, making mention of you always in my prayers, hearing of your love and faith which you have toward the Lord Jesus and toward all the saints, that the sharing of your faith may become effective by the acknowledgment of every good thing which is in you in Christ Jesus.

—PHILEMON 1:4-6

Generous Lord Jesus, I read Paul's words of affirmation to Philemon, and dedicate this to be a day of positive affirmation of others and what You have done in my life.

I remember Paul's reason for writing his friend Philemon in Colosse on behalf of Onesimus, the Colossian's runaway slave whom the apostle had met and led to Christ in Rome. I am moved by the way Paul affirmed Philemon before he asked him to receive Onesimus back not as a slave but as a brother in Christ.

Lord, remind me first to affirm the people I want to help act on some aspect of Your truth or guidance. May my affirmation not be some solicitous schmoozing to manipulate people, but a genuine expression of how much You love them and have done for them. Free me to communicate that I enjoy and cherish them for who they are. When I want to influence people who believe in You, may my desire be that their faith will become effective by the acknowledgment of every good thing which is in them because of You.

SEPTEMBER
4

Who sees anything different in you?
What have you that you did not receive?

—1 CORINTHIANS 4:7 (RSV)

Gracious Lord Christ, You have called me to live life to the fullest and exemplify to others life as You meant it to be lived. Today I sense Your nudge to think about the kind of example I am to others. I wonder: If all they knew of what it means to be a Christian were dependent on what they see, hear, and feel from me, what would be their perception of Christianity? If they had to write a 30-word definition of a Christian from my life, what would they write?

My mind darts to how I can be more strong and perfect in my example. Then I realize that is not the issue. I'm not to get the glory for my growth in You; You are to receive the glory for Your grace at work in me. Thank You for giving me the crucial questions to ask: What will people learn from me about how to deal with difficulties, how to have courage in problems, and how to express joy when circumstances are frustrating? What will others learn about Your peace and hope?

Paul's questions to the Corinthians, "Who sees anything different in you?" makes me wonder about the difference others may observe that You have made in me. Lord, help me to think about the awesome power of what can be Your influence on others through me.

SEPTEMBER
5

Nothing will be impossible for you.

—MATTHEW 17:20

Lord Jesus, I begin this day with a renewed and unreserved commitment of my life to You. Fill me with Your Spirit. Think Your thoughts through my mind. Express Your love to the people around me through my words. Energize my will to do Your will.

Focus my attention on all the opportunities of the day ahead. I'm thankful for the challenges that will make me trust You more completely. I surrender each of these and ask for Your supernatural power, wisdom, and guidance. Thank You, in advance, for displaying Your majesty and might in the mundane duties of life. Life is meaningful when I remember that I'm here to love You by serving others.

Lord, nothing makes me love people more than talking to You about them. Thank You for the gift of intercessory prayer. The more I pray for people, the more I am able to love them as You do. I'm amazed by the way You change my attitudes. Help me to pray in Your name, Your perspective, purpose, and power. Help me to move through this day with Your watchword, "Nothing is impossible."

September
6

Give thanks to the Lord for His goodness.

—Psalm 107:21

Dear Father, there is no shadow of turning with You. You do not change; Your compassion is consistent; Your presence never leaves nor forsakes. Today I praise You for Your goodness, the composite of all Your attributes of righteousness and truth. Your goodness is Your outpouring, generous love.

The ultimate expression of Your goodness is Your Son, my Savior Jesus Christ. Your consummate, stunning generosity was revealed in His life; He has shown me Your incredible goodness and what You intended humankind to be. I shrink back confessing I can never be good enough to deserve Your love. I could not dare to come to You without the imputed goodness of my standing with You through my Savior and His cross. My status with You is only because of His reconciling atonement. Father, look at me only through the focused lens of Calvary!

Out of unqualified goodness, You have offered me the fruit of the Spirit in goodness. Through the infilling of my mind and heart with the Holy Spirit I am empowered to emulate Your consistent compassion and overflowing generosity. You enable me to be good, to accomplish the purpose for which I was born: simply to be Your loved, cherished, chosen person through whom You can communicate Your generosity.

SEPTEMBER
7

He will baptize you with the Holy Spirit.
—LUKE 3:16

Spirit of the living God, I confess the banked fires of faith in the hearth of my heart. White ash covers the burned-down embers.

The danger of burnout is very real to me. When I become too busy, there is little time to be refueled by Your love, joy, peace, and patience. I start living on my own resources and forget that You are the source of wisdom, knowledge, discernment, vision, and the power to lead others. I never was meant to make it on my own. Forgive me for trying.

Today, my responsibilities are too great to face without the constant replenishment of Your inspiration. Bellow the flickering embers of my heart until they are white-hot again with the fires of passion for discipleship. May I glow with Your radiance. Be glorified in my life today. I long for the authentic spirituality I see displayed on the pages of the book of Acts: love for Christ, loyalty to fellow disciples, contagious faith, unreserved commitment, and expectation of great things.

Holy Spirit, I need You. I open the hearth of my heart to You. Thank You for setting me ablaze with Your fire.

SEPTEMBER
8

O LORD my God, I will give thanks to You forever.

—PSALM 30:12

Lord, I want to acknowledge with praise and gratitude the countless good things which are mine because of my life in You and Your abiding in me. I look back at the person I was before You took control of my life and gave me the privilege of being Your disciple. And best of all, You are not finished with me. So today as I gratefully acknowledge the character and personality transformation You have performed in my life. Help me communicate affirming hope to others.

You inspire what You desire. May I listen intently now as You show me what is Your best for each person or perplexity. It is very exciting to realize that You have called me to this quiet moment because You want to reveal Your plan and release Your power through me. I am so grateful for the privilege of being Your disciple.

You do not ask me constantly to take my own spiritual pulse, but rather to become more aware of the pulsebeat of Your Spirit working in and through me. Light of the world, shine on my face, sparkle in my eyes, illuminate truth through my words, radiate Your glory in my attitudes.

SEPTEMBER
9

*Now may the God of peace who brought up
our Lord Jesus from the dead, that great Shep-
herd of the sheep, through the blood of the everlasting covenant, make you complete in every
good work to do His will, working in you what
is well pleasing in His sight, through Jesus
Christ, to whom be glory forever. Amen.*

—HEBREWS 13:20-21

Dear God, so often I feel incomplete. I feel like I've
barely begun to grow into maturity in Christ. My self-improvement promises and bootstrap programs make very
little difference. Then I read a promise like this one from
Hebrews.

Father, I accept this stupendous assurance as the
source of a lively confidence and courage for this new day.
It's amazing and awesome: The identical force You exer-
cised in taking Jesus out of the tomb can be at work in and
through me today. I am uplifted out of any mood of
discouragement about my progress by the tremendous
promise that You want to make me complete in every way,
whole and liberated to be all that You intended me to be.
In response, I accept the crucial condition: I surrender my
life to You and I am willing to take up my cross of obedience and servanthood. You will provide me with exactly
what I need to be strong and brave today with resurrection power. Thank You in advance for guiding me in what
pleases You so that all I do today will be pleasing in Your
sight.

SEPTEMBER
10

Call upon Me in the day of trouble; I will deliver you, and you shall glorify Me.

—PSALM 50:15

Almighty God, You are a very present help in trouble. Today, I want to remember all the times You have helped me in trouble. I am quick to cry out to You for help, but I am slow to remember the countless times You intervened to meet my deepest needs. Especially I remember _____ and _____. Thank You, Lord.

I sense a new confidence stirring in my heart. I can say, "Though I walk in the midst of trouble, You will revive me" (Psalm 138:7). When I think of troubles I'm facing right now, the psalmist again gives wings to my thoughts: "Hear my prayer, O LORD, and let my cry come to You. Do not hide Your face from me in the day of my trouble; incline Your ear to me; in the day that I call, answer me speedily" (Psalm 102:1-2).

Bring to my mind the people I know who are troubled or are confronted with adversity. I name them and their needs one by one. Do for them what You have done for me repeatedly. For Your glory, resolve problems, give guidance, provide strength.

Lord, I'm also aware of some problems You won't solve until I'm ready to be used by You in working out the solutions. Sometimes You wait until I am ready to be part of the miracle You want to perform. Show me what You want me to do. I will leave the results to You.

SEPTEMBER
11

Therefore I exhort first of all that supplications, prayers, intercessions, and giving of thanks be made for all men, for kings and all who are in authority, that we may lead a quiet and peaceable life in all godliness and reverence. For this is good and acceptable in the sight of God our Savior.

—1 TIMOTHY 2:1-3

Dear God, the word "godliness" stands out in this familiar verse. You have called me to intercede for leaders so that I may lead a "godly" life. Though the word is used frequently in the New Testament epistles, it has an archaic ring to me. What would it mean for me to be godly, exemplifying "godliness" in today's world? I take a closer look at the word in the Greek New Testament and I'm amazed: *eusebeia*—from *eu*, well, and *sebomai*, to be devout; God-centered, God-inspired; God-motivated living. When I think about that, a godly life is exactly what I want to live today. I want a God-ward attitude and a desire to do what is pleasing to You. Reverence for You will never go out of style.

I note that Paul speaks of the "mystery of godliness" in 1 Timothy 3:16, incorporating the truths of Your Son, my Savior. That gives me the secret: The more I know Christ and am filled with His Spirit, the more I will be able to know Your will and glorify You in everything. I dedicate this day to living in the quiet trust and tranquility of true godliness.

September
12

The Son of Man did not come to be served but to serve, and to give His life a ransom for many.

—MARK 10:45

Almighty Lord, the same yesterday, today, and forever, You have been my help in ages past and are my hope for years to come. The sure sign of an authentic relationship with You is that I believe in the future more than the past, and that my previous experiences of Your grace are only a prelude to Your plans for me.

Give me a fresh burst of enthusiasm for the next stage of the unfolding drama of my life and the work You have given me to do. You have called me to serve You. Your power is released for service. Help me focus on my high calling to communicate Your love to the people with whom I come in contact today. May I put You first, others second, myself last. May all that I do and am today be so obviously an expression of Your truth, righteousness, and justice that I can press on with the confidence of Your blessing.

I relinquish my worries to You and my anxiety drains away. I take courage because You have taken hold of me. Now I know that courage is fear that has said its prayers. I spread out before You the challenges of the day ahead and see them in the proper perspective of Your power. I dedicate myself to doing things Your way under Your sway. And now, Your joy, that is so much more than happiness, fills me. I press on to the work of the day with enthusiasm. It's great to be alive! Amen.

SEPTEMBER
13

I am the LORD, I do not change.

—MALACHI 3:6

Gracious God, my Father, give me the diligence to seek You, the patience to wait for You, the understanding to know You, and the willingness to do Your will.

Forgiving God, from whom to turn is to fall, to whom to return is to rise again, in whom to trust is to abide secure: grant me strength in my duties, guidance in my perplexities, protection in any danger, and peace in turmoil.

You created me in Your own image with a mind to understand You, a heart to love You, and a desire to serve You. Increase in me today my comprehension of Your goodness and grace, my response to Your presence, my gratitude for Your caring, that I may grow in the likeness of Jesus Christ my Lord. Guide the thoughts of my mind, the words I speak, the work I do, the attitudes I hold, the countenance I communicate, and the impression I have on others. In good times may I give You the glory and in troubled times may I trust You more.

You do not change. May Your changeless love and reliability give me the courage to change what needs to be changed in my life. Now in this quiet moment, I ask You to give me strength to change_____ in my life and _____ in my relationship with _____. Thank You, Lord, for today!

September
14

*Rejoice always, pray without ceasing, in every-
thing give thanks; for this is the will of God in
Christ Jesus for you. Do not quench the Spirit.
Do not despise prophecies. Test all things; hold
fast what is good.*
—1 THESSALONIANS 5:16-21

Holy Spirit, I long to be a spontaneous person
today—one who is open, free, expectant, and willing to
be surprised. There is an uncalculating, unaffected, un-
bounded excitement in me when I give You complete
freedom within me to help me respond to life's opportunities and challenges with "All-signals-go!" immediacy
and intensity. That's the way I want to live today.

It is so easy to get sucked into the eddies of stagna-
tion, resisting the new, the innovative, and the different.
Sometimes I thoughtlessly repeat the mottos of the stag-
nated: "We've never done it that way"; "We're not ready
for that"; "We tried that before"; "It just won't work!"

Instead of all that negative thinking, I want to base
my life on today's Scripture: I will accept Your gift of enthusiasm, I will welcome life expectantly, I will dare to be
an open person, I will be thankful in advance for what
You will do today to help me, I will consider the future as
a friend, I will set courageous goals, and I will overcome
the negative confronting me by doing a specific, positive
good. With these resolves as my commitment, make me
an authentically spontaneous person today.

SEPTEMBER
15

Who touched me?. . . Somebody touched Me,
for I perceived power going out from Me. . . .
Be of good cheer, your faith has made you well.
Go in peace.

—LUKE 8:45,46,48

Lord Christ, Great Physician, You are the healing power of the world. You use doctors and nurses and medicine, but You are the healing power.

Lord, I long for Your physical, emotional and spiritual healing. I want to be whole.

I picture the woman who pressed through the crowd around You, whispering, "If I can only touch Him!" She exemplifies my yearning to get in touch with You. It is awesome to me that You are concerned about me and respond to my touch of faith. Now what I need is the touch of Your healing hand upon my body, mind, emotions. Here in the quiet I ask for Your healing touch.

My desire to reach out to You has been initiated by You. Your touch upon my desires precedes my reach. My longing for Your healing power is because You are more ready to give than I am to ask.

Now, in touch with You, I realize that anything You do for me is secondary to the greater gift of fellowship with You. I love You for Yourself, not for what You can do for me. Grateful for this wondrous gift, I place my total life in Your healing power. Now I hear Your whisper, "Go in peace." Thank You, Lord.

SEPTEMBER
16

*If you abide in My word, you are My disciples
indeed. And you shall know the truth, and the
truth shall make you free. . . . Therefore, if the
Son makes you free, you shall be free indeed.*

—JOHN 8:31-32,36

Lord Christ, You came to set me free. You are my
emancipator, liberator, and redeemer. Today I want my
mind to be filled with the truth of the status I have with
the Father because of Your reconciling death on the cross,
Your victory over the grave, and Your reigning presence in
my life. May the truth dominate my thinking that there is
no condemnation to those who believe in You and are
filled with Your Spirit. May this liberating conviction,
rooted in fact, break the syndrome of self-condemnation
and reorient all my thinking. To be justified in You is to
be set free!

Thank You that this clear conviction enables emotional freedom. I feel the wonderful emotions of true lib-
eration. My attitude about today changes. As a loved and
forgiven person, I want to love and forgive. Free me from
judgmentalism and negativism. Help me be as gracious to
the people in my life as You have been to me.

Bondage to You breaks the bondage of my willfulness. I am not free until You are my Master and Lord. Like
Paul, I want to be Your bond-servant. You have set me
free to know and do Your will. Ah, freedom at last!

SEPTEMBER
17

Beloved, I pray that you may prosper in all things and be in health, just as your soul prospers.

—3 JOHN 2

Gracious God, who constantly is seeking my spiritual prosperity, I thank You for Your care for every aspect of my life. When I am in a right relationship with You, everything else works better. I am healthier emotionally and physically when I relax and trust You to guide and strengthen me. Amazingly, my relationships are more harmonious. When I do things Your way, You work things out for Your glory and my growth. It's really liberating to claim that You are for me and not against me. You are working night and day to accomplish Your very best in my life. So I claim Paul's promise to the Philippians as my personal assurance today: "My God shall supply all your needs according to His riches in glory by Christ Jesus" (Philippians 4:19).

Thank You for this quiet moment to reorient my thinking and reform my attitude about today in the light of the spiritual prosperity in the riches of Your grace and power. I confess that I often think about what I must do with the challenges and relationships of a day without thinking about how You will accomplish Your will by Your power through me. You do not want me to fail at life today. You are by my side in circumstances and dwell inside to give me courage. I'm spiritually wealthy for the expenditures of working for You today!

SEPTEMBER
18

Jesus Christ is the same yesterday, today, and forever.

—HEBREWS 13:8

Christ, my Lord and Savior, You are light in my darkness, food for my hungers, peace in my pressures, forgiveness for my failures, strength in my weakness, guidance in my confusion, health in my sickness, assurance that death has no power and heaven has begun for me now, and security in all the ups and downs I will face today.

I vacillate, people are unreliable, circumstances fluctuate, but You remain stable as the Rock of Ages. This gives me an unchanging center of quiet strength to deal with the tensions of the day ahead. You set me free of hurting memories so all my energy may be used creatively. I can live with confidence in each moment because You are with me. Fear of the future is over because You will show the way.

Knowing all this, it seems absurd that I should still feel burdened by the cares I carry. I've gotten so used to the weight that it is difficult to shift them to Your shoulders. Or, sometimes I shift them, and before long, take them back. I confess that I've not learned how to be creatively carefree: to trust You to guide me in dealing with my concerns. I want to do Your will, in Your way, in Your timing, and by Your strength.

SEPTEMBER
19

. . . the word of knowledge through the same Spirit.

—1 CORINTHIANS 12:8

Almighty God, help me be a creative thinker today. I know that beyond my education and experience there are solutions to problems I will not think of without Your gift of knowledge.

I think of times in the past when I've received this supernatural gift. You revealed answers to problems that I had not achieved with my own analysis. As I prayed faithfully and waited patiently, the startling "Ah-ha!" dawned on me. You gave me insight I could never have grasped by myself. By divine inspiration You helped me know what was happening beneath the surface of perplexities or relational conflicts. You allowed me to see what You see. I gave You the credit and the glory.

Now as I begin this day, once again I confess how much I need the gift of knowledge. People I love are troubled by complex problems. I want to give them more than my limited advice. Unsolved problems have a way of piling up. Please use me to discover and communicate Your answers.

Thank You for transforming my imagination so that it can be a holy riverbed through which You can pour Your creative ideas. Help me picture reality from Your perspective and then claim what You want. I look forward to an inspired day.

SEPTEMBER
20

He who dwells in the secret place of the Most High shall abide under the shadow of the Almighty. He is my refuge and my fortress; My God, in Him I will trust.

—PSALM 91:1-2

Almighty God, Most High, I come to the secret place of prayer. Here there is peace and serenity. My lowest moods can be transformed by Your highest joy. My deepest needs can receive Your highest hope, and my suppressed longings can be released by Your highest power.

I'm so thankful that the secret place in me can be brought to Your secret place. When the two meet, profound conversation takes place. You speak the first word of invitation and I respond with gratitude that You, the Creator and Lord of all, want me to abide in Your presence. I praise You. As I do, my mind and heart become open to your love. You guide my confession so there is nothing in my secret place hidden from You. Thank You, Father, for the assurance of forgiveness through the blood of Your Son, my Savior. Free me from repetitive patterns of sin and failure.

Direct my prayers for others. Especially _____ and _____. I give over to Your control the problems and difficulties that confront me today, particularly _____ and _____. Reveal Your will for the decisions I must make. I commit myself anew to You, Lord. Because of Your greatness, it's going to be a great day!

SEPTEMBER
21

*And now, Lord, what do I wait for? My hope
is in You.*

—PSALM 39:7

Father, so often we hear the old shibboleth, "Where
there's life, there's hope." You have shown me that just
the opposite is true: Where there's hope, there's life. Lord,
I need fresh hope today. There's a pall of hopelessness
today. Who can be trusted? Movements falter, political
parties wrangle, leaders stumble. There's a breakdown of
confidence in one another. Our shallow hopes in progress,
institutions, and businesses often are disappointed.

I come to You for authentic hope, lasting hope that
is a by-product of an assurance of Your grace, goodness,
and faithfulness. You are the source of my hope because of
Christ's resurrection. This is the hinge of hope for me. You
have acted to open the cul-de-sac of human futility and
give me a "living hope through the resurrection of Jesus
Christ from the dead" (1 Peter 1:3).

My unquenchable hope is that You, in Your Son
my Savior, have defeated death and the devil and have
elected me to share in Your plan for the world and
someday, to live with You in heaven. With hope like that,
I can face the future unafraid.

God of hope, make me a confident, resilient communicator of hope. May it be the source of a vibrant, vital
quality of abundant life.

SEPTEMBER
22

Now to our God and Father be glory forever and ever. Amen.

—PHILIPPIANS 4:20

Father Almighty, Maker of heaven and earth, I praise You.

Thank You for the privilege of living in Your world. You created me and I am accountable to You. I am not my own; I belong to You. You made me for Yourself; I am not complete without You. With infinite wisdom You set the standards of how I am to live obediently as Your person. I have Your commandments and Christ's commandment to love as Your irreducible demand. I submit to Your authority.

It is out of love that I want to know and do Your will. You gave me freedom to choose to love and obey You. You also revealed Your grace in Christ and the cross. "Love so amazing demands my life, my soul, my all."

Father, in this time of prayer, once again I come home to Your heart. I cherish the thought of my value to You. Here with You I can value myself as You do. May this assurance spill over to others today and give me the courage to share Your love. Grant me freedom from grudges and resentments over hurts of the past, and from double standards by which I require more of others than of myself.

Today, Father, I rejoice in being part of Your interracial, intercultural, international family of faith.

SEPTEMBER
23

. . . that Christ may dwell in your hearts through faith; that you, being rooted and grounded in love, may be able to comprehend with all the saints what is the width and length and depth and height—to know the love of Christ which passes knowledge; that you may be filled with all the fullness of God.

—EPHESIANS 3:17-19

Lord Christ, Your love passes knowledge. I can't grasp the whole of it with my intellect alone, but I can open my heart to experience it.

Thank You for the width of Your love. When Your arms were outstretched on the cross, You suffered for the sins of the whole world—all sins before and after Calvary. Your love now embraces all who come to You. You love me just as I am, but You will not allow me to remain as I am.

Thank You for the length of Your love. There is no limit to the lengths You will go to find me when I wander from You. Your love outdistances my efforts to run from You. There is no failure You won't forgive.

Thank You for the depth of Your love. When I say with the psalmist, "Out of the depth I cry to You," You hear my call and lift me out of discouragement and disappointment.

Thank You for the height of Your love. I will not limit the heights to which I can soar by Your power. Because of You I live today as a part of heaven, which physical death cannot end.

SEPTEMBER
24

We are His workmanship, created in Christ Jesus for good works, which God prepared beforehand that we should walk in them.

—EPHESIANS 2:10

Dear God, I praise You for this new day, a page in the present chapter of my life. I am very challenged by the fact that You have good works planned for me to do and that today I will have an opportunity to do some of them for Your glory.

Lord, don't let me miss what You have prepared beforehand. Make me aware, attentive, and accountable. There will be places today You want to enter through me, situations that require the impact of Your presence through me, wrongs to be righted, justice to be declared and done by me. I'll meet lonely people who need me to listen, worried people to be comforted, distressed people to be consoled, and suffering people who need healing. When I meet people who need prayer, give me the courage to pray for them immediately.

Today, I will meet agnostics who are not sure about You, religious people who don't have a personal relationship with You, and troubled people who feel You have not heard their prayers. Help me to be sensitive and responsive in the way I share how much You mean to me. The best of the good works You have prepared for me are to help people become sure of Your love, forgiveness, and care.

SEPTEMBER
25

Men will be lovers of themselves . . . rather than lovers of God.

—2 TIMOTHY 3:2,4

Dear God, today, I want to see self-centeredness for what it is: apostasy, the departure from loving You, the inordinate, obsessive and eventually compulsive focus on self, what I want, how others treat me, my rights, and my feelings. It's a direct opposite of healthy Christ-centered esteem, loving myself as loved by You that turns me outward toward others and not inward on myself. There is so much self-centeredness in our culture. I see it in people around me. I abhor what it does to them and want to get rid of any vestige of it in me. You have shown me what the proclivity to this problem does to cripple effectiveness, relationships, and people's character.

I've witnessed the results of bogus leaders in all walks of life who worship at the shrine of themselves, seeking to make themselves great rather than doing great things for Your glory. Self-centeredness disrupts churches, denigrates politics, debilitates friendships. I commit myself to shifting my focus from self-centeredness to You and the needs of others. Lord, I know that the self is to be a container and transmitter of Your Spirit. Again I pray for the fruit of the Spirit to flow through me today: love, joy, peace, long-suffering, kindness, goodness, faithfulness, gentleness, self-control.

SEPTEMBER
26

*I fled previously to Tarshish; for I know that
You are a gracious and merciful God, slow to
anger and abundant in lovingkindness, One
who relents from doing harm.*

—JONAH 4:2

Almighty God, there's a bit of Jonah in me at
times. You called him to go to Nineveh to proclaim Your
sovereign power; instead, he headed off to Tarshish on the
coast of Spain. Even when You intervened and got him to
Nineveh and gave him success, he complained. I've been
reminded again of how easy it is to use Your kindness and
goodness as an excuse to resist what You have revealed is
Your will for me. It doesn't help a bit that I see the same
thing in most people. We all take Your love for granted at
times and presume on Your forgiveness. Repetitive patterns result: resisting Your guidance can become a habit.

Today, I want to have Your grace motivate a greater
willingness rather than be an excuse for willfulness. Never
again may I trivialize Your forgiveness. May the joy of
living in obedience to You give me profound satisfaction.
No longer do I want to put up with injustice around me,
procrastinating because of a false confidence in Your patience.

Lord, I repent of anything in my life that I know
You cannot bless or is blatantly inconsistent with Your revealed will for me. Today I will trust and obey, for I know
there's no other way.

SEPTEMBER
27

Wait on the LORD; be of good courage, and He shall strengthen your heart; wait, I say, on the LORD!

—PSALM 27:14

Dear God, Lord for the long pull, I ask You for staying power. My need is not for brash impulsiveness, but for fortitude. You do give strength for the single battle, but You also give me a resolute faithfulness for the long campaign. You have taught me that this stick-to-it-ness comes from a consistent relationship with You. I echo David: "One thing I have desired of the LORD, that will I seek; that I may dwell in the house of the LORD all the days of my life, to behold the beauty of the LORD. . . . When You said, 'Seek My face,' my heart said to You, 'Your face, LORD, I will seek'" (Psalm 27:4,8).

Lord, You have shown me that so many battles in life are lost because people give up just before victory. Along with others, I need not to give up when the going gets rough. Again David articulates my feelings: "I would have lost heart, unless I had believed that I would see the goodness of the LORD in the land of the living" (Psalm 27:13). Patient Father, show me again that the process is the product. I like neat, finished packages, but when I get one thing finished, another opportunity or challenge comes along. I need long-lasting fortitude. What I do want to finish well is my life here in this portion of my eternal life. Today is only one day in a succession of days and years to come. Give me exactly what I need to live victoriously today. That's all I need. Tomorrow is up to You. We'll tackle that together when it comes. What a super way to live!

SEPTEMBER
28

*My God will hear me. Do not rejoice over me,
my enemy; when I fall, I will arise; when I sit
in darkness, the LORD will be a light to me.*

—MICAH 7:7-8

Almighty God, for whom nothing is wasted, not
even the difficult, dark times of life, I thank You for reminding me that You never leave me nor forsake me. Like
everyone, I know times of failure. Help me make this
verse from Micah my motto of might: When I fall, I will
arise!

Father, help me to take life's little defeats as a part of
a bigger process on the way to final triumph. Give me a
faith that defies defeat. Help me get up and press on. Ultimately, the only thing that is important is my relationship
to You. Nothing is more crucial than trusting You. You are
the only one I have to please. Lift me up when I get down
on myself. Help me learn from life's difficulties, but keep me
from brooding over them. I rise to fight again!

Today is a new chance, a new beginning. I commit
to You the new challenges today offers. Especially I ask for
fresh courage to face _____and new wisdom to solve
_____ and deeper love for people I sometimes perceive as adversaries: _____. Also, I thank You for
those faithful loved ones and friends who have been Your
agents of encouragement in times of need. I name them
one by one with a grateful heart. Help me to care for others
who are battling discouragement and share with them the
password to a fresh start: When I fall, I will arise!

SEPTEMBER
29

He who has My commandments and keeps them, it is he who loves Me . . . I will love him and manifest Myself to him.

—JOHN 14:21

Gracious God, in a world of qualified love it is so encouraging to hear those five wonderful words You greet me with as I begin this moment of prayer: "I will always love you." I'm amazed at all the territory that word *always* covers. It spans the full spectrum of all that I've ever done or said and extends to difficulties, problems, and failures of the future. It also includes those times when I forget that You are the source of my strength and take the glory that belongs to You. Amazing love! You love for keeps.

You come to me at the point of my need, but You also help me come to the point about my needs. You encourage me to confess my hopes and hurts to You. You wait for me to ask for what You are ready to give. It's a mystery: Your willingness, coupled with my willingness to ask, make for dynamic prayer.

And yet, I have an immense proclivity to hang on to my needs or try to handle them myself. I wonder why I wait so long before I turn them over to You. Sometimes I simply endure them, pushing them down inside. Thank You for this honest, open time of prayer in which I can relinquish my control and claim Your power.

Help me express to the people around me the quality of indefatigable love You have given me. May I express in word and attitude, "I will always love you."

SEPTEMBER
30

Though I walk in the midst of trouble, You will revive me.

—PSALM 138:7

Gracious Father, as nature abhors a vacuum, You deplore deadlocks that debilitate progress. Everywhere I look I see people hammer-locked and pinned to the mat by seemingly unsolvable differences. I see people unable to work toward creative compromises because they are determined to win arguments, always be right, and be superior to others. Marriages are crippled, families are hurt, friendships are destroyed, companies are unproductive, cities are blighted by unresolved social problems, and government is often debilitated by people who become party to acrimonious discord because of loyalty to their parties rather than what's best for the nation.

At the same time, I tire of racial conflict and prejudice—tensions between religions and battle between different philosophies. I'm part of a very intolerant time. Judgmentalism is rampant.

I claim today's Scripture verse as my motto for today. You *will* revive me when I walk in the midst of trouble. You are the only one who can! Revive my spirit with positive goodwill to others, renew my love for the most cranky people I meet, replenish my inner security so I will have a tender heart and a tough skin. You have allowed me to live in a time like this because You want to enter into the places I'll be today. You and I can take anything together. Don't let me forget that!

OCTOBER
1

By this we know that we are of the truth, and shall assure our hearts before Him. For if our heart condemns us, God is greater than our heart, and knows all things. Beloved, if our heart does not condemn us, we have confidence toward God.

—1 JOHN 3:19-21

Dear God, as I begin this new day, I want to praise You especially for the assurance that when my heart condemns me, You are greater than my heart. You know that sometimes I begin a day with my heart in reverse. It wants to revisit some mistake of the day before and incriminates me with reminders that I'm not free to enjoy a new day. Then You invade my heart with the conviction that if there is anything to forgive, You have forgiven it and if there is any vestige of self-condemnation left, You will cleanse it. You don't want me to play god by holding myself captive to a bad mood when you have cleansed the slate. You alone have the right to judge.

Now Lord, help me to claim that You have and will continue to overcome my perfectionistic heart all through this day. When good things happen I want to praise You, when difficult things happen I want to trust You, when failures occur I want to accept both Your judgment and absolution. Today I will bless You for Your grace rather than be a brooder over my goofs.

OCTOBER
2

Beloved, let us love one another, for love is of God; and everyone who loves is born of God and knows God.

—1 JOHN 4:7

Gracious God, thank You for the freedom to begin this day with an assurance of Your unqualified love and acceptance. Thank You for the liberating experience of Christ-esteem. I know I am special to You and dedicate this day to making others aware that they are special to You and to me.

A deep sense of gratitude for the talents and abilities You have given me surges through my heart. I feel a freedom to love myself as loved by You. You have broken the bind of self-negation and freed me to enjoy being me.

My daily challenge is to accept Your attitude toward me as my own attitude toward myself. Repeatedly I have heard You say, "I know all about you, the needs and failures. I love you just as you are. You belong to me. I have blessed you through the years. Why? Because I knew that someday You would receive my love, be reborn to a new life, and be liberated. Accept the special person I've created you to be!"

Thank You, Lord. Today I want that affirming love to spill over to others. Help me glorify You by really enjoying them. May my Christ-esteem be the motive of communicating esteem to others.

OCTOBER
3

Whatever is born of God overcomes the world. And this is the victory that has overcome the world—our faith.

—1 JOHN 5:4

Blessed reigning Christ, take Your position on the throne of my heart. Abide in me so I can overcome the forces of evil in the world. Thank You for the conviction of the apostle John that "He who is in you is greater than he who is in the world" (1 John 4:4). I take that as my motto and move on into this day as an overcomer.

Throughout the day Satan will try to intimidate me. There will be evil people who will try to enrage me, neutral people who will upset me, and good people who do little who will alarm me. I'll be confronted by corporate and collusive evil in institutions. The news will have evidence of the virulent infection of the forces of evil.

So before I go into the battle of the day, I fortify myself with truth. I am a reborn person—begotten of God, called, chosen, and given birth as a cherished child of the Father. I have been given the mighty weapon of the shield of faith for the battle. It gives me a bold quality of spirit that meets danger or opposition with intrepidity, calmness, resoluteness, and determination. Your gift of faith will overcome the world. I'm ready for the day!

OCTOBER
4

This is the testimony: that God has given us eternal life, and this life is in His Son. He who has the Son has life; he who does not have the Son of God does not have life.

—1 JOHN 5:11-12

Dear God, I live this day as one more day of eternity. Thank You for helping me know that eternal life is not reserved for after physical death, but is Your life in me through the indwelling Savior. By Your grace and the abiding of Christ in me, I am alive forever. Death has no power over me. There is no distinction between abundant life now and eternal life forever. Heaven has begun!

That conviction changes my attitude toward today. I can see people and circumstances from an eternal perspective; I am totally free to do what You guide because only Your will matters. I have only You to please. Today is not an examination to decide my eternal destiny but an expression of my assurance of where I will spend the next phase of eternal life after this physical life on earth.

Thank You in advance for another great day. I have nothing to win or lose; I am free to love You unreservedly by serving others unselfishly. Everything can matter creatively because nothing matters ultimately, except discovering and doing Your will.

OCTOBER
5

Now this is the confidence that we have in Him, that if we ask anything according to His will, He hears us.

—1 JOHN 5:14

Father, Son, and Holy Spirit, once again I give praise for being drawn into the glory circle of the Trinity. Father, You glorify Your Son, He came to earth and now reigns to glorify You. He glorifies the Holy Spirit, the Counselor, whose ministry reveals Your will and enables me in my glorification of Christ, who leads me to the heart of the Father.

Thank You for this time of prayer in which my needs may be clarified so that my petitions may be directed according to Your will. Jesus, I take Your words seriously; "I say to you, whatever things you ask when you pray, believe that you receive them, and you will have them" (Mark 11:24). With a power like that available, I need to be sure of what I ask. Holy Spirit, thank You for helping me to ask for what boldly can be prayed in the name of Jesus—in keeping with His message, authority, and plan. Christ, You are my Advocate with the Father, ready to state my case to Him. I know You will ask for only what is best for my life.

So I lay out before You all my needs, concerns, projects, loved ones, and friends. Teach me to listen.

OCTOBER
6

Keep yourselves from idols.

—1 JOHN 5:21

Holy Lord God, who has commanded Your people to have no other gods before You, I pray for the honesty to face any idols in my life that compete with You as absolute Sovereign of my life. I confess that I slip into the idolization of the approval of people, the accolades my work can produce, the success that becomes addictive, the human power that becomes a seduction of the secondary.

I can identify the idols of my heart when I consider what I use to gain the satisfaction and security that only You can give. My problem is not that I eliminate my belief in You, but that I add idols to my personal pantheon.

As I begin this new day, I want to clear out the throne room of my heart and evict all those people, things, and commitments that clamor for the first place in my life. I belong first, foremost, and always to You.

With my priorities clear, I now seek to glorify You in the very relationships and responsibilities that have competed for Your place in my heart. I don't need them so I can serve You in them. Their chains of control have been wrought so I can worship only You.

OCTOBER
7

The love of money is the root of all evil.

—1 TIMOTHY 6:10

Lord of all life, source of all that I have and am, I praise You for the healing of that spiritual virus that the apostle Paul called *philarguria*, the love of money. Today in this quiet moment I want to open myself to a probing inventory. Help me to be honest with myself and with You, Lord.

- Do I ever worry over money . . . having enough and keeping what I have?

- Is bill-paying time a stressful time for me?

- Has money ever been the focus of an argument or misunderstanding with people I love?

- Do I experience twinges of competition or envy over what others earn, have inherited, or are able to do because of money?

- Do I ever spend money to solve hurt feelings, setbacks, or disappointments?

- Do I worry excessively about inflation or what's happened to crack my nest eggs?

- Do I tithe my income to glorify You and enable Your work in the world?

Lord, guide me in the earning, tithing, spending, and saving of money.

OCTOBER
8

Peace to you. Our friends greet you. Greet the friends by name.

—3 JOHN 14

Prince of Peace, whose peace cannot be kept unless it is shared, I seek to receive Your peace and communicate peace to others throughout this day.

I confess anything that may be disturbing my peace with You as I begin this new day. I know that if I want peace in my heart, I cannot harbor resentment. I seek forgiveness for any negative criticism, gossip, or destructive innuendos I may have spoken. Forgive any way that I may have brought acrimony to my relationships instead of helping to bring peace into any misunderstandings or angry hostility among or between people around me. You have shown me that being a reconciler is essential for a continued, sustained experience of Your peace. Most of all, I know that lasting peace is the result of Your indwelling Spirit, Your presence in my mind and heart.

Very specifically, I pray for people who need Your peace: _____, _____, _____. Show me how to be a communicator of the peace that passes understanding and is Your precious gift. Help me picture the people with whom I am to be a peacemaker today, bringing healing reconciliation, deeper understanding, and open communication. Use me, Lord!

OCTOBER
9

He has sent Me to heal the brokenhearted.

—LUKE 4:18

Lord Christ, penetrate the protective layers I put around my heart to keep from being known as I really am. You know me as I truly am and want me to know You as You are: present, powerful, loving, forgiving, encouraging. Thank You for breaking the cycle of the strain, stress, and struggle of life.

Repeatedly in the Gospels I read the words, "He had compassion." You helped people identify their struggles with this disarming question: "What do you want Me to do for you?" So I identify my deepest needs today. I imagine how You would have dealt with people with those needs. Help me to ask for what You want to give. You know what is best for me. Some things You will help me to endure and You will bring my good and growth and Your glory out of difficulties. Other things You can and will help me solve. In either case, You will enable me to live victoriously.

Thank You, Lord, that You have resources, people, and unanticipated strength to unleash to help me today to do what I have not imagined possible. Break through with blessings I could not anticipate. Then, send me to the brokenhearted to communicate Your healing power.

OCTOBER
10

*The grace of our Lord Jesus Christ be with you.
Amen.*

—1 THESSALONIANS 5:28

Gracious Lord Jesus, Master of things great and small, I need to talk to You about how often I sweat the small stuff. I pray about the big challenges and receive Your guidance and power. Then little annoyances blow my cool and I get suited up with Your full armor only to fight little skirmishes over trifles. It's good to know that Your grace is sufficient for all things, but I have to admit I do a better job with big problems than I do with the minuscule, mundane details that bug me.

Lord, today as an act of will, I commit myself to practicing Your presence in the lackluster, little details of life. Grant me a sense of humor to laugh at myself.

Give me the assurance that poet Annie Johnson Flint found in experiencing Your grace to meet troubles great and small. Thank You, dear Lord, for Your grace.

> His grace is great enough to meet the great things,
> The crashing waves that overwhelm the soul.
> The roaring winds that leave us stunned and
>   breathless,
> The sudden storms beyond our control.
> His grace is great enough to meet the small
>   things,
> The little pin-prick troubles that annoy
> The persistent worries, buzzing and persistent,
> The squeaking wheels that grate upon our joy.

OCTOBER
11

*Looking unto Jesus, the author and finisher of
our faith.*

—HEBREWS 12:2

Blessed, living Lord Jesus, the author and finisher of
my faith, the best days are those days in which I focus my
attention on You. Today, I renew my dedication to keeping
my eyes on You as the only lasting source of security and
strength. No human being is meant to give the ultimate
meaning to my life; no material possession or achievement
is capable of giving me profound inner peace.

So I look to You, Alpha and Omega, the way, the
truth, and the life who gives me direction, revelation, and
abundant life. You are the light who dispels darkness, the
bright and morning star of the dawn of a new day and
thousands of second chances, the Bread of Life to feed my
spiritual hungers, the door to safety in a dangerous world,
the true vine in whom I abide with fruitfulness as a branch,
and the resurrection and the life who has defeated death
and makes this another day of heaven already begun.

I love You, Lord Jesus. You are my Master and I am
Your disciple, You are my Savior and I am Your forgiven
follower, You are my Lord and I am Your servant. Life is
great because it is filled with great opportunities to love
You by caring for people. Author of my faith, write this
page of my life today as You see is best; finisher of my
faith, I will never finish praising You.

OCTOBER
12

My soul, wait silently for God.

—PSALM 62:5

Dear God, airports, train stations, and hospitals are not exclusive in having waiting rooms. Sometimes it seems like a lot of life is one large waiting room, an anteroom of expectation for some longed for event or dream. As I wait I tire of the trite reminder from people, "All things come to those who wait." When I turn to the Bible, from psalmist, prophet, and apostle comes the same challenging word: wait. "Wait on the LORD; be of good courage, and He shall strengthen your heart; wait, I say, on the LORD!" (Psalm 27:14). "Those who wait on the LORD shall renew their strength" (Isaiah 40:31).

Waiting on You is not so You can catch up with me, but a conditioning to receive You who are always ahead of me calling me on. You Yourself are the answer to my deepest need. Waiting is not passive but active. It's responding to Your call to intimate communion with You.

In this time of prayer, I report in for a renewed relationship with You, Father. You have been waiting for me to realize how much I need You. Abiding in You is the essence of waiting on You. Thank You for giving me patience to wait for Your perfect timing to release power for me to respond to the guidance You give while I wait.

OCTOBER
13

The Congress has designated the third week of October as "Character Counts" week. During this week, six pillars of character will be emphasized. A prayer for each is arranged so you can pray for these pillars to be a part of the structure of your personal character and of our society.

Dear God, trustworthy Sovereign of this nation, and Lord of my life in whom I trust, I join with others throughout this land in seeking to have *trustworthiness* a pillar of my character and an essential mainstay of our culture. I know that I should not pray for a quality of life like this for society unless I am willing to begin with myself.

Lord, You desire to implant Your character in me. Everything I know about being trustworthy I've learned from You. Your faithfulness never fails; You are consistent in Your lovingkindness; You are always true to Your Word. May my trust in You as my God be the inspiring motivation of trustworthiness in me. May integrity be the basic fiber of my character. I dedicate myself to speaking the truth, to saying what I mean and meaning what I say. Make me totally dependable to keep my promises. May others be able to count on me and always be able to say, "What you see is what you get." I pray that my actions will build a confidence of trust in others. I commit myself to making trustworthiness the reliable, consistent quality of my character. Help me, Lord, to keep this promise to You.

OCTOBER
14

Show respect for everyone . . .

—1 PETER 2:17 (TLB)

Holy God, may my reverence for You give me authentic respect for people, the world You have entrusted to me to care for, and the values and traditions that are sacred in America's history which I am called to revere.

Dear God, I learn about the character pillar of *respect* from You. You created me and respect my uniqueness. You give me esteem and security and help me live at full potential. I know I am of value to You. Help me to communicate respect for the dignity of other people. May I respect their gifts and talents, and encourage them to be all that You created them to be. Free me from self-centeredness so I can be a cheerleader of their successes and an empathizer in their failures. Make me a defender of the rights of people to be distinctive, to honor differences of race and religious practices.

Lord, I pray for the character pillar of respect to be expressed in the way I live in Your creation. May I behold and never destroy the beauty of the natural world You've given me to enjoy.

Sovereign of this nation, remind me that patriotism has not gone out of style. May my gratitude for living in this free land give me profound respect for the constitution, our flag, and the genuine American spirit of mutual respect for the rights of individuals to life, liberty, and the pursuit of happiness.

OCTOBER
15

. . . as responsible to God . . .

—1 CORINTHIANS 7:24 (NIV)

Almighty God, I am accountable to You. You have given me life, loved and guided me, and entrusted to me responsibilities to be assumed and done for Your glory. In all my ways, I will acknowledge You and You shall direct my paths.

Today, I continue these "Character Counts" prayers and thank You for the pillar of character called *responsibility*. I praise You that You have given me a mind to know Your thoughts, goodness to strengthen my emotions, and resoluteness to motivate my will. The central purpose of my life is to listen for Your commands and to obey with passion. Help me to do the best I can with all that I have so that I may serve You with excellence.

Lord, You have given me my own realm of responsibility. I am a steward of the blessings You have given me. All that I have and am is a gift from You to be used for the relationships You have given me. Help me to be generous and kind as I assume responsibility for loved ones, friends, people for whom I work or those who work for me.

Lord, help me never forget that I must account for how responsible I was to You in carrying out my responsibilities.

OCTOBER
16

Doing what is right and just and fair.

—Proverbs 1:3 (NIV)

Father, You always are right, just, and fair. Your fairness is the result of Your righteousness and justice. Today I pray for the character pillar of *fairness*. Help me to play by Your rules of absolute honesty, purity, and love. I not only want to do to others what I would want them to do to me, but I want to treat others as You have treated me.

Thank You that I have Your commandments and Your truth in the Bible as my guide. In Jesus You have taught me not only to meet but go beyond the just standard. May I be distinguished for my generosity in exceeding what is expected.

May my expression of the character trait of fairness also include my judgments of other people and what I say about them. Forgive me when my evaluations of people are polluted by pride, envy, or competitiveness. Remind me of the power of words to assassinate other people's character. When I can say nothing positive, may I say nothing.

Lord, You know that the times the strength of this pillar of character is tested is when people are unfair in what they say about me or are unfair in their dealings with me. My temptation is to retaliate, but I know that resentment fired by retaliation usually results in recrimination. Help me break that cycle by being fair by Your standards and with Your strength.

OCTOBER
17

He cares for you.

—1 PETER 5:7

Dear Lord, in a world where people often say, "I couldn't care less," help me to remember how much You care for me and then may I say, "I dare not care less!" I can cast all my cares on You for I know You care for what ultimately is best for me.

Thank You for the character transplant that takes place when You take up residence in me. I cannot achieve the traits of true character on my own. Thank You for giving me the secret: You come into my mind and heart with reorienting, recreative power. You do through me what I long to do. It is liberating to know this secret when today I seek the character pillar of *caring*. I accept Paul's reminder to Timothy, "I want to remind you to stir into flame the strength and boldness that is in you . . . for the Holy Spirit, God's gift, does not want you to be afraid of people, but to be wise and strong, and to love them and enjoy being with them" (2 Timothy 1:6-7 TLB).

Lord, may I follow the motto "A knowledge of a need is Your call." Today, like the Good Samaritan, I will come across many opportunities to care for people in need. May I cooperate with You in caring. I want to be prepared for what You have prepared. Caring is everything. I can't care less!

OCTOBER
18

For the Lord's sake obey every law of your government.

—1 PETER 2:13 (TLB)

Almighty God, Sovereign of the United States and Lord of my life, You have lavished Your love in the natural resources and expressed Your providential care in the blessing of this nation. Thank You for the privilege of living in this land of liberty and justice, opportunity, and promise. Lord, You have made *citizenship* a character trait. You call Your people to be loyal in their patriotism and diligent in their active involvement in seeking Your very best for their land. There is so much for which we can be thankful, but there are problems that debilitate Your plan for America.

Today, I make a new commitment to love You by serving as an active citizen. You have shown me that this begins with daily prayer for my local, state, and national leaders. You wait to bless them with supernatural wisdom, discernment, vision, and leadership ability . . . until I will join Your people in prayer.

Lord, may the citizenship characteristic of my character actively involve me in the political process. Help me exercise the privilege of citizenship not only by my vote but also by my support of leaders who trust in You and seek Your will.

So, in everything from praying to paying taxes, help me to express my gratitude for my nation. God, bless America!

OCTOBER
19

You know his proven character.

—PHILIPPIANS 2:22

Blessed Lord Jesus, I read Paul's commendation of Timothy and it clarifies a deep longing in me. These past days of prayer for the pillars of character have made me take an honest inventory of my own character. I want to be consistent, dependable, loyal, and trustworthy. Make my character like Yours, and then may I be faithful.

I think of the transformation You performed in Timothy's character. You helped him overcome timidity and fear to become a faithful disciple and loyal friend. His character was proven, tested in the challenges and difficulties. It became like refined gold that had been through the fires. That's what I want, Lord.

Then I think of Epaphroditus, whom the Philippians sent to help Paul in his time of need. His character was tested by illness in Rome, and he almost died. In it all, his greatest concern was that he might not cause his fellow Philippians worry. It is encouraging to me to read Philippians 2:25-30 and feel Paul's affirmation of Epaphroditus as a brother in Christ, soldier of the faith, fellow worker, and one who set aside his own needs to care for the apostle. I prayerfully reflect on what the refining fires of life have produced in my character. Lord, give me a proven character that people can count on.

OCTOBER
20

There we saw the giants. . . and we were like grasshoppers in our own sight, and so we were in their sight.

—NUMBERS 13:33

Lord God, I smile as I read the report given by the majority of those sent in by Moses to spy out the Promised Land. They saw only the problems and dangers that would confront the people of Israel if they went in to possess the land. In the presence of the tall descendants of Anak, the reconnaissance team felt like grasshoppers. The Israelites felt and acted like grasshoppers, saw themselves as nothing more, and their limited self-image was transferred to the sons of Anak. They saw the Israelites as the Israelites saw themselves.

Lord, I want to overcome any vestige of this tendency in human nature to project self-defeating prophecies. I'm willing to admit my inadequacies, but forgive me when I focus on those to the exclusion of the new person in Christ I am, the gifts of the Spirit You have given me, and the character You have developed in me. Rather than expect difficulties and talk about them, help me to remember that "I can do all things through Christ who strengthens me" (Philippians 4:13).

You have shown me that I become what dominates my self-image. I am what I am because of Your grace. Free me of the fear that hides behind false humility and makes me less than You intend me to be.

OCTOBER
21

Caleb quieted the people before Moses, and said, "Let us go up at once and take possession, for we are well able to overcome it."

—NUMBERS 13:30

Lord, give me "Caleb courage" to hold a positive attitude toward the challenges of this day. Yesterday the furtive report of the Israelites who thought of themselves as grasshoppers in comparison to the giant sons of Anak motivated me to pray about self-defeating prophecies. Today Caleb inspires me to factor in Your presence and power in any analysis of the possible. He was courageous in his vision because he knew You would strengthen Your people to accomplish what You already had promised.

Help me linger in my prayers until I feel sure of what You want me to do in the opportunities ahead of me today. Then with an assurance of Your power, may my attitude be filled with enthusiasm. I'm not asking for "Can do!" self-generated bravado, but "God is able to help me do!" courage.

Lord, help me to have a contagious courage today. Enable me to infuse hope in others—not in what they can do, but what You can do through them. Fear can so easily cripple people. Some end up safe and sorry. Give me Caleb-courage to come alongside them and encourage them with a vision of what extraordinary things You can do with ordinary people who trust in You.

OCTOBER
22

Our brethren have discouraged our hearts, saying, "The people are greater and taller than we."

—DEUTERONOMY 1:28

Lord God of encouragement, forgive me when I get discouraged and spread the discouragement to others. Moses' own analysis of the negative report from the ten on the reconnaissance team sent in to spy out the Promised Land was that they discouraged the hearts of others. I note that the original Hebrew word translated "discouraged" means "melted." Their negative attitude melted the iron in the hearts of the people.

I think of people like that. They dissuade courage in others with their discouraging attitudes. They get down on themselves and are down on possibilities of progress. Lord, seeing the impact of people like these brings me to a new commitment for today. I pray for people who need me to encourage them to be bold in grasping Your blessings to press on. Help me to be one of the first persons others think of when they need a positive boost to trust You more.

I know that being a positive encourager is dependent on receiving a fresh flow of Your enabling power for the problems of each day. I can share only what is a fresh experience in my own life. So here are things that could cause me discouragement: _____, _____, _____. Help me to experience hope so I can be an uplifting example of courage.

OCTOBER
23

Joshua did as Moses said to him, and fought with Amalek. And Moses, Aaron, and Hur went up to the top of the hill. And so it was, when Moses held up his hand, that Israel prevailed; and when he let down his hand, Amalek prevailed.

—EXODUS 17:10-12

Almighty God, make me a member of the royal, loyal order of Aaron and Hur. I want to be faithful to those who serve as my leaders. May I hold up their hands by my faithful prayers and unswerving support in good and bad days. Help me to learn from this biblical example that You give victory when we pray for those whom You have appointed to leadership.

Today I hold up the arms of the President, the Vice President, the leaders and members of both houses of Congress, the Governor of my state, and the Mayor of my city.

With the same prayerful commitment I pray for spiritual leaders and teachers and ask for a fresh anointing of Your Spirit today. Dear Lord, help me lift up the arms of loved ones and friends who may be exhausted in battles with illnesses, difficulties, or discouragements. Especially I pray today for _____ and _____. When I too become weary in battle, help me accept the Aarons and Hurs You send me. Remind me that the battle for righteousness and justice is Yours, and You are going to win!

OCTOBER
24

*Sanctify yourselves, for tomorrow the LORD
will do wonders among you.*

—JOSHUA 3:5

Almighty God, thank You for the privilege of co-operating with You in accomplishing Your plans. You called the people of Israel to consecrate themselves. I look with interest at the Hebrew root word for "sanctify," meaning "to cut" or "to be bright." Both meanings apply to what the people had to do to be ready to move forward and cross over the Jordan River into the Promised Land. They had wandered in the wilderness for forty years after they had procrastinated entering. Now at last they were ready.

I picture how You involved the people in the wonder of crossing the River Jordan. I put myself in the skin of one of the priests who were called to shoulder the Ark and move down toward that overflowing river. You promised that when the soles of the feet of the priests got wet, You would roll back the river. Those priests waded into the water, probably up to their necks, and waited patiently for hours before You stopped up the waters nineteen miles away at Adam, and eventually the river around them receded and the people were able to cross over the dry riverbed. Lord, help me be as obedient and patient as I wait for the manifestation of Your promises. The first step is the hardest: I have to get my feet wet, trust You, and wait. I thank You for involving me in Your wonders today.

OCTOBER
25

The Spirit of the Lord came upon Gideon. (Alternative translation: "The Spirit clothed Himself with Gideon.")

Behold, I send the promise of My Father upon you; but tarry in the city of Jerusalem until you are endued [clothed] with power from on high.

—JUDGES 6:34 AND
LUKE 24:49 *(parentheses added)*

Spirit of the Living God, fall afresh on me. The day ahead will require more than my strength or talent can bear. Like Gideon, I need You to clothe Yourself with me to accomplish what You want done in my life today. Enter into me and empower me to attempt great things by Your power. Gideon faced impossible odds, but You gave him Your strategy and sagacity to lead Israel to victory.

Shifting the metaphor of might a bit, the disciples were told to wait until they were clothed with power. When You came upon them at Pentecost, they received Your supernatural strength.

Holy Spirit, I claim both aspects of Your empowering: take possession of my inner self and transform my whole being. Like the disciples, I cannot be the person Christ has called me to be without Your empowering. As the day stretches out before me, I know I cannot make it without a fresh endowment of Your divine enabling.

OCTOBER
26

Entreat me not to leave you, or to turn back from following after you; for wherever you go, I will go; and wherever you lodge, I will lodge; your people shall be my people, And your God, my God. Where you die, I will die, And there will I be buried. The LORD do so to me, and more also, if anything but death parts you and me.

—RUTH 1:16-17

Gracious Father, whose lovingkindness never fails, thank You for Your unchanging loyalty. In response, I seek to be loyal to You and become a person who is known for indefatigable loyalty in all the ups and downs of life.

I am deeply moved by the book of Ruth and the loyalty Ruth expressed to her mother-in-law, Naomi. Today's oft-quoted Scripture expresses undying faithfulness. It's the kind of loyalty I want to be able to offer to and receive from loved ones and friends. Out of a shared, common grief, the bond of loyalty was forged between Ruth and Naomi. Both lost their husbands. Naomi offered Ruth freedom from the responsibility of remaining with her and caring for her. Instead, Ruth committed herself to staying with Naomi. You eventually rewarded this loyalty with Ruth's marriage to Boaz.

Lord, You have made loyalty the golden thread of the fabric of authentic relationships. I wonder, Lord, who needs to know and feel my loyalty? Help me express it today!

OCTOBER
27

I have found David the son of Jesse, a man after My own heart, who will do all My will.

—ACTS 13:22

Dear God, like David, You created me to be a person after Your heart. Today's Scripture reminds me that You have a heart, You have endowed me with a heart, and the secret of an abundant life is receiving Your heart in mine.

Lord, when I speak of my heart I am identifying what the Bible identifies as the seat of the intellect, will, and the whole range of emotions. Then I think of Your heart as Your essential nature. I praise You for Your divine intelligence, indefatigable lovingkindness, plus Your sovereign will. You have created me to think Your thoughts after You, receive and express Your love, and will to do Your will.

Thank You for reminding me that the word "after" in Acts 13:22 means "in succession to, responding to, in search of, molded in a likeness of, and complete harmony with." As a sculptor sculpts clay "after" a likeness, or a painter paints a portrait "after" a person's likeness, so when my heart is "after" Your heart, it is one in which Your heart is reproduced—intellectually, emotionally, and volitionally. As David was distinguished because he longed to know and emulate Your heart, so too, my life goal is to be moldable clay for Your hand to shape into Your likeness.

OCTOBER
28

*Do not cast me away from Your presence, and
do not take Your Holy Spirit from me.*

—PSALM 51:11

Gracious God, there are times I am stunned by the Bible's honesty about its heroes and heroines. Yesterday I was moved by the example of David as a man after Your heart. Today I read Psalm 51 prayed by David after confrontation by Nathan about his sin of adultery with Bathsheba and the arrangement of the death of her husband. No wonder David has been called the greatest saint and sinner of the Old Testament! A man after Your heart? Rather, a man who did what he had promised himself he would never do.

Lord, was there a danger that You would remove Your Holy Spirit from David? Or was it because of the movement of Your Spirit in his tumultuous heart that he longed that You would forgive him and not turn Your back on him? Thank You that You never give up on Your people and that a fear of Your departure is the result of a fresh realization of how much You mean to us.

Father, David's sin is not mine, but I have my own idea of the worst sin I've promised myself I'd never do. It may not seem all that serious to others, but for me it's the big one. Stay by me, Holy Spirit, that I may never commit it or any other grievous sin, but on a daily basis convict me of my sins, and remind me of both the cost and the forgiving power of Calvary.

OCTOBER
29

I am the light of the world.

—JOHN 8:12

Lord Jesus, light of the world, Your light shows me the truth about myself and Your strength gives me courage to change those things that need to be changed. Your light also reveals the things You want to affirm.

Today, I am very thankful that You know about another person inside me who is greater than my faults or weaknesses. There's a hero in my soul waiting to be set free.

In Your presence, the miracle happens again; Your light shines on the deepest aspect of the inner person within me, someone I often neglect. You bring out of hiding the person You want to liberate and affirm. It's wonderful to know that You know the most profound longing of my heart: to love and serve You, to be loyal and faithful to You, and to love others as You have loved me.

I think of the old saying, "If each person's internal care were written on his brow, those who have our envy would have our pity now." Lord, make me empathetic, sensitive, and compassionate.

I'm ready to be Your manifest intervention in situations to infuse joy, affirm people, absorb pain, or help relieve anguish. I will do battle for truth and justice. I plan to live this day and the rest of my life in the reality of Your life in me. Thank You for making it so!

OCTOBER
30

O God, my heart is steadfast.

—PSALM 57:7

Lord of time, may I not be distracted from what's important today by the tyranny of the urgent. Help me prioritize the demands of this day. Give me the courage to live on what You will show me is on Your agenda for today. May I deem urgent only what glorifies You, brings me into a deeper relationship with You, and serves the needs of people. My desire is to live with an inner serenity about the pressures of the day. Carry me in the currents of Your Spirit. Rather than thrashing about to keep afloat, free me to float uplifted by the blessed buoyancy of Your power. Guide me through the rocks in the river, some of which are hidden beneath the surface.

Lord, I want to be an inner-directed person rather than one who is pulled in all directions. Make me so secure in You that I will have the courage to discover and do Your will. Give me courage to say no to some things and yes to others on the basis of Your guidance in my mind and heart.

Lord, I press on to this day with my only concern being that I might miss Your best in the busy schedule of the day. So, now in this quiet moment, quiet any dissonance in me, overcome any resistance in my will, and fill any emptiness in my heart. Living this day to the fullest is part of a life lived at full potential.

OCTOBER
31

. . . that their hearts may be encouraged.

—COLOSSIANS 2:2

Gracious Lord, I commit this day to making other people happy. So often my prayers are for what I need You to do to make me happy. Now in this quiet time, inspire me to think imaginatively about how I can bring nothing but happiness to those You have given me to love and those whose friendship I enjoy.

Lord, help me to think of ways I could make life easier for the people in my home, among my friends, and at work. My tendency is to think of some big, grand thing I could do and then because of the immensity of it, I never get it done. Help me forgo these grandstanding feats of heroism and do something that simply makes life more of a joy to the people in my life. I want to make this a day free of uncreative, unproductive criticism. Today I will not be a nagging, fault-finding source of distress. Whatever I do that causes anxiety, help me to change.

Often Lord, it's what I fail to do that causes unhappiness. People need encouragement and affirmation. Today I give up the control I get by withholding the attitude or the words of approval not just of what people are trying to do, but what they are striving to become. May the end of this day be a time for remembering the happy memories I gave others. That's what it's all about, and that's what I'm going to be about today!

NOVEMBER
1

I delight to do Your will, O my God; Your law is within my heart.

—PSALM 40:8

Dear God, liberate me from my attachment to the reward system. The whole fiber of human relationships is woven by the back-and-forth movement of the shuttle of deeds and expected rewards. Sometimes I project onto this barter of give and take. I slip into thinking that You will bless me more if I'm good, effective, and efficient. I catch myself thinking that I should do loving and forgiving things to be sure I can count on Your approval. Sometimes prayer is like a negotiation session for the best deal I can get.

Remind me that You own me; You do not owe me anything. I cannot manipulate Your blessings by my beneficence. I should not expect a citation because I pray, seek to be faithful, serve others, and care for the suffering world around me. When I finish all this, I'm still at the starting line ready to begin adventuresome discipleship.

Thank You for showing me that beyond duty is delight. I delight to serve You because of the limitless love You have already given rather than trying to earn Your love. Saturate my heart with Your wondrous love. May my status as a forgiven sinner saved by grace, loved to the uttermost, filled with Your Spirit, blessed beyond imagination, destined to live forever and headed for heaven—be the inspiration of living this day to the fullest.

November
2

Do everything without complaining.

—Philippians 2:14 (NIV)

Lord, today I want to stop complaining and start confessing my trust in You. I think of what life would be if every time I want to complain about circumstances, I took that moment specifically to ask for Your intervention, inspiration, and instruction.

Complaining can become a habit. I've learned that when I complain I put off on to someone else, or even to You, the responsibility to fix things for me. There's a great difference between enlisting the help of a loved one or friend in tackling a problem and simply standing around complaining. With You, Lord, it's so easy to tell You how You ought to have done better running my life, and handling events that impact my life. Often I expend my energy asking, "If You know everything, why do I still have problems?"

Complaining is contagious. We often infect our friends with the virus. Forgive me, Lord, when I spread this spiritual illness to others. There is a great difference between complaining and creative analysis of problems. Make me a hopeful thinker with a mind You can inspire with solutions. Take away that "poor me" attitude and replace it with a positive expectation of Your blessing and power in the very things about which I've been complaining.

NOVEMBER
3

No one puts a piece from a new garment on an old one; otherwise the new makes a tear, and also the piece that was taken out of the new does not match the old.

—LUKE 5:36

Blessed Christ, fellowship with You is an adventure that's never completed. You are never finished with me; therefore I am never finished growing. You are engaged in a momentous transformation of my life. I know that I have barely begun to become the person You are ready and able to liberate me to be.

Your parable of the new patch on an old garment reminds me that new life in You is not a tattered, patched, and restyled old self but a completely new character made in Your likeness. When You take up residence in me, a dynamic process begins by which everything is made new. My mind is transformed. Memories are healed and liberated. Values and goals are reoriented. My image of myself is changed. You are satisfied with nothing less than molding me into Your image. Thank You that the miracle of the new creation never stops.

You want more than a patch on an old garment. Any false security of the familiar must be replaced with the garment of trusting You completely with the complexities and uncertainties confronting me today. Lord, make me a new person for a new day.

NOVEMBER
4

Election Day

Almighty God, Sovereign of our nation, thank You for the privilege of living in a free land where I have the opportunity to vote. Today leaders at various levels of government will be elected. Work through the votes cast today so that the people will be elected who will glorify You and live the motto of this nation, "In God We Trust," and the affirmation of the Pledge of Allegiance, "One Nation Under God." Strengthen their commitment to trust You to guide them as they confront the problems and claim Your best for their realm of leadership. May they never forget that they are in office by Your choice and are accountable to You for how they lead. May the immense responsibilities they assume, and the vows they make when sworn into office, bring them to their knees with profound humility and unprecedented openness to You.

Save them from the seduction of power, the addiction of popularity, and the aggrandizement of pride. Lord, keep their priorities straight: You and their families first; the good of the nation second; consensus around truth third; party loyalties fourth; and personal success last of all. May they never forget that they have been elected to serve and not be served. Consistently replenish the reserves of strength and courage so often drained by pressure and stress. Anoint their minds with Your Spirit and guide them as they seek to know and do Your will in the crucial issues before my city, state, and nation. I firmly believe that this can be America's finest hour awaiting leaders imbued with Your power.

NOVEMBER
5

For everyone who asks receives, and he who seeks finds, and to him who knocks it will be opened. . . .

How much more will your heavenly Father give the Holy Spirit to those who ask Him. . .

—LUKE 11:10,13 (emphasis added)

Dear God, I ponder Jesus' words. The purpose of asking, seeking, and knocking through prayer is to refine my ability to request what You want to give most of all. The one blessing You do not give until I ask is the fullness of Your own indwelling Spirit. You surround me, protect me, watch over me, arrange life's circumstances for my good and growth; but You do not give the fullness of Your Spirit until I cry out for nothing less than an infusion of Your very life in me.

I know that You constantly are at work preparing me to realize that my deepest need is for the power of Your Spirit. I acknowledge that need now. Father, anoint my mind and heart with Your Spirit. I open myself completely. Grant me the strength, joy, peace, and power of Your indwelling Spirit for the challenges of today. Imbue me with the wisdom, insight, and understanding I will need for today's problems. Especially, fill me to overflowing with the gift of love. I think of particular people to whom I need to communicate love today. When I remember the sheer delight of being loved by You through another person, I want to love in that healing, helpful, hopeful way today.

NOVEMBER
6

These are murmurers, complainers.

—JUDE 16

Strong Father, mighty to save and to sustain, take the wimp out of my heart and the whine out of my voice. Put a "no whining" sign on the walls of my mind and a "no whimpering" badge on my shoulder. Forgive me, Lord, when my prayers have that plaintive, high-pitched sound of a whiner. You must tire of hearing me and so many others whine to You. But then, I know You've endured the sound all through human history. You heard the murmuring of people of Israel against Moses and You during and after the Exodus from Egypt. Christians have not done any better through the ages. So often we have the annoying edge of a whine to our voices and attitudes when we criticize You for not doing better for us, or rail away at people who have not done what we want when we want it.

Lord, lift up my heart and put a new lilt in my voice. Warm me with the depth of Your love so that I will speak to others with warmth and not a whine. People have it hard enough without having to deal with the noise pollution of my whining. Help me to listen carefully to how I sound when I do more fussing than inspiring faith in You. Then give me the courage to change the tone and tenor of what I say. Thank You, Lord, for speaking through me the words of affirmation and encouragement You want communicated today.

NOVEMBER
7

Now thanks be to God who always leads us in triumph in Christ, and through us diffuses the fragrance of His knowledge in every place.

—2 CORINTHIANS 2:14

Blessed Lord, yesterday I asked You to help me stop adding to the negative noise pollution with my whining. Today, I ask You to enable me to clean up the distorted thinking that pollutes the air with untruth and half truths. Instead, I want to spend my entire day today giving thanks for the way You lead me in triumph and spread the fragrance of the knowledge of You.

Christ, there is a delightful fragrance that is spread when You are communicated in Your victorious power. You dispel the odors of doubt, envy, hatred, and greed. Change me so I may have no stinking attitudes to pollute the atmosphere of my relationships.

May the thoughts that I think and express be room deodorizers to freshen up the atmosphere and give others healthy, positive air to breathe.

I think of the countless times You have led me in triumph over trouble. Then I think of those people who brought the fragrance of the knowledge of You into my life, clearing away the polluted air of fear and anxiety. Help me to spread the fragrance of Your truth and love wherever I go today.

NOVEMBER
8

Jesus: "I do not want to send them away hungry."

—MATTHEW 15:32

Almighty God, You have chosen to do Your work through Your people. I have been called to communicate Your love by caring for the spiritually and physically poor and hungry of the world. You press my heart next to the heartbeat of those caught in the syndrome of poverty and those millions who feel hunger gnaw at them day and night. Help me respond to their cry as individuals and as participants in united efforts to care for those who suffer.

Father, motivate me by the memory of Your generosity to me, but also by the bracing truth that I can't continue to grow in grace without obeying Your command to feed the hungry and care for the poor.

As I pray this prayer, I realize how easy it is to talk to You about the poor and end up doing nothing, or very little, as Your agent of relieving suffering. So today, I ask for the opportunity to give love, care, and a gift to one person who is hungry. I need to do this even if I question how the person will spend the change or bills I give him or her. Most important, today I make myself available to work in some cause for the poor and hungry. Also, help me make a generous gift to those organizations You have raised up to confront the immense problems of hunger in the world. Lord, help me act!

NOVEMBER
9

I will carry you! I have made, and I will bear;
even I will carry, and will deliver you.

—ISAIAH 46:4

Lord God, I picture Isaiah watching the beasts and cattle carrying the heavy Babylonian idols. As he watched the burdensome practice of their religion You reminded him that You did not need to be carried but You carry Your people.

I need to remember that today. Sometimes the rules and regulations, duties and obligations of religion become a burden to fulfill. Added to these are all the man-made traditions and customs that take on obligatory weight. Today I need to recover the dynamic fire of a relationship of love with You. When I'm motivated by love, I feel carried by You rather than feeling the musts and oughts of a strained relationship.

Remind me that I don't need to carry the heavy burden of defending You, or religion, or tradition. The best witness I can make is to communicate the joy of knowing Your uplifting, carrying power.

Keep me from being a person with a heavy attitude others feel must be carried or dragged along. When I allow You to meet my deepest needs, I don't have to transfer to others the responsibility of making me happy. You do that so well with Your faithful supply of love and encouragement.

NOVEMBER
10

For what is your life? It is even a vapor that appears for a little time and then vanishes away. Instead you ought to say, "If the Lord wills, we shall live and do this or that."

—JAMES 4:14-15

Almighty God, without whom I could not take a breath, or think a thought, I am accountable to You for the way I live the precious days of my life. Often I hear people who have escaped from some accident or some life-threatening illness say, "God must have some reason for saving my life. I want to find out what it is and get on with it." May I be no less grateful for life and no less intentional in living out the special purpose You have for me. You have protected me so I could live this new day.

Suddenly, I feel differently about the relationships and responsibilities of the day ahead. You have plans for me and I don't want to miss them. There are things You have appointed me to do and if I don't do them, they will not be done.

Lord, fill me with Your Spirit and give me an enthusiastic, positive attitude for today. Help me to express delight in the people of my life. They have enough burdens to carry; may I not be one of them. I can choose whether I will drag my feet today or walk with a spring in my step because You are the unseen but loyal Friend who holds my hand.

NOVEMBER
11

Veteran's Day Prayer

Every good citizen makes his country's honor his own and cherishes it not only as precious but as sacred. He is willing to risk his life in its defense and is conscious that he gains protection while he gives it.

—ANDREW JACKSON

Gracious God, all through our history as a nation, You have helped us battle the enemies of freedom and democracy. Many of the pages of our history are red with the blood of those who paid the supreme sacrifice in just wars against tyranny. Those who survived the wars of the past are all our distinguished living heroes and heroines. They carry the honored title of veterans.

Today, on Veteran's Day, I want to express my debt of gratitude for them and to make this a day of prayer for our nation. I commit myself anew to the battle for the realization of Your vision for this nation.

You have helped us conquer external enemies; now give us the same urgency in our internal battles against racial divisions instigated by any race or group. Renew our strength as we move on toward a truly integrated society with equal opportunity for all people. Make us one. Help us to press on in the American dream to banish vociferous expressions of hostility and hatred in our society. Make me and all Americans seasoned veterans in the daily struggle for righteousness in our land.

NOVEMBER
12

With eyes wide open to the mercies of God, I beg you . . . as an act of intelligent worship, to give your bodies, as a living sacrifice, consecrated to Him and acceptable by him.

—ROMANS 12:1 (J.B. PHILLIPS)

Dear God, this is one of those days when I really need two alarm clocks: one to wake me up, and the other to remind me of why I'm up. Give me a two-alarm wake-up call every hour of today—an alarm to go off inside to wake up to the wonderful privilege of being alive, and the other to claim the wondrous power You offer to do Your will in all the circumstances and challenges in which I will find myself.

Help me to see You alive in the world around me, active in the lives of people, and abundant in Your blessings. Astonish me with evidences of Your intervening in my life. When I least expect You, You are there. The outward evidence of Your indwelling Spirit is that I never lose the capacity constantly to be astonished by what You are up to in my life and the lives of people around me. You have taught me that a bored, bland, unamazed Christian is a contradiction of terms.

So Lord, give me courage to attempt what only You could help me achieve. Renew my enthusiasm, invigorate my vision, replenish my strength. I'm wide awake now, Lord!

NOVEMBER
13

Happy is he . . . whose hope is in the LORD *his God.*

—PSALM 146:5

God of hope, thank You for the incredible happiness I feel when I trust You completely. The expectation of Your timely interventions to help me gives me stability and serenity. It makes me bold and courageous, fearless and free. You have shown me that authentic hope always is rooted in Your faithfulness in keeping Your promises. I hear Your assurance, "Be not afraid, I am with you." I place my hope in Your problem-solving power, Your conflict-resolving presence, and Your anxiety-dissolving peace.

Lord, You have helped me discover the liberating power of an unreserved commitment to You. When I commit to You my life and each of the challenges I face, I am not only released from the tension of living on my own limited resources, but also a mysterious movement of Your providence begins. The company of heaven, plus people and circumstances begin to rally to my aid. Unexpected resources are released; unexplainable good things start happening. I claim the promise of Psalm 37:5: "Commit Your way to the LORD, trust also in Him, and He shall bring it to pass."

November
14

You are my God, and I will praise You;
You are my God, I will exalt You.
Oh, give thanks to the LORD, for He is good!
For His mercy endures forever.

—PSALM 118:28-29

Gracious God, I want to be so committed to you, so filled with Your Spirit, so open and expectant of Your blessings, and so willing to be surprised by Your interventions, that I will be a positive person today. Keep me from being navigated by negativism into the whirlpools of judgmentalism. Instead, I want to step into the fast-moving currents of the river of Your Spirit and be carried along by Your supernatural power. You will guide my thinking, unravel my difficulties, and empower my decisions.

Today, my desire is not just to do different things, but to do the same old things differently: with freedom, joy, and excellence. Give me new delight for matters of drudgery, new patience for people's problems, new zest for unfinished details. Be my lifeline in the pressures of deadlines, my rejuvenation in routines, and my endurance whenever I feel enervated. May my communication with You throughout the day give me deep convictions and high courage to defend them. Give me a special measure of wisdom, insight, and discernment as I tackle the challenges of this day.

NOVEMBER
15

For though I am free from all men, I have made myself a servant to all, that I might win the more.

—1 CORINTHIANS 9:19

Gracious Father, You created me to need and love You, and then to love people but not need them. Sometimes, I get that all mixed up. I edge You out of Your place as first in my life whenever I inordinately need people for my security and self-worth. The focus tends to be on myself and my needs rather than on others and their need for Your love expressed through me.

Remind me again that You are the only person I have to please. And when I know of Your pleasure in me not because of my performance but because of sheer grace, I am free not to have to please anyone else. The amazing thing is that this realization releases me to focus on really loving people. My deepest concern becomes how to communicate Your grace rather than using people to fill my emptiness.

You have shown me that I am not free until I serve. The outward expression of that freedom is when I commit my time, energy, resources and thought to caring about them rather than worrying about how they care for me. The need beneath all my needs is not for people, but to serve people. That's the way You meant abundant life to be lived, and that's how I'm going to live today.

NOVEMBER
16

You have been given fullness in Christ.

—COLOSSIANS 2:10 (NIV)

Lord Christ, when I experience Your fullness in my emptiness, I receive Your mind for my thoughts, Your nature for the formation of my character, Your person for the shaping of my personality, Your will for the direction of my will, and Your power for my discipleship. Each day as I yield my inner life to the formation of Your character in me, I am able to face the struggles of my outer life.

Today I can face the three most troublesome struggles of life. First, thank You for helping me overcome the struggle with my human nature. When I admit the impossibility of changing myself with resolutions and self-improvement disciplines, You take control and perform the continuing miracle of making me like Yourself. Second, You free me from the struggle to be humanly adequate. I know I am insufficient for the demands of life, but I also know of Your all-sufficient adequacy. I can't imagine any problem You can't help me solve, any person You can't love through me, any challenge You can't give me strength to tackle. Third, I don't have to struggle with worries over what the future holds. I can relax. Whatever I face today will be an opportunity for new dimensions of Your character to be formed in me.

NOVEMBER
17

If you bring your gift to the altar, and there remember that your brother has something against you, leave your gift there before the altar, and go your way. First be reconciled to your brother, and then come and offer your gift.

—MATTHEW 5:23-24

Lord, I came to this time of prayer thinking I was ready to present You with the gift of myself. Then I read Your admonition about what You want me to do before I can truly have this prayer be an authentic communication with You. You want me to be reconciled with people who may have something against me. So often I talk to You about people who have offended or hurt me. Now You've turned it all around and want me to think about the people I may have harmed in word or action. Then I read Your instructions more closely. You're concerned about even those who have a perception of having something against me when I may not agree that I did anything wrong. What You want is reconciliation.

All this gives me marching orders for today. Before this day is out, You want me to do everything I can to seek and establish right relationships with all the people in my life. Now I can see how serious You are that I do more than say my prayers. You want me to live out my prayers in being a reconciler. Give me courage, Lord!

NOVEMBER
18

Love . . . hopes all things.

—1 CORINTHIANS 13:4,7

Lord of all creation, Sovereign of this universe, in the revolution of the earth around the sun, You brought into being another day. As the sun rises, may Your Son rise in my heart. He, indwelling in me, is my true self. This is the self I want to be out this morning and shine all through this day. It is wonderful to know that it is Christ in me who will face the delights and difficulties of this day. I am fortified from within; I can face anything with Christ to strengthen me.

Indwelling Lord, make me expectant of what You will do in and through me today. How easily I lose a sense of excitement about a new day and what You have planned. With the psalmist I want to sing a new song for this new day because You have made all things new, including me. Just as You have made me a never-to-be-repeated miracle of Your grace, so too this day will be like no other day past or to come.

Lord of new beginnings, I don't want to drag through this day with dullness and drabness. Make me fully alive to greet the day with enthusiasm and spread a spirit of expectation to others. Make me aware of the people You will call me to love and encourage today and alert me to those tasks that You want me to accomplish for Your glory.

November
19

You have an anointing.

—1 John 2:20

Holy Spirit, there are times my imagination gets layered with the negative varnish of reserve and caution. I need Your anointing that acts like turpentine. What turpentine does to the layered varnish and paint on a wood surface, I need You to do with my lacquered imagination. You are able to soften the hard layers, scraping them clean, so that my imagination may become an instrument of receiving clear guidance in vivid, dramatized pictures of Your plans for me.

Today I long to receive a picture of my life completely under Your control. Dramatize in my imagination Your solutions to my problems and opportunities in my relationships. I want to see You at work in troublesome situations. Help me to think clearly and process these guided thoughts through my imagination. Keep my imagination so busy picturing what You want me to be and do that there's no time to misuse my imagination to activate emotions of panic, pumping adrenaline into my bloodstream in an agitated state of stress.

Holy Spirit, I ask for Your fullness to fill, heal, and use my imagination to help me see my self, others, and situations with Your inspiration and live at full potential today.

NOVEMBER
20

He breaks the power of cancelled sin,
He sets the prisoner free. . .

—CHARLES WESLEY
Hymn, "Oh for a Thousand Tongues to Sing"

Lord Jesus, two thousand years ago, You died on the cross for my sins. Therefore, I claimed Your breaking power over the binding power of what You have already forgiven. I dare to ask the crucial question: When is Your forgiveness given? Before I sin, when I am sinning, or when I finally confess my sin? The answer comes thundering through. It's astounding, but true. I am forgiven now even before I fail, miss the mark, rebel against You, or hurt someone else by what I say or do. But the strange thing is that this realization has tremendous liberating power. I want all the more to do what pleases and glorifies You. What no "ought" or admonition could do, Your grace does.

Can I apply this wondrous truth to my relationships? Do people know that my forgiveness has no limits and that it is given before and not after they fail You, themselves, or me? I wish I could answer that this is always true. But You know me, Lord—sometimes it's difficult to love others the way You love me. Then it dawns on me: even this reluctance is forgiven. I am gripped with a desire to make this a day in which I communicate unqualified forgiveness to those who do not deserve it. Thank You, Lord.

NOVEMBER
21

You have heard that it was said, "You shall love your neighbor and hate your enemy." But I say to you, love your enemies, bless those who curse you, do good to those who hate you, and pray for those who spitefully use you and persecute you.

—MATTHEW 5:43-44

Gracious Christ, Your words have an awesome ring. Who can live out this quality of love? No one! Except by Your power . . .

I picture the people I categorize as enemies in my secret heart: adversaries, critics, opponents. Bless them Lord? I know the answer before I ask. When I invite You to live in me, You give me the power to love my enemies. It's impossible to do without You. The sure sign that You are in control of my life is that I can do what I could never do on my own: love, bless, forgive, and pray for the very people whom I reject because I have experienced their rejection.

So, here in this quiet moment I list out those I perceive as enemies and intercede for each of them. Lord, give me insight into what they do and say. Help me see beneath the surface to the inner causes of their behavior. You have shown me that praise and gratitude in everything is the sure way of release. I thank You that these people have caused me to trust You more profoundly. Love through me today, dear Lord!

NOVEMBER
22

. . . that their hearts may be encouraged.

—COLOSSIANS 2:2

Dear Lord, as I look back over the years, I realize how faithful You have been strategically to place people in my life who believed in me and spurred me on. I have seen Your goodness expressed through these people. When I was discouraged, they affirmed my potential; when I was tempted to give up in some challenge, they communicated hope.

You balance the scales. When the going is rough, You send someone to encourage me. Now when I'm going through a tough time, I actually anticipate with expectancy the person You will use to mediate Your uplifting love. You've never let me down.

Having had that kind of help through the years, I long to be an encourager to others. There's no lack of opportunities. When I'm attentive, people express their needs in their tone of voice, the expression on their faces, and their body language. Life is difficult for many people. Just as You have sent the right people to me when I have needed strength and courage, today I feel You are calling me to a ministry of encouragement. I think of specific people You already have put on my agenda. Added to these, make me aware of others with whom I come in contact today. Shine Your accepting love through my countenance. May I really want an answer when I ask, "How are you?" Lord, help me to listen!

NOVEMBER
23

I will hear what God the LORD will speak.

—PSALM 85:8

Dear Lord, I want to listen to some of Your promises as my quiet moment today.

> *Fear not, I am with you. I will never leave nor forsake you. You are Mine for eternity.*

> *Seek to please only Me, and you'll have nothing and no one to fear.*

> *Face your fears, retrace them to their root in your soul, displace them with My indwelling presence, and erase them with an assurance of My forgiving love.*

> *Love yourself as I love you. I have healed your frightened memories. My love casts out fear.*

> *You don't have to worry about being inadequate ever again. I am your strength, wisdom, and courage.*

> *When others reject you, be sure of My unqualified love for you.*

> *Let go of your own control and humbly trust Me to guide you each step of the way.*

> *You have the gift of imagination to picture and live My best for your life.*

> *Don't spend your life worrying about sickness and death— live your life to the fullest now.*

> *You don't need fear to manipulate people any more. You are free to motivate them with love.*

> *And be sure of this—the "good work" I have begun in you will be completed. You have nothing to fear. I love you!*

NOVEMBER
24

I am the light of the world. He who follows Me shall not walk in darkness, but have the light of life.

Lord Christ, You have invited me to walk in Your light. Just as physical light makes objects visible in their real character, so Your light exposes everything in the moral and spiritual order in its true essence. Your light forces me to see myself compared with Your absolute moral purity. You are not an impossible standard; You are an undeniable inspiration. You have called me to live and love, give and forgive, care and dare as You did and do.

Shine Your light into my inner self, the wellspring of my motivation, attitudes, actions, and reactions. Penetrate the inner depths. A vital encounter with You enables me to see things as they are. Your light exposes my pride, self-will, and desire for control. You see the content of my inner thoughts, illusions, and fantasies played out on the stage of my private mind. Most of all, Your light reveals my inner reserve and reluctance to really follow You. The shadows of fear become evident in Your light.

I could not bear to see myself without Your gift of confession. It is wonderful to talk to You about what's going on inside me and receive Your forgiveness. You are a Friend who can know everything and not go away.

NOVEMBER
25

This is the secret: that Christ in your hearts is your only hope of glory.
—COLOSSIANS 1:27 (TLB)

Living Lord Jesus, yesterday's prayers lingered in my mind all through the day. It has brought me to a realization of my need to claim again the awesome mystery of Your indwelling presence and power. Your post-resurrection home is in the minds and hearts of Your disciples. Nothing else could explain the transformation of Your followers through history. They became new creatures as You took up residence in their inner lives. The challenge of loving, forgiving, serving, and caring is not my responsibility for You, but Your ministry through me. You have elected me to be one through whom You reach out to an estranged, sick, and suffering world. I don't have to do it on my own. I am to allow You to flow through my countenance, words, expressions, compassionate acts, and empathetical involvement.

So, Lord, here is my mind, think Your thoughts in me. Be the source of my wisdom, knowledge, and insight. Here is my voice. You told me not to worry about what I am to say, but it would be given me what to say and how to say it. Free me to speak with silence or with words, whichever is needed. Give me Your timing and tenderness. Now, Lord, here is my body. Strengthen me. Release creative affection in my face, my eyes, my touch. If there is something I am to do by Your indwelling presence, however menial or tough, empower me to do it.

NOVEMBER
26

Let us come before His presence with thanksgiving.

—PSALM 95:2

Lord, on the eve of Thanksgiving, I want to prepare my heart for the festivities of tomorrow. You remind me that thanksgiving is the memory of the heart. You desire it, I require it, and others never tire of it.

It amazes me that You desire my gratitude. You have made it the language of love. It's the way I can say, "I love You, Lord, not just for Your blessings, but for all You have been to me."

Then I realize how much I need to express gratitude. It breaks the illusion that I am in charge of my life and can provide for my own needs. I am not self-sufficient. I humble myself before You, dear God, and praise You for all that You have given me and enabled me to become.

Further, I'm reminded that the people of my life never tire of my expression of gratitude for them and what they mean to me. An attitude of gratitude is absolutely essential to deep relationships. People need to hear me say, "Thanks for being you!" May I say those affirming four words to people with whom I celebrate Thanksgiving. Also, help me make time for a phone call or a written note of gratitude to others. Tomorrow will be a day for my thankful heart to overflow, spilling over with Your love.

NOVEMBER
27

A Prayer for Thanksgiving

Oh, give thanks to the LORD, for He is good!
—PSALM 107:1

Almighty God, Sovereign of this nation, my Lord and the source of the manifold blessings of life, today on Thanksgiving, my heart is bursting with gratitude. I want to recapture an aspect of what happened when the Pilgrims celebrated the first Thanksgiving. The children were given plates with five kernels of corn to remind them of the difficult year they had endured. It was only after prayers of gratitude that the full meal was served.

This leads me to think of the five blessings for which I am most thankful today. Where else can I begin but with You, dear Lord? I'm profoundly grateful for who You are as my loving Father. You are faithful, Your loving kindness never fails, and Your goodness is always consistent. Thank You for the gift of salvation and new life in Christ. I praise You for His atoning death, His triumphant resurrection, and His reigning power. Thank You for the Holy Spirit and His gifts of wisdom, knowledge, discernment, vision, and love. Thank You for loved ones and friends. You have blessed me with people who love me and whom I am privileged to love. And thank You, dear God, for Your timely interventions in need. I want all the days of my life to be one continuous thanksgiving!

NOVEMBER
28

Samuel took a stone and set it between Mizpah and Shen, and named it Ebenezer, saying, "Thus far the LORD has helped us."

—1 SAMUEL 7:12

Here I raise my Ebenezer; hitherto by Your help I've come, and I hope by Your good pleasure safely to arrive at home.

—ROBERT ROBINSON
Hymn, "Come Thou Fount of Every Blessing"

Fount of every blessing, on this day after Thanksgiving, the profound gratitude lingers. As I read the verse about Samuel, I was reminded that after a victory or a time of special blessing, the prophet built an altar and called it *Ebenezer*, which in Hebrew means, "stone of help." Samuel exclaimed, "Thus far the Lord has helped us." The stone marked the place where You had brought the people of Israel.

This has been an Ebenezer kind of Thanksgiving week. I have been able to look back and gratefully build an altar of praise saying "Ebenezer, You have brought me thus far." Daily, I have prayed for Your guidance and You have shown me the way each day. You have intervened with timely provision.

Reflecting on the Ebenezer stones of the past has given me courage for today and expectancy for the future. Thank You for preparing me for the today's evidence of Your grace and goodness. Tune my heart to sing Your praise.

NOVEMBER
29

Let all those rejoice who put their trust in You;
let them ever shout for joy, because You defend
them; let those also who love Your name Be
joyful in You. For You, O LORD, will bless the
righteous; With favor You will surround him as
with a shield.

—PSALM 5:11-12

Almighty God, thank You for the privilege of living in this land You have blessed so bountifully. You have called this nation to be a providential demonstration of the freedom and opportunity, righteousness and justice You desire for all nations. Help us be faithful to our destiny. May my response to Your love be spelled out in dedication to serve. Enable me to grasp the privilege of the blessing of being an American.

Lord, empower the women and men of Congress as they seek to keep their eyes on You and what ultimately is best for our nation. Guide and direct the leadership of both parties to work toward creative solutions to the crucial issues before them today. "Righteousness exalts a nation" (Proverbs 14:34). "And when the righteous are in authority, the people rejoice" (Proverbs 29:2).

Bless the President and First Lady of our land, the Congress, the Chief Justices, and all who seek Your guidance in the government of the cities and states across our country. God, bless America. I trust in You! Blessed be the name of the Lord.

NOVEMBER
30

St. Andrew's Day

Lord Christ, as Andrew the fisherman left his nets to become Your disciple, so too today I recommit my life to answer Your call, "Come, follow me!" He took You seriously when You promised him and the other disciples, "I will make you fishers of men."

In this quiet moment I think of the people in my life who desperately need to meet You, know You, and experience the adventure of the abundant life: people in my family, among my friends, at work. Their faces pass before my mind's eye. I see the need for Your love and forgiveness, Your strength and courage, Your hope and vision.

I confess my reluctance to talk to people about how much You mean to me. Forgive my silence when I have opportunities to communicate the peace of trusting You, the joy of following You, the confidence of knowing that I will spend eternity with You.

Today I want to make a bold promise. Give me another chance, Lord, to put in a good word for You. Cure my lockjaw and loosen my tongue. When the opportunity comes, help me share Your love with enthusiasm. Free me really to care about what concerns others so that I can earn the right to be heard when I talk about You. I want my faith to be contagious and my witness on social issues to be consistent with Your righteousness and justice. Today is my day to stand up and be counted . . . so help me, Christ!

DECEMBER
1

*The things which are seen are temporary, but
the things which are not seen are eternal.*

—2 CORINTHIANS 4:18

Eternal Father, sometimes I feel hemmed in by
problems, lost in the labyrinth of life's enigmas, and
wonder if I can cope. The things which are seen captivate
my attention. Newspapers and television constantly remind me of the violence and vandalism, the crimes and
conflicts, the economic and ecological problems. At the
same time, You call me to see the things which are not
seen—Your eternal presence and power at work.

Sometimes, the things which are seen blur my vision of the things which are not seen. It's difficult to live
in both worlds at the same time. And yet, I know I can't
deal with what is temporal unless I am sure of the tran-
scendent. So, here I am again at prayer seeking to find beyond the ongoing drama of secular life—with all its
sinister and alarming possibilities—the communion with
You that will help me see what You are doing in my life
and society. I don't want a simplistic "God's in His heaven
and all's right with the world" nostrum for my anxiety.
Rather I need a "Lo, I am with You always" cure for my
loneliness for You.

Thank You that in Jesus Christ You invaded the
world that is seen with the world that is unseen and
eternal. United to Christ by faith, eternal life has begun.
Now I can cope with the temporal with the conviction of
the eternal.

DECEMBER
2

And Enoch walked with God . . .

—GENESIS 5:24

Gracious God, how did they know that Enoch walked with You? What were the undeniable signs? Was it his serenity, composure, and attitude? Did it produce a radiance on his face, a lilt in his voice, a strength in his character? There's only a one-line epithet in Scripture, a single-sentence biography. And yet people knew that he walked with You. That makes me wonder how people will know today that I have dedicated my life to walking with you. Who will see any difference and why?

Lord, I renew my commitment to walking in the light of Your truth. Thank You that I don't need to stumble about with no sense of direction. Your Word is a lamp to my feet and a light for my path. I can live by the absolutes of Your commandments; I know right from wrong.

Master, I want to walk in Your love. May the assurance of Your love and forgiveness in my life give me that undeniable security and confidence only You can provide.

Today I will walk in the Spirit. I know I am not capable of handling the demands of this day on my own. Dwell in me and provide the wisdom, insight, vision, and hope that I need.

DECEMBER
3

On every tongue was the Healer's name
Throughout all the country they spread His fame
But doubt clung tight to his wooden crutch
Saying, "We must not expect too much."
Down through the ages a promise came
Healing for sorrow sin and shame
Help for the helpless and sight for the blind,
Healing for body and soul and mind
The Christ we follow is still the same
With blessing that all who will may claim.

—ANONYMOUS

Blessed Lord Christ, in this Advent season in preparation for the celebration of Your birth, I praise You for the healing power released in Your incarnate life, atoning death, victorious resurrection, and abiding presence.

Most of all, I rejoice that You are the same yesterday, today, and tomorrow. What You did to heal the minds, bodies, and souls of people in Your earthly ministry so long ago, You now do in me and in those for whom I pray.

In this quiet moment of prayer, I surrender to You all my problems and perplexities, my physical pain and emotional disturbance, my confused thinking and distorted attitudes, my anxious worry and strained relationships, and my lack of faith and trust in Your power to heal my needs. Stretch forth Your tender, strong, uplifting hand and make me whole!

DECEMBER
4

Come to Me, all you who labor and are heavy laden, and I will give you rest.
—MATTHEW 11:28

Lord, I long to live a full and abundant life. I want each day to count, each relationship to be free and loving, each opportunity to be used fully for Your glory.

But You know what I do with the gifts of life! You know me for what I am, deep in my inner self. You know the hours that have been blighted with doubt and distorted by lack of self-affirmation. Forgive me when I fail to love myself as much as You love me.

Often I miss the joy of living because of memories of the past and unguided wish-dreams for the future. I get hemmed in by the demands of life and miss the freedom You desire for me.

I come because of Your gracious invitation, "Come to Me!" and Your admonition to love others as You have loved me. I thank You for Your forgiving love, which frees me now to tell You about any way that I have resisted or refused to say "Yes!" to life.

DECEMBER
5

Be strong and of good courage.

—DEUTERONOMY 31:6

Oh Gracious Lord, in the midst of the temptations of compromise and cowardice, often I step back from loving and forgiving. Sometimes I join the chant of the "Me" generation when I want everything for myself rather than serving, and when I think in terms of only what You can do for me rather than what You have called me to do through me. I desperately need a fresh touch of Your Spirit.

Lord, give me courage for facing life's challenges. Right now in the quiet of this moment, I want to put You first in my life. I want to make a covenant with You to serve You first and then serve others as a part of Your mandate to me.

Gracious Lord, guide me and give me power. All around me are people who urgently need You and who need to come to know You as Lord and Savior more than they need their next breath. Forgive my dumbness and my insensitivity. You have called me to make an impact on the problems and the suffering of my time. Lord, I am so often afraid. Forgive me, and grant me courage.

Bring me back to a realization of the power of my words—how my careless gossip and my negative criticisms hurt, maim, and frustrate others. Gracious Lord, give me the courage to be different. Pour out Your Spirit that I may be bold in my faith, unreserved in my witness, uncalculating in my love, and unreserved in my dedication.

DECEMBER
6

Do not worry about tomorrow, for tomorrow will worry about its own things. Sufficient for the day is its own trouble.

—MATTHEW 6:34

Gracious God, for tomorrow and its needs I do not pray, but keep me, guide me, love me . . . just for today. Help me to be faithful and obedient to You by living only in this new day which You have given me. Yesterday is a memory, and tomorrow is uncertain. But today, if I live it to the fullest, will become a memorable yesterday and tomorrow will be a vision of hope.

Help me to remember that a great life is an accumulation of days lived, one at a time, for Your glory and by Your grace. Anything is possible if I take it in day-sized bites. Help me make today a day to be that different person I've wanted to be, to start doing what I've put off, and to enjoy the work I have to do. I want this to be a special day to love You, serve You, be faithful to You, and be an encourager of others around me.

One day to live; Lord, it will go so fast; please make it a good memory, before it's passed.

DECEMBER
7

God, who is rich in mercy, because of His great love with which He loved us, even when we were dead in trespasses, made us alive together with Christ.

—EPHESIANS 2:4-5

Dear God, thank You for confronting the sins of the world. Because You cared, You came in Jesus Christ to reconcile us to Yourself. You did not tolerate our rebellion, but invaded us with love and forgiveness.

Sovereign Father, give me the courage to do more than tolerate people. Help me to remember what life was like before I knew You personally. May that shock me out of bland aloofness from the peril in which people around me are living. Thank You for giving me joy and hope to share with them.

In the quiet of this moment, Lord, clarify for me the people in my life who have been prepared by You for a loving and decisive communication of Your judgment and Your forgiveness. Help me to rely on Your Spirit for the right words to speak with a gracious attitude. Free me to be vulnerable to share what You have done in my life. I continue this prayer interceding for those I know who urgently need to receive the gift of faith to trust You completely.

DECEMBER
8

Wait on the LORD; be of good courage, and He shall strengthen your heart; Wait, I say, on the LORD!

—PSALM 27:14

Lord God, You are the light of truth for those who know You, the security of those who love You, the strength of those who trust You, the patience of those who wait on You, and the courage of those who serve You.

May all that I say and do today be said and done with an acute awareness of my accountability to You. Help me to ask, "What would the Lord do?" and then, "Lord, what do You want me to do?" I think of the people about whom I am worried or troubled. Show me what You want me to do to express Your love and practical help. I reflect on the list of problems I face. Lord, I am willing to do Your will. But You know that sometimes I am hard-of-hearing when You talk to me. Unstop the ears of my heart so I can hear and follow Your guidance. Give me courage to act on however little I know so that my knowledge of Your will can grow.

Hear my prayer, oh Lord, now as I submit to You each concern that troubles me.

DECEMBER
9

*In everything give thanks; for this is the will of
God in Christ Jesus for you.*

—1 THESSALONIANS 5:18

Gracious Sovereign of my life, my help in ages past
and my hope for years to come, I enter into this day with
a mind in great need of your direction and a heart filled
with gratitude for Your provision. In the midst of the
problems I'm facing at this time, I need the refreshing rejuvenation that comes when I turn from my trials and
focus on thanking You for Your great faithfulness in every
circumstance of life.

You have shown me that gratitude is not only the
greatest of all virtues, but the parent of all others. Any
achievement without gratitude limps along the road of
life; anything I accomplish without giving thanks becomes a source of pride. You desire my gratitude because
You know it enables me to grow, and helps me to avoid
being self-serving and arrogant.

Oh God, I praise You for what You have made me
and what You have given me. I repent of any pride that
entertains the idea that I am in charge of my own destiny.
Grant me the true humility that comes from acknowledging that You are the source of all that I have and am.

December
10

*Examine yourselves as to whether you are in
the faith. Prove yourselves.*

—2 Corinthians 13:5

Gracious Father, in the welter of human words, my
soul cries out, "Is there any word from the Lord?"

I wonder what You have to say about my present
crisis. In the deepest reaches of my heart I know all too
well. You call me to absolute honesty with myself, to
mean what I say and to do what I promise.

Yet so often my words are not backed by my heart,
and my promises are not backed by actions. Though my
intentions may seem right and honorable, I realize they
have no value if they remain unfulfilled. And in the wake
of that unfulfillment are people whom I've let down, or
even hurt.

Oh God, I am fully accountable to You. Remind
me that when I speak or make a commitment, Your name
is at stake as well as mine. Help me to take my intentions
and vows seriously, and to make them cautiously.

And when I move to fulfill what I have committed
to do, may I do it not in my human frailty, but in Your divine power.

DECEMBER
11

I will give you a new heart and put a new spirit within you; I will take the heart of stone out of your flesh and give you a heart of flesh. I will put My Spirit within you.

—EZEKIEL 36:26-27

Dear God, I need a new heart for this new day. Remove from me any hardness of heart and give me a moldable, flexible, free heart ready to receive Your Spirit. Help me say with the psalmist, "Praise the LORD! I will praise the LORD with my whole heart" (Psalm 111:1). Forgive my halfhearted response to You, Lord, and the gift of life You give me today. I think of Your attributes, Your nature, and Your glory, and my heart begins to soar. My enthusiasm for this day increases as I accept Your forgiveness. Thank You for all Your blessings. Thanksgiving is the memory of my heart.

Now I picture my life completely under Your control. I commit myself to You to live out the picture You have given me of what I would be like filled with Your Spirit and exuding Your love, joy, and peace.

You have called me to be an intercessor and wait for me to pray so I can be a partner with You in the blessing of others. Specifically, I pray for family members, friends, people at work, the President and First Lady, Members of Congress, and the Justices of the Supreme Court.

December
12

*Continue earnestly in prayer, being vigilant in
it with thanksgiving.*

—Colossians 4:2

Dear God, You have shown me that gratitude is the
secret of receiving Your grace. I commit this day to be vigilant in my thanksgiving, constantly on the watch to be
sure that gratitude is my consistent response to what happens to me and around me. I know that when I give
thanks in everything, I claim that You are in charge of my
life and will bring good out of even the most difficult and
baffling situations. When I let go, the blessings flow.

In this quiet moment, I want to thank You for Your
limitless blessings. Especially, thank You for _____.
I also want to thank You for the tough times in which I
experienced great relief and release, when I finally could
thank You for a problem and what I would discover
through facing it with Your help. Today I thank You for
using me as a part of Your solution to challenges I have
ahead of me today. Particularly, I surrender _____ to
You, thanking You in advance that You will provide me
insight and wisdom.

Thank You for the people of my life: those I love,
those I need to learn to love, those who get on my nerves,
those who need my forgiveness, and those whose forgiveness I need to seek. I will be anxious for nothing, but in
everything by prayer, with thanksgiving, will make my requests known to You, dear Father.

DECEMBER
13

I wait for the LORD, my soul waits and in His word I do hope. My soul waits for the LORD.

—PSALM 130:5-6

Loving Father, who allows waiting times so I can place my hope in nothing other than the word You speak in the depth of my soul, I confess that waiting is not easy for me. Often I turn to false hopes for quick easy answers. Graciously You wait for me to realize again that nothing or no one can be a source of lasting hope except You. Now it dawns on me that what I thought were my waiting times are really times during which You wait for me to want You and Your guidance above all else. Help me to realize that there are no unanswered prayers. A delay is not a denial if it brings me closer to You in deeper trust.

In this world of instant everything, fast foods and shallow relationships, there are times I become very impatient with anything or anyone who causes me to wait. I hate long lines, delayed flights, tardy friends. Sometimes I get stressed out with exasperation. Then I worry about burnout. Neither the pout nor the shout seems to get things moving the way I want and when I want them.

Now in the quiet of this moment, I need to experience a hush instead of a rush. Your timing is perfect. An inner glow comes from living in the flow of Your peace.

DECEMBER
14

I am . . . the Life."

—JOHN 14:6

Christ, You are my life. Christianity for me is life as You lived it, life as I live it in You, life as You live it in me, and life as You communicate it through me. In Your incarnate life on earth as Jesus of Nazareth, the Messiah, You not only revealed the Father, but also what life was meant to be for humankind. You revealed eternal life, the life of God lived in human flesh, and showed us how we too could enter into eternal life through beginning again with a new birth. You gave me the secret of abundant life through complete trust.

In Your death and resurrection, O Christ, You revealed the power available to me. I want to live as a person in You, fully engrossed in what You have done for me. May Your cross give me an assurance today that I am forgiven and Your victory over the grave give me the conviction that I am alive forever.

In this quiet moment, also help me to rejoice that You have kept Your promise to abide in Your followers. I ask You again to fill me with Your Spirit. Infuse my mind with Your mind so I can think clearly with Your perspective and purpose. Love through my emotions. Command my will. Throughout this day help me exemplify the abundant life overflowing with Your grace, joy, peace, patience, kindness, and hope. Show the people in my world what You can do for them because of what they see You have done for me. This is a day to really live!

DECEMBER
15

I am the bread of life.

—JOHN 6:35

Lord Christ, the Bread of Life, what physical bread is for the body, You are for my hungry heart. You alone can save, satisfy, and strengthen my inner being. My hunger to know You better is a sure evidence that I belong to You. My heartaches are an indication of how much I need You. You are the source of healing.

Living Bread, You have promised me eternal life, both a new quality of life now and a limitless quantity of life forever. You have saved me from fear of death, worry over my welfare, frustration over my failures, anxiety about my status and success, fears about the future, panic about death. Your living presence dwells in me; I am saved!

Bread of Life, You also satisfy my deepest needs for love, self-esteem, significance, affirmation, a reason for living, involvement in a calling that counts, an assurance that there is meaning in daily living. You give me security no one else can provide.

Strength of my life, thank You for the spiritual sustenance You infuse into me moment by moment. You provide abundant energy, wisdom, and power to do what You ask. I'm sure of this: The deeper I go in an intimate relationship with You, the more I experience a flow of insight, creative ideas, love, empathy, and energy to endure!

DECEMBER
16

I can do all things through Christ who strengthens me.

—PHILIPPIANS 4:13

Holy Lord God, I confess that I have tried to live my life within the narrow, limited dimensions of my own wisdom and strength. I am painfully aware of my inadequacies: My love is shallow and sometimes selfish; my feelings are often distorted and easily hurt; my patience has a short fuse and my disposition often reflects my inner tensions; my disappointment with life and people is reflected in my attitudes; my anxiety over social and world conditions reveals how little I trust You. As a result, I often order my life around my own abilities and skills and miss the adventure of life that You have prepared for me.

I confess to You all the things I dared not attempt, the courageous deeds I contemplated but was afraid I could not do, the gracious thoughts I had but never communicated. Forgive me Lord, for forgetting that You are able to do in and through me what I could never do myself, and for settling for a life which is a mere shadow of what You had prepared for me.

Now in the quiet of this time of honest confession, plant in me the vivid picture of what you are able to do with a life like mine, and give me the gift of new excitement about living life by Your triumphant adequacy!

DECEMBER
17

Do not be afraid, but speak, and do not keep silent; for I am with you, and no one will attack you to hurt you; for I have many people in this city.

—ACTS 18:9-10
(The answer to Paul's prayer in Corinth)

Lord, I want to live this day in the confidence You gave to the apostle Paul there in Corinth. In a difficult time You reminded him that he was not alone: You were with him and there were many people there who believed in You who would be Your agents to help him.

I think of the faithful friends You have given me and pause to name them with gratitude. They have faith in You and pray for me. So at every moment You are answering their prayers in practical ways I can see and in mysterious ways that are unseen, but felt in the depth of my heart. You have been so good to me to give me fellow disciples to share the adventure of living for You. They are there in times of need to remind me that You are the source of my strength, and they are ready to give themselves to care for me in so many amazing ways.

As I think about the people You have given me as gifts of grace, I also wonder about the ways You may want to use me in the lives of those who count on me to help them in the ups and downs of life. Lord Jesus, make me aware, available, and accountable. Live in me and love through me. I dedicate myself to that privilege today.

DECEMBER
18

Without Me you can do nothing.

—JOHN 15:5

Gracious Lord, I confess I have periods of rebellion when I hold You at arm's length. My will has had to be softened and remolded until I am willing to trust You. Help me to graduate from that impersonal level of religious rules and regulations as the only basis of relating to You. Bring me into an intimate and personal relationship with You in which I can know You face to face, eye to eye, heart to heart.

Dear Lord, show me what I am to be and do. Give me Your specific guidance so that I can obey and follow.

You have all authority in heaven and on earth. I submit my life to Your authority. Possess my mind with clear convictions that You are in charge of my life and the lives of those about whom I am concerned. I surrender myself and them to You.

Brand in my heart and on my mind the great truth that Paul wrote while he was in prison: *"I can do all things through Christ who strengthens me"* (Philippians 4:13). Let me have that kind of faith, which enabled Paul to run the race that You had marked out for him, no matter what difficulty or suffering befell him.

Oh Lord, may that courage result in a new, positive attitude that exudes joy and hope about the present and the future. I trust in Your impossibility-defying name!

DECEMBER
19

I am . . . the Bright and Morning Star.

—REVELATION 22:16

Lord Jesus Christ, the bright morning star, I need Your powerful assurance spoken to the apostle John on the island of Patmos. You revealed Your supremacy over life and death, frustration and pain, loss and loneliness. In this quiet moment, I praise You for being the bright morning star in the spiritual darkness that comes at high noon as well as in the dark night of the soul.

Just as the morning star appears and shines brilliantly in the sky right before the dawn, shine with hope in my heart in the darkness I experience: those times of discouragement and disappointment, failure and fear, indecision and indecisiveness, grimness and grief. Give me the courage to hold out until Your morning star rises in my heart (2 Peter 1:19). Remind me that the darkest time is just before the morning star appears in the sky and often the times of deepest darkness in my soul are just before You break through with the light of Your truth and guidance. Grant me the light of Your discernment and insight. Bless me with the illumination of Your plan and purpose. Make me radiant with the light of Your indwelling Spirit.

My prayer is not just for myself, but also for the impact of my life on others. Some people around me live in spiritual darkness. Give me fresh hope to share with them Your faithfulness as the morning star of my life.

DECEMBER
20

If I had not come . . .

—JOHN 15:22

Gracious Christ, Lord and Savior, I stumble on your words, "If I had not come," and am stunned by the realization of what I would not know and have if You had not come. Just to think about it sends a chill up my spine. And yet, each thought becomes a source of profound thanksgiving. You have exposed my need and met that need through Your life, death, and resurrection.

Thank You for revealing the true nature of grace. Through You I know about the width, length, depth, and height of love that passes understanding. Through Your teaching I know how to put first the kingdom and God's righteousness. In the cross I experience the forgiveness and cleansing of my sins. Your death defeated the power of death so I can be sure that this life is only a small part of eternity and that I shall live forever. You are reigning Lord of history and are able to take what I commit to You and bring Your best. You understand my confusion and give me calmness, You see my stress and give me serenity, You invade my perplexities and infuse Your peace. Praise You, Lord; I am a new person filled with the Spirit.

Guide me today as I think prayerfully about what life would be like . . . if You had not come. Most of all, help me claim all that is mine because You came and continue to come.

DECEMBER
21

Continuing steadfastly in prayer. . . .

—ROMANS 12:12

Almighty God, I'm so grateful for this time of prayer. It is a privilege to intercede on behalf of my family, friends, and people with whom I work. Bless them with Your love and strength.

Now, in this Christmas season, Lord, I feel led to ask You for a very special gift. This gift is one I know You want to give.

You have told me in the Scriptures that there are blessings You grant only when I care enough to pray for others. I also know how my attitudes are changed when I pray for others. I listen better and conflicts are resolved. I discover answers to problems because prayer has made it easier to work out solutions.

Also, when I pray for others, You affirm that caring You've inspired by releasing supernatural power. Added to this, working together with people for whom I've prayed becomes more pleasant and more productive.

Knowing all this, I make a renewed commitment to pray for the people around me, those with whom I disagree, and those with whom I sometimes find it difficult to work. Today when I meet people, shake their hands or have a conversation, help me to whisper a silent prayer for each of them. Then guide what I say so that I may be Your special blessing to him or her. Thank You for this day to spread Your joy.

DECEMBER
22

For unto us a Child is born
Unto us a Son is given;
And the government will be
Upon His shoulder.

—ISAIAH 9:6

Blessed Christ, my Savior and Lord, may my celebration of Your birth this Christmas be an expression of praise for all You have done for me and are to me moment by moment. I am stunned when I think about all that is mine because You came: abundant and eternal life, love and forgiveness, peace and power.

It's strange: most people know the accomplishments of the great personages of history but know little of the circumstances of their birth; in contrast, people know the intricate details of where and how You were born and remember so little of what You said and did.

You are my reigning Lord. Today as I celebrate Your coming in Bethlehem of Judea so long ago, help me joyously expect Your coming to me today. I think about Isaiah's prophecy, "And the government shall be upon His shoulder," I wonder if the prophet had on his mind Exodus 28:29, "So Aaron shall bear the names of the sons of Israel on the breastplate of judgment over his heart." You are infinitely greater than Aaron; You are my Emmanuel, God with me. Your broad shoulders can take my burdens and carry them. I'm moved as I discover that the Hebrew word translated as "government" here means, "the burden of authority." I really want to place the hopes and fears of my life on Your shoulders.

DECEMBER
23

How silently, how silently
The wondrous gift is given!
So God imparts to human hearts
The blessing of His heaven.
No ear may hear His coming;
But in this world of sin,
Where meek souls will receive Him still,
The dear Christ enters in.

—Phillips Brooks
Hymn, "O Little Town of Bethlehem"

*D*ear God, in my quiet moment today I want to think about the awesome mystery of Christ's conception and birth in and through Mary. I never cease to be amazed by the announcement to her by the Holy Spirit that she would conceive and give birth to Your Son. Her words in response are on my mind right now: "Let it be to me according to Your word."

In the same way spiritually the indwelling Christ is received by people today. All that's required is that we accept the gift. May it be done, Lord, according to Your will! May my open heart receive the conception of Your indwelling presence. Christ, grow in me until all my thoughts are inspired by You, all my emotions controlled by You, all my will instigated by You.

I think of Paul's longing for the Galatians, that You be formed in them (Galatians 4:19). That's my deepest longing this Christmas. Just as You revealed the perfect union of God's glory and human nature in Your incarnate life, may that miracle be recapitulated in me in a diminutive but dynamic way as I am made a new creation in You.

DECEMBER
24

Christmas Eve

*Do not be afraid, for behold, I bring you good
tidings of great joy.*

—LUKE 2:10

Dear Father, I don't want to miss the true joy of
Christmas. I long for the authentic quality of joy that's an
outward expression of an inner experience of Your grace.
Today, on Christmas Eve, help me to receive the full measure of Your unqualified love that will result in a day
bursting with joy. I hear the words of the angel translated
with the true meaning: "Glory to God in the highest, and
on earth peace, among men in whom He is well pleased."

Now I can repeat the familiar words from John
3:16-17 using the personal pronouns: "You so loved me
that You gave Your only begotten Son, that believing in
Him, I should not perish but have everlasting life. For You
did not send Your Son into the world to condemn me, but
that through Him I might be saved."

My heart leaps. Joy is the ecstasy of heaven for those
who know they are loved and forgiven. It's so much more than
happiness that's dependent on circumstances. Real joy cannot
be dampened; it lasts regardless of whatever has happened.

Thank You for giving me down-to-earth joy in Jesus.
I don't want to leave Your Christmas gift unwrapped. I
hear His whisper in my heart: "I came for you, lived for
you, died for you, defeated death for you, and am here for
you now." Joy! Sheer joy!

DECEMBER
25

Christmas Day

When they had come into the house, they saw the young Child with Mary His mother, and fell down and worshiped Him.

—MATTHEW 2:11

Lord Jesus Christ, the world is quiet now. All the rush of the busy Christmas season is over. I feel an overwhelming desire to worship You. I join with the wise men who rejoiced with exceeding great joy and fell down on their knees and worshiped You. They had prophetic Scripture and a star to guide them in their worship of You as a child in a house; I have the awesome truth about what You did as my redeeming Savior and what You are as my reigning Lord.

Thank You for the peace that floods my being as I worship You. It is a peace of a forgiven heart, a surrendered heart, a willing heart. Fill me with Your Spirit, Lord, so that I may experience Your serenity. The more I worship and adore You, the more at peace I feel.

A profound sense of humility sweeps over me as I realize that all that I have is Your gift and all I have accomplished is because of Your blessings.

Now uncontainable love supersedes all other responses. I love You, Lord, for who You are and linger in this sublime moment of unfettered adoration. Today, on Christmas, I want to tell You how much You mean to me.

DECEMBER
26

The shepherds returned, glorifying and praising
God for all the things that they had heard and
seen, as it was told them.

—LUKE 2:20

Lord Christ, You are the same yesterday, today, and forever. At Christmastime the diamond is touted as the gift that never stops giving. Only You can fulfill that kind of promise. Your faithfulness knows no end; Your love is indefatigable. The joy of Christmas is for every day of the year.

Thank You for promising me strength for whatever comes in the passing moments of every hour of the New Year. Knowing this, I plan to live each moment to the fullest. You have banished worry about tomorrow; now the future is a friend.

Like the shepherds who went back to work as different people because of beholding Your glory in the manger, I want to go back to my daily routines as a different person because of Christmas. I accept the gift that changes everything. With Christmas love, joy, hope, and peace, I can go back to old relationships, pressing responsibilities, the troubled world, and those problems I set aside until after the holidays. Nothing has changed, and yet everything is different. The difference is inside of me. Nothing can ever be the same again! You have recruited me to be a Christmas angel, a messenger, to the world around me. Some people will be disappointed that Christmas made so little difference. Today help me to communicate to uptight, tired out, done-in people what it means to receive Your strength each moment.

DECEMBER
27

Behold, I stand at the door and knock. If anyone hears My voice and opens the door, I will come in to him and dine with him, and he with Me.

—REVELATION 3:20

Lord Christ, You stand at the door of my heart knocking. Once again You make the first move. You come to me in a new way each day. I have learned that yesterday's experience of fellowship with You will not be sufficient for today's challenges. You seek entrance into every facet of my life. The latch always is on the inside. Daily, I have a choice to open the door or leave it shut in Your face.

As I look back over this past year, I am alarmed by the number of days I spent in self-propelled effort. I was too absorbed in myself to hear You knocking. Forgive me and open my ears to hear Your knock at the beginning of each day of the New Year.

Suddenly, again, I'm struck by the startling realization that You know and care about me. I'm amazed: You have chosen and called me and are not about to let a day go by without knocking and waiting for an invitation to come in and take control of my life. Who am I to deserve such attention from the Savior of the world? Then I remember that it is Your grace and not my goodness that motivates Your persistence. You have work to do where I live and work and, wonder of wonder, You plan to do it through me. Come in; You are welcome!

DECEMBER
28

If you ask anything in My name, I will do it.

—JOHN 14:14

Blessed living Lord Jesus, I reaffirm my commitment to be Your disciple today. I take up my cross and follow You by serving others.

Fill me with Your Spirit. Use my mind to think Your thoughts, my emotions to express Your love, and my will to discern and do Your will for me. I surrender the challenges, relationships, and responsibilities of the day ahead.

Grant me Your power. I take seriously Your promise that Your disciples are to expect supernatural power for the work You give them to do. Awe and wonder grip me as I reflect on Your promise that "He who believes in me, the works that I do he will do also; and greater works than these he will do, because I go to My Father" (John 14:12).

In these days, as I prepare for a New Year, my commitment is to seek to love as You love, forgive as You forgive, inspire others as You inspire me, give hope as You give me hope. Help me to confront the physical, emotional, and spiritual illness and suffering around me with prayers for healing. Give me a renewed sense that nothing is impossible for You. Replace my insecure grimness with an inexhaustible graciousness. Help me to envision a new year totally surrendered to You and triumphantly supplied with Your strength and courage.

DECEMBER
29

Do not remember the former things, nor consider the things of old. Behold, I will do a new thing . . .

—ISAIAH 43:18-19

Forgiving Lord, the healer of hurting memories, I am deeply concerned about the way I carry the burden of troublesome memories from year to year. Repeatedly I dredge up from the past unforgiven hurts and unfulfilled hopes. I have a sharp memory for my failures. Just thinking about them brings back all the pain. Also, the memories of what people have done or said to cause me anguish lurk and stalk about the corridors of the ever-present past.

You have promised to liberate my memories of the syndrome of repetitive reflection on distressing memories. A New Year is at hand. Will I carry into the future the same old unresolved, unforgiven, unhealed memories?

In this quiet moment, I realize how urgently I want to have a good memory of Your faithfulness and a poor memory about the sins You have already forgiven. Liberate me so I need not remember regretfully what You have forgotten. Help me to list out on a piece of paper the memories that hinder my progress, and then tear up the list and claim the healing of Your Spirit. It's really exciting to think about a New Year that's truly new, because right now Your healing power is moving through my memory, sorting out what I dare not forget about Your goodness and what I dare not keep if I want to be whole.

December
30

See I have set before You an open door . . .

—REVELATION 3:8

Dear Lord, there's a lot of talk this week about New Year's resolutions. I guess we all want to be different and change those habits and attitudes we know hold us back from being what You want us to be.

As this old year draws to a close, I open my mind to Your guidance about Your vision of what You want me to be and do next year. Help me become the person You desire. Give me a vivid picture of myself filled with Your Spirit and empowered to discover and do Your will.

I think of my relationships. Inspire my imagination with ways You want me to be Your person to those around me. In this quiet moment I picture what life would be like if I acted and spoke under Your guidance. In the realm of my responsibilities, help me take the cap off my reservations about what's possible. Show me Your maximum plan and my part in it. Please be very specific, Lord, so I can make resolutions that are more than generalities.

As thoughts are formed into hopes, I realize again that You know me very well. You guide me to attempt what I could not do on my own strength. Thank You that I don't have to remain as I am, nor does life have to be the same. Now I am really excited about the New Year!

DECEMBER
31

New Year's Eve

Have I not commanded you? Be strong and of good courage; do not be afraid, nor be dismayed, for the LORD your God is with you wherever you go.

—JOSHUA 1:9

Almighty God, Sovereign of my life, my help in this past year and my hope for the year to come, I praise You for these quiet moments You and I have had together at the beginning of each day. Daily, You awakened me with the desire to have a personal time with You. These prayers have been conversation starters. Often the conversation of prayer has gone on all through the day. The best days of the year have been when I claimed Your presence and lived by Your power.

Thank You for the way You answered my prayers for Your guidance and courage. I'm amazed at the thoughts You placed in my mind, the desires You planted in my heart, and the willingness You produced in my will. You have given me what I asked: wisdom beyond my understanding; knowledge greater than my learning; discernment more penetrating than my analysis; vision that outstretches my fondest expectation.

Now I'm ready to face a new year without fear. I press on with Your assurance for the future, "Fear not! I am with you." That's all I need to know!